SO MANY FREAKIN' SECRETS

The real story behind the "perfect" family - and the healing truths that can set anyone free

JANET BERNICE CHENEY

So Many Freakin' Secrets

Inspired Legacy Publishing is a division of (DBA) Inspired Legacy, LLC
PO Box 900816
Sandy UT 84090-0816.

ISBN 979-8-9904401-0-4 (paperback)
ISBN 979-8-9904401-1-1 (hardcover)

Printed in the United States of America.

"You own everything that happened to you. Tell your stories.

If people wanted you to write warmly about them, they should have behaved better."

-----Anne Lamott

WHAT PEOPLE ARE SAYING

"In this journey of personal discovery laid bare, Janet Bernice Cheney reminds us that all families have secrets. Struggling to discover her real origin story, Janet lets us follow along on her hero's journey of understanding, healing, cutting ties, and forgiveness. You'll walk away inspired to look deeply into your own life.

—Jennifer Utley, Executive Story Producer, *Ancestry.com*

"In spite of all the above issues of interpersonal, marital, several children, with a husband who didn't have any idea of responsibility or maturity, Janet took control and she has developed a great amount of insight, sensitivity, and spirituality that will be helpful in reaching others who have had similar experiences."

—John Waterbury, CMHC, Therapist Retired

"We should all appreciate the raw and transparent view that Janet shares about her life, in her book, So Many Freakin' Secrets. A motivating and inspiring read for anyone in difficult situations."

—Georgia Carpenter, Book Promoter and Publicist

"It's disheartening to realize how many children are adopted for the wrong reasons only to be abused emotionally and physically. So Many Freakin' Secrets is a well—written story about the author's healing journey. This poignant narrative serves as a beacon of hope for those who have experienced similar circumstances."

—Madison Frederick, International Best—Selling Author of *Untangle The Web of Narissism*

"I absolutely loved So Many Freakin' Secrets and was so impressed by Janet's strength and courage for how she lived her powerful and inspirational story. My heart ached right along with the author during her struggles and I cheered as she made her comeback. Very well done!"

—**Brita Peterson, International Best–Selling Author of *Getting Through Today. How Chronic Illness Taught Me, The Beauty in Being Broken***

DEDICATION

To those who helped me save my life: John Waterbury, CMHC, and Rhoda Weber, LMFT.

But most of all, to Alex and Sonya, Chris and Mel, and Eric and Kirsty, darling sons and remarkable women who serve as their wives. And to so many dear friends who have encouraged me to write for years and years and years.

If you are reading my story and have experienced life trauma of any kind, know that you have the power to make your life wonderful! If I can, you can too.

ACKNOWLEDGEMENT

Wolverton Mountain words and music by Merle Kilgore and Claude King Copyright © 1962 Painted Desert Music Corporation, New York. Copyright renewed, all rights administered by Reservoir Media Management, Inc. International Copyright secured all rights reserved. *Reprinted by Permission of Hal Leonard LLC*

DISCLAIMER

These are *my* memories...

CONTENTS

Prologue 1

Chapter 1: Accelerant..3

Chapter 2: Snakes Really Are Everywhere............................. 11

Chapter 3: Don't Talk, Don't Share 21

Chapter 4: First and Second Love 29

Chapter 5: Everything Has to Change 39

Chapter 6: Let the Games Begin.. 49

Chapter 7: Let's Be Disobedient 59

Chapter 8: Come What May 69

Chapter 9: Us Versus Them..77

Chapter 10: Out of the Frying Pan..87

Chapter 11: You've Made Your Bed 95

Chapter 12: You Can't Always Get What You Want 101

Chapter 13: Drugs, Babies, and Going to Church.................109

Chapter 14: Peace, Love, and Priesthood? 121

Chapter 15: Hippies Call It "A Happening"........................... 131

Chapter 16: It's Called Labor for a Reason 139

Chapter 17: Turmoil and Bliss 149

Chapter 18: It's Only for a Little While 157

Chapter 19: Down the Rabbit Hole..167

Chapter 20: I Made It Stop 177

Chapter 21: Grenadine and Rocky Road 185

Chapter 22: God Is in the Details 195

Chapter 23: A New Beginning 207

Chapter 24: Geographical Cure? 219

Chapter 25: Who Knew? 229

Chapter 26: After All 239

Chapter 27: Thomas Wolfe Was Right 247

Chapter 28: Putting Me Together 257

Chapter 29: I Woke Up 263

Chapter 30: Accelerating 269

Chapter 31: Ascending 273

Epilogue 281

Final Thoughts 287

Photo Gallery 289

About the Author 293

Full Reviews 295

Reviews 297

PROLOGUE

My two-year-old older brother watched the car drive away, with me in it, then ran into the street shouting, "Don't take my sister, don't take my sister!" I was 13 months old.

That's what my birth mother told me fifty-one years later. What? I have an older brother? There were more disclosures to come—all exciting, unexpected, and frightening. My past was a closely guarded secret. That was adoption in the 1950s. I had no knowledge of anything, I had no knowledge of me.

In 2003, I met my mother for the very first time in the San Francisco airport. She hobbled toward me with a cane, holding onto a man's arm. Her short gray hair, tired smile, and sad brown eyes affirmed her hard life. But she was *my* mother; she'd birthed me. We had a quick shoulder-to-shoulder hug, then sat together on a cold, metal bench. I held her thin-skinned hand in mine as she looked at the floor tiles.

I was all wild blonde hair, anxious eyes, and a neediness I was sure radiated out of every pore. I took in every inch of this woman. Did I look like her? Was she happy to see me like I was to see her? How and why was I put up for adoption?

"Hi, I'm your brother, John," Mother's escort said. At five-foot eleven, he was taller than us both, and he had a warm, open smile. His eyes twinkled behind black-framed glasses and his short, straight hair fell across his wide forehead. "We've been looking for you for years."

From no family connection to five half-brothers and sisters, their spouses, and children,. . . my head was spinning. I could hardly process it all.

I'd been searching myself for over twenty years. I had a copy of my adoption papers with the father's name, Vasco Leitao, but only a last name for the mother, McGill. When a friend with her own adopted child offered to help in the search, I jumped at the chance. She knew how to run the gauntlet of sealed adoptions. It only took her three days. "I found her. Do you want to speak to your mother?"

On that Tuesday in August 2003, I took the phone in my trembling hand as adrenaline pumped through me like gasoline. Talk to my mother? Yes! Questions had been swimming in my brain all my life.

Questions—Do I call you Mother . . . Mama? Why did you give me away? Is there something wrong with me? Why to a family in Prescott, Arizona? Is Vasco really my father? Didn't you want me? Didn't you love me? Do you love me now?

So Many Freakin' Secrets . . .

CHAPTER 1

ACCELERANT

I woke in the middle of the cold November night in 1958, catching my breath. *Something's wrong. Why am I awake in the dark?* Then I realized our dog was barking outside.

"What the Sam's Hill is wrong with that dog?" Daddy yelled as he stomped down the hall and slammed open the back door to go find the mutt.

Suddenly Dad's voice turned from anger to panic. "Mildred!" he bellowed, "the neighbor's house is on fire! Go to the Jensen's and call the fire department!"

Mama ran into our bedroom and grabbed Connor out of his crib. "Put on your bathrobe and slippers, Janet!" she ordered.

I wrapped the robe around me fast and jammed my feet into some slippers. Mama took my hand and yanked me out the front door. I moved as fast as my now-straight legs would carry me, without rickets bowing them outward any longer. As we ran to the car, a smoky haze hurt my eyes, almost blinding me, and I heard glass shatter somewhere behind me.

An ear-splitting roar filled the air. It sounded like thousands of pieces of paper being scrunched up all at once. I looked back to see where the noise was coming from. Through the smoke, orange and red fire shot into the sky like rocket flames. My mouth dropped open in shock and a cold shiver ran through me.

"Move it, Janet!" my mother shrieked, her dark hair wild and uncombed in the night air. "Get in the car—NOW!"

I jumped into the passenger seat and slammed the door as Mama put baby Connor, in his carryall, on to the floor by the back seat. How could he sleep through all that noisy explosion? Hot air rushed across my face as I stared out the open window and watched pine trees near our house turn black. A rush of adrenaline-fueled fear raced through me and hot tears cascaded down my face. Confused and terrified, my sobbing quickly changed to all-out wailing.

"Stop that blubbering!" Mama roared as she yanked me back in. "Your father's risking his life so the least you can do is shut up! Do you hear me? I mean it. Stop that crying or I'll give you something to *really* cry about."

I clamped my mouth shut, swallowed the lump in my throat, and huffed uneven breaths.

Mama started the DKW station wagon and backed us out of the dirt parking area as fast as she could. Without fully stopping, she yanked the car into drive and violently peeled out, which threw me back against my seat. We accelerated down the road to the close-by neighbor's.

Will the fire catch me? Will I burn up too?

Soft amber light from the Jensen's house spilled out onto the dirt road as we turned into their drive.

The lights were on in the kitchen and I saw the neighbors sitting at their table. The smell of fresh brewed coffee filled the air as we rushed in. The familiar aroma made me a little less nervous. With a few quick words from Mr. Jensen, Mama deposited Connor and me in the front room. She charged into the kitchen and dialed the black wall phone. I heard her talking frantically: "Yes, fire, fire! 49A Clubhouse Drive!" Then she made one more frenzied call.

"It's insane!" Mama's shrill voice spoke into the phone. "Yes, of course! Joe's doing all he can to help! So," Mama took a breath, "Bernice, I need to bring the kids over so I can run back and help him. I can't manage a hysterical kid, feed the baby, and help remove everything from our house in case the fire doesn't quit. You can't imagine the blaze, sky high . . ."

Sirens screamed past the Jensen's house and suddenly Connor's eyes flashed open in alarm. Even I sucked in a strangled breath at the piercing sound as my baby brother and I stared at each other. Neither of us cried.

Mama ran to us, picked up Connor in his carrier, grabbed me by the wrist, and we rushed out the door. Ten minutes later, we were in Grandy and Gramp's driveway.

Grandy stood in the doorway, her face creased with worry. I ran up the porch stairs and into her warm embrace, holding on to her tightly. She held the door open as Mama rushed into the living room with Connor, lulled asleep once again by the car's movement. She placed him on his side against the back of the sofa and wedged pillows around him to hold him in place.

With a few words to Grandy about feeding the baby, she disappeared out the door.

"Mama!" I screamed, running to the door as it banged closed. I sure loved my grandparents, but I didn't like being left by anybody. For some reason, it hurt deep inside my six-year-old heart more than anything.

"Come here, sweetie," Grandy whispered. "Let's be quiet, Gramps is sleeping. Sit here with me, we can cuddle up for a little while."

Gasping back my good-bye tears, I let my grandmother take my hand and pull us together onto the chaise lounge. My body trembling, I tucked in against her shoulder, cocooned in her lilac talcum fragrance. As her fingers gently stroked my hair, I let go with the sobbing I'd been holding in since the car ride. Around 2:00 a.m. we snuggled into Grandy's large bed. Safe at last, my nerve flutters quieted and I drifted off to sleep holding my grandmother's soft, warm hand.

I dreamt.

I sat again in the Jensen's darkened living room and watched Mama jabbering into the wall phone, silhouetted in the kitchen light. The front door opened and a fireman in a black coat and bright yellow helmet slipped in without a sound. He carried a charred bundle wrapped in a dirty gray blanket and gently settled the form on the couch near me, then left silently.

Peeking out of the blanket, scared blue eyes stared up at me from a little girl's face. Her blonde hair singed, her white skin soot-streaked, she was a startled little mouse. The child reached out for me, then let out a pained moan, her face scrunched into a wince.

My heart hurt to see her in so much agony. I wanted to help, to tell her she would be okay, but I was afraid of this blackened heap of flesh. I pressed myself back into the couch and crossed my arms against my chest. I covered my face with my hand.

She's all burned up. Where's her daddy?

Mother came in then, grabbed my arm, and dragged me toward the door. As we passed the burned child in her scorched clothes, she gave me a haunting look. I reached out to take her hand, but her eyes were closed. Her face had gone still.

I woke up in a startled flash and stared at the ceiling as gray light filtered in through Grandy's gossamer curtains.

Half-awake and confused, I rubbed my temples and tried to remember the dream.

Did I really see a burned child on Mr. Jensen's couch? I need to ask.

Grandy's body was warm next to me in the darkness, but the sheets under me were damp. I closed my eyes tight; I knew what this meant, but I didn't want to.

"Grandy, I—"

"I know, dear. It's okay. Sometimes I wet the bed too."

Though I was surprised that she was awake, I was glad, too; her words comforted me. She wasn't mad at all and I loved her for that. "Let's get you into something dry and we'll put some towels down so we can sleep a little more." It was a relief to sleep as long as we needed. It was a much-needed first.

Sunday afternoon, I got to hold and feed Connor. He goo-gooed and smiled at me. My heart melted. Grandy fed Gramps and me a Swanson's pot pie, with coffee for him, 7-Up for me. I never got soda or this kind of food at my house. I felt like special company.

We settled into the chaise lounge to watch *Pollyanna* on "Walt Disney Presents" as Connor napped. Gramps sat in his overstuffed chair really close to the TV so he could see it better. He loved to smoke his pipe, and I loved the sweet woody scent that drifted over us. It was peaceful and my heart was calm.

I loved Pollyanna. She had lost both her parents and had to go live with her stern, controlling aunt. "May I kiss you good night, please?" she asked the sour-faced woman. In a strange place, trying to feel loved . . .Pollyanna was in *my* life story and I was in hers.

I didn't think about the fire. I didn't think about going home.

On Monday, Gramps drove my brother and me back to our house that was still standing and untouched by flames. We lived a mile outside Prescott, so Gramps drove us past groves of aged pine trees and crossed over a small creek surrounded by the yellow blooms of pussy willows. Manzanita bushes with their bright red berries glinted in the morning sun as we pulled onto the gravel driveway. I got out of the car, closed the passenger door, and stared, shocked.

The neighbor's house was now a skeleton of a blackened frame. Anxiousness burned my stomach as I took it all in. The small plot of grass in front of the house was scorched down to nothing. What were once trees surrounding the home were now just black trunks glistening in the sun. All that remained from the original was the concrete foundation and five cement stairs that led to where the front door used to be.

To the right of the burnt-out house was a small wooden building with our shared well. The side of the building closest to the neighbor's house was charred black, but our side of it remained unscathed. Our house was fine, with the sign that said 49A Clubhouse Drive. I sighed in relief.

I held Gramp's hand as we walked into the living room. That was when I second-guessed everything: this couldn't be *my* house! Living room furniture was stacked up catty-wampus near the stone fireplace and an acrid smoke stench hung in the air. Mama's normal spic-and-span housekeeping was nowhere to be seen. There was even ash floating in the open window. Fear rose up in me.

This isn't where I live! What is this place? I want to go home with Gramps.

We entered the kitchen and Gramps gave Mama the baby carrier with Connor in it. Daddy sat at the red Formica table, his eyes closed, a Chesterfield cig dangling from his lips, and a cold cup of coffee within arm's reach. Mama sat down next to him and placed Connor's carrier near her feet.

No one said anything. It was an eerie silence I could almost taste.

Instead, Gramps put his arm around my shoulder and I walked with him back to the front door. "You be a good girl," he said kindly. "Your folks have had a hard couple of nights." He kissed me on the top of my head, then pushed open the screen door, letting it bang closed behind him. I watched him walk to his green Chevy Bel Air, get in, and drive away.

Don't leave me, Gramps! Everything's a mess . . . I don't like it here.

I watched him go 'til a dust cloud rose up from the back tires as he disappeared.

My bedroom was just as big a mess with toys, books, and bed clothes piled in a heap on the mattress. The bed was still by the screened-in window, one bit of familiarity at least. I sat on top of the pile and lay my head on the windowsill. All the weirdness made me tired. I closed my eyes and the burnt child dream appeared again in my mind.

Where are all the kids from next door? We could have played together, except they thought my being six was too little.

On Monday, Daddy went to his American history teaching job at the high school, but came home early, his eyebrows and mouth drooping. Mama made me stay home from first grade to put my room in order, but I was glad for it. My insides were still shaking.

"Don lost his life trying to save his kids," my dad shared over lunch, his shoulders hunched over. "I wish I could have done more to help him." He took a bite of his cheese and ham sandwich and shook his head in despair. "Only his wife and one child escaped."

Maybe I really did *see a little burned girl on Jensen's couch.*

My stomach cramped.

"I'll see if we can get some folks out here to help with cleanup. Just terrible." He looked at me then, his eyes sad. I came and stood next to him and he wrapped his arms around me. "But you're okay, Tiger, aren't you? You're safe, Connor and your mother are safe, and our home is still here. I'm glad for that, anyway." Daddy looked at the floor and tightened his hug. "But I sure am bone-tired."

We were tummy to tummy now, his breath soft on my face, his eyes moist. My stomach turned to mush. His hugs were as good as Grandy's. I didn't want to let go.

"It's okay, Daddy. When I'm tired, I take a nap," I offered with all the cheerfulness I could muster. "You could do that and then you'll feel better."

Daddy held me at arm's length, gave me a surprised look, and broke out in a smile. I smiled back with all my teeth showing. "That's a good idea, Sug."

He gave me a quick squeeze, then headed to his bedroom.

Mama walked to the table, dripping a bit of milk on her arm from Connor's bottle to test its warmth. "Go back to your room, Miss, and don't bother your father. Go on, I have to feed Connor."

A throb started behind my eyes and made my face sore.

"Okay, Mama, I love you," I said, looking at her with eagerness, but she had already turned her back to me.

CHAPTER 2

SNAKES REALLY ARE EVERYWHERE

I *wanted* to be good for Mama like Gramps said, but no matter what I did, I couldn't make her happy. Her face was always cranky when she was around me.

Maybe I can get her to say I love you if I kiss her good night.

With the house back to normal, Mama and Daddy planned to go out to a Christmas dinner. I sat on Mama's bed and watched her get ready. A touch of red lipstick and some eyebrow pencil, then she patted her hair under in a perfect bob. She turned to me. "You don't need to do more than that to look your best, just a touch of color. More than that and you look like a floozy."

"What's a floozy?"

"Nothing for you to worry about. Go get on your coat," she snapped with a touch of annoyance. "Quit asking questions."

That Friday we drove down our dirt road to my grandparent's house once more. Mama's face was full of light as she chatted with Daddy, her full attention aimed at him like a flashlight. As we turned onto the driveway, tiny snowflakes began to fall on our windshield. Daddy switched off the engine, then shifted toward me in the backseat.

"Bundle up, Janet, and let's make a run for it!" He took me by the hand and we skipped in the front door with Mama behind us with Connor. She settled him on the couch next to me and went to stand by the front door. I bounced up and down with excitement as I watched Grandy and Daddy smile at each other. Their joy for each other filled the room and filled me. I'd get to stay a whole weekend wrapped up in it, two full days without feeling like a bad girl.

Daddy gave me a hug and joined Mama at the front door. "Thanks for sitting the kids, Mom. We'll be back later to pick up Connor." He held the door open for Mama, who pushed open the screen door and stepped on to the porch.

No cranky faces, no nasty smoke-stench rooms. I looked around at the warm adobe walls, the seafoam-colored carpet, and the heavy dark green drapes that held in the warmth. I leaned back and let the quiet surround me, like a hot bath on a cold night.

I flipped through the brightly colored pages of fairy tales in *My Bookhouse* books, Grandy's favorites from the 1920s. The evening hours ticked away. I even got to hold Connor and give him a bottle. His toothless grin and milk dribble made me giggle.

After Daddy and Mama took Connor home, I nestled down on the couch that Grandy had fixed up for me as a bed. The sconce lights above the couch and around the room made eerie slithering shadows all around the walls near the ceiling. I crunched down under the thick wool blanket and closed my eyes tight. Fiery blazes burned up in my memory, eating through all the foliage and trees in our neighborhood.

Think of something good—QUICK, QUICK! Um . . . maybe the fire killed off all the lizards, mosquitoes, and snakes. I can go play and not get bit . . . right?

I took a deep breath, then another, and willed my heart to slow down.

When I opened my eyes, it was Saturday morning. The nutty aroma of brewed coffee floated in and bacon crackled in the nearby kitchen.

Please God, let me stay here forever. It actually felt like "home": a place where you were listened to and given love and shown praise and shared answers with . . . none of that happened at my house, and especially *not* with Mama.

Later that morning, I opened Grandy's big white leather Bible as she washed and rinsed dishes in the kitchen. I dragged the heavy book off of a table near her favorite chair. I turned the pages of columned print, some of the words in red. The pages fell open easily to a painting of a man with light around his head talking with a woman.

The next page was the same man helping a ragged old man to stand up and, finally, Jesus hugging a little child. Wide-eyed, I flipped back and forth between the images, wondering why there was always a circle of light around the man's head.

Grandy came toward me, wiping her hands on her apron, then sat beside me.

"Who is that?" I asked.

"That is Jesus. He was kind, understanding, and did good things. That's what the paintings are about. You know, we talk about Him at Church."

"Oh, yeah, the pictures we color where he's knocking on a door with no handle."

I smiled up at Grandy and she put her arm around my shoulder. "Jesus knew how to love people, especially those who were having a hard time. He especially loved children and still does. You can talk to him anytime you want. That's what praying is; He's always there."

Grandy wouldn't tell me a fib, but I wasn't sure about praying, especially when I couldn't see who I was praying to. But mostly, I was glad Grandy let me ask questions. Asking Mama questions was scary. I wrapped my arms around my grandmother's plump middle. It made me feel warm all over, especially inside.

That afternoon, Uncle Ted sauntered in the front door from his job in Bagdad to check on his parents. He smelled like stale cigarette smoke and horse sweat.

"Hey, Janet," he said with a grin, "we should go find us some road apples."

He laughed a big laugh and I laughed with him. "Got some coffee for me, Mom?"

Uncle Ted talked in ways I'd never heard from Daddy. It was confusing and made me shake my head. He was an adventure all by himself. He made me laugh, but he also made me feel nervous.

When I turned nine, Mama let me go with Uncle Ted for the afternoon. We rode in Uncle's turquoise Chevy pickup to downtown Prescott. It was still the old West with cowboys riding their horses into town and tying them to hitching posts next to rancher's pick-up trucks.

We took the two-lane street past the railroad station where railroad cars with the blue-eyed Indian painted on their sides were being unloaded. Black men in undershirts threw boxes from those cars onto pallets. Their big muscles bulged with each throw and sweat dripped down their faces. Focused on their work, they never talked, not even to each other.

"Those niggers are good workers," Uncle Ted observed. "Even in dubaya dubaya II, you could always depend on them, though we didn't like 'em much."

"You say nasty words, Uncle Ted." I scrunched my face into a tight frown, scooted closer to my rolled-down window, and looked out.

"I do, honey?" he questioned with a laugh. "I just calls it as I see it."

He pulled in at The Palace Saloon on Montezuma Street and parked. "Hey, when I get back, let's get you a snow cone, okay?" he offered, his eyebrows lifted up, in a hopeful question. I scowled and refused to look at him. But when he returned with his brown paper bag, I broke into a smile. A snow cone *would* be nice on a very hot July day. I couldn't wait for Uncle Ted to get us moving so the breeze would flow in through our open windows.

We motored to the outskirts of town, passed the baseball diamond with its yellow patch of scrubby grass, then up and around and across the street to the back of the Smoki Museum. As we pulled in and stopped the truck, I saw a concrete pit in the ground with wire grating across the top. I'd never been *behind* the museum, only inside when Grandy came to volunteer and brought me with her. We hopped out of the truck and Uncle Ted went to the back, pulled down the tailgate, and dragged out a cardboard box with holes in the top. I walked with him, curious about the box that jostled against his arms. I could hear scratching noises mixed with twittering. Butterflies in my tummy flitted around at top speed.

I squinted my eyes up at my uncle in suspicion. Something bad was coming, I knew it, but I couldn't stop myself from walking onward to find out what was coming.

"I've got to feed these critters," Uncle Ted chortled as we stopped near the pit. Below under the wire grating, in the cool shadows, I saw fifty or more snakes, slithering around and over each other. They *looked* like rattlesnakes—what Daddy had warned me about since I was little. The chilling scene made me hold my breath. I was mesmerized and couldn't stop looking.

"They're just bullsnakes, honey," Uncle Ted said as he opened the top of the box. "They're not poisonous." He pulled up a corner of the grating and tipped the box over. A cascade of fluffy yellow chicks fell into the dark, chirping in alarm as they fell.

"UNCLE TED!"

Horrified, I ran, jumped back into Uncle Ted's truck, and buried my face in my hands.

I heard Uncle jump in and start the engine. I couldn't look at him. "Listen, sweetie, those wigglers won't hurt anybody . . . it's the human snakes you need to be careful of," he added as he lit up a Kent.

When we got to my house, I ran to Mama at the ironing board. It would be a long time before I let Uncle Ted take me anywhere again. How could Daddy and Uncle Ted be brothers?

"Mama, Mama, Uncle Ted fed baby chicks to snakes!" I screamed. Tears dripped off my chin as I grabbed her around her knees.

"Let go of me, Janet! I almost dropped this hot iron on you," she yelled as she pushed me away. "That's what snakes eat," she replied, turning back to straighten out the shirt she was ironing. "If you don't want surprises, don't go with Ted. Now go outside and play."

I went out to the sandstone patio where the picnic table and chairs were. Daddy would be here soon and he'd know what to say. I slapped the tears off my face, hard breaths pushing my stomach in and out. Catching my breath, I looked over my summer clothes and saw the hole in my jeans surrounded by pine pitch . . . that stuff never came out. Relief rushed through me, glad that Mama hadn't seen it. She'd be mad and I'd get punished.

When Daddy showed up from work, his hair was singed, he had sweat rings under his arms, and he smelled funny. Sunburned arms were speckled with dirt, but his eyes twinkled with mischief as I wrapped my arms around his middle.

"Hey, Tiger. Do you want to go with me up to Joshu's? I promised to help him throw the gravel out on his driveway."

"Yep! Let's go, Daddy."

I jumped in the Jeep beside Daddy. He got in, pushed his black-framed glasses up his nose, gave me a wink and a smile, and drove up a hill to the Joshu's house. The Joshu kids and I played on the Slip and Slide on a strip of cherished Arizona grass, next to the driveway, the only grass in the neighborhood. Daddy and his friend dug their shovels into the gravel and heaped it out onto the dirt driveway, talking and joking, perspiration soaking their shirts. Suddenly Daddy stopped and stood completely still.

"Well, look at that!" he exclaimed.

We all looked.

Neatly coiled in the bowl of Daddy's shovel was a baby rattler, hissing. Daddy held the far end of the shovel's handle while the shovel bowl and snake floated in the air at a distance.

"How'd you get in there, little fella? We must have disturbed your sleep."

"Kill him, Daddy!" I demanded, eyes wide. "Chop its head off!"

"Ah now, this little guy's more afraid of us than we are of him," he said, chuckling.

That's wrong! Snakes slither over each other in dark concrete pits and eat baby chickens. Doesn't he know that?

"All right, Tiger, you come with me, now," Daddy said as he carefully slipped the snake into a burlap sack. He gave me that "do what I say" look as he put the sack in the back of the Jeep. I grudgingly got in and we drove into the hills on a Forest Service dirt road.

" So, what's the problem with snakes?" Daddy asked as we passed through a thicket of pine trees.

I bit my lower lip and looked at the floorboard. "I hate them. They bite you when you're not doing anything, and they swallow baby chickens whole. They're slimy and poisonous."

"Well," Daddy began, his forehead wrinkled, his eyebrows drawn together, "if a snake sees you, it'll usually crawl away and hide. They curl up in shady places so's they don't get sunburned, and they eat field mice out in the forest, not children. True, some are poisonous but that's just to kill their food. The little critter back there is scared to death, that's why he coiled up and hissed. It's instinct for a snake. You understand?"

"Yes, Daddy," I sighed hesitantly. "Okay. But if I find one, will you kill it for me?"

He chuckled. "Of course; I'm always here to protect you, scamp."

When we got back, it didn't take Mama long to find my jeans with the knee hole. In fact, it was just the next morning. She smacked my bare rear end four hard times with the metal pancake turner as I jumped around and tried to twist out of her grasp, my tears flying everywhere. It hurt as bad as I imagined snake bites would—maybe even worse.

"It's for your own good, Miss! Now get busy and scrub those pants." Mama gave me a stern stare, then left me in the bathroom with a red face from crying, trying to catch my breath.

I worked on the jeans for an hour, but the pine pitch wouldn't come out.

Why does Mama have to be so mean? She could have just yelled at me and that would have been enough. Where is Daddy when I need him?

When school started, I wore the jeans as cutoffs under my skirt when other girls wore dresses and black and white saddle shoes. I'd come to the Ingalls with rickets and bowed legs, so I had to always wear solid shoes with good support. That was the way it was; it was no good begging. Mama said it was her way of taking care of me and I should be grateful.

Most of the time I liked being different from other people, especially when I was away from Mama. I was my own person then. Independent, chattery all the time, and a bit stubborn, being different felt good . . . well, until people made me feel bad about it. At school, being different was a pain. It was just like when I was at home alone with my mother. No matter how hard I tried, I couldn't do what the other students did with my drawings, even though I tried hard to create the way the teacher wanted.

I did okay with reading, but even then, I had to practice—a lot.

"You want to be smart like your father, don't you?" Mama asked after school one day. "So, sit there and practice. If you do that, maybe I'll let you help me cut up potatoes."

I nodded to that with a big grin, excited that Mama might let me do something with her.

The truth was, I was fascinated with stories—movies, music, books, I loved them all. The characters and plots, all the adventures in strange wonderful places, I could disappear into the scenes and forget what made me sad or unhappy. That part of schoolwork never felt like "work" to me, but I certainly couldn't share that love with Mama.

As she prepared a chicken for the oven, I tried to read the book Uncle Ted loaned me, *Smoky the Cowhorse,* but I was too distracted to read. I watched Mama scurry around the kitchen instead. I so much wanted to help, especially because she seemed to be mad at me most of the time. I needed to find a way to show her I wasn't always "a pain in the neck."

Connor started to whimper in the next room, so Mama shoved the chicken in the oven, took the bottle out of the warming pan on the stove, and hurried away.

Here's my chance! I'll cut up those potatoes before she gets back. Won't Mama be surprised and happy I helped!

Quietly, I tiptoed over to the sink and found the paring knife in the dish drainer. The potatoes were already washed and peeled, so I pulled out the wooden cutting board, placed a potato on it, and proceeded to try to do what I'd seen Mama do hundreds of times: hold the potato with your right hand, position the knife above it, and push down. With my left hand, I began to cut, pushing the knife through as hard as I could . . . but the knife went sideways and only cut off a *small sliver!*

Ackkk! My mouth twisted with frustration. *Try again.*

I chopped at the potato. Small, slivered pieces fell onto the board. Then I made another attempt at the remains. Each time I got a little better and managed to cut bigger pieces. I pushed the wrecked potato pieces aside, and placed another bigger potato on the board.

I'll do better now that I've had a little practice.

But after ten minutes, I still had only a pile of thin potato slivers and wet, starchy hands. I couldn't get my fingers to work like Mama's. Before I knew it, Mama was standing next to me.

"What are you doing?" she shouted with irritation. She scrutinized my sorry potato pile. "What's this mishmash? You can't do anything right!"

Eyes narrowed, jaw clenched, she pushed me aside with her hip and took over. "You'll have to learn to cut things with your right hand, Miss, like this . . ." She grabbed the remains of my potato and cut it into nice, even slices with her right hand, using her left hand only to hold the vegetable steady.

"I wanted to do *something* to show I could help," I replied softly. "Can I grease the pan and layer the potatoes in it? I've watched you do it lots of times."

"Oh, you've *helped* enough for one day," Mama declared. "Go read."

I slumped back on to my chair with my head drooped, my heart beating hard. I was still sitting there when Daddy got home, sadness a cloud on my face. For a moment, I hated being left-handed, being different. I couldn't do anything right.

"Hey, Tiger," Daddy said, as he saw my opened book. "How's you're reading? Real proud of you! Now, what's that face all about?"

I looked up at my father and made my face smile. "I don't mind the reading. It's just, well, I can't draw well at school or cut up potatoes for Mama, because I'm left-handed, Daddy. I didn't think being different would make people not like me."

He nodded in understanding, then wrinkled up his forehead in thought.

"Everyone has different skills and talents. Yours are just more specialized, Hon," he offered, not seeing the glance my mother threw at me. "It'll take time to learn how to do things in a world made for right-handers, but I'm sure you'll figure it out. Besides, didn't you know? Only left-handed people are in their right minds."

He let out a massive laugh, then pulled me out of my chair and gave me a big hug. I didn't have a clue what he meant, but his hug made my misery fade.

Daddy went over and put his arms around Mama, even though her back was to him. "Go on, Joe. I'll have dinner ready soon," she remarked, annoyance in her voice.

Now that I was in the third grade, I spent every weekend at my grandparent's house. That very next Saturday I stood next to Grandy at the kitchen sink and watched her smoothly cut up vegetables and throw them in a pot for soup. She handed me a knife. "Here, cut this sandwich in half and take it to Gramps."

I took the nasty thing and looked at it, then stared at the sandwich for a long time.

"What's the matter, Janet?"

"Cutting . . . I'm not good at it."

"Oh! Yes, I see; you're left-handed. Well, it's different, but it's all just cutting. Look, do this . . ." Grandy placed her right hand on my left and guided the knife back and forth in a sawing motion. The knife sliced through the bread, meat, and cheese like it was warm butter.

My eyes got big and my mouth curved into a smile. She was right; different wasn't wrong. It was, well, just different. I had to tell Mama.

"Mama doesn't like the way I cut," I murmured. "Maybe I cut different cuz I'm adopted."

"Well, honey, left-handed takes some time to learn. With Connor to take care of, your mama probably doesn't have much time to teach you right now. Besides," she added, "your being adopted means I get to have you in my life and that's a wonderful thing."

CHAPTER 3

DON'T TALK, DON'T SHARE

Grandy made me feel good and I wished I could be with her all the time. Being with Mama made an ache creep up the back of my neck.

Maybe she just loves Connor better cuz he's a baby and cute.

In October 1960, Mama, Daddy, Connor, and I drove down Highway 69 through desert scenery to Phoenix to see Mama's parents. The desert was wide open freedom, a feast for the senses, unlike anything I'd seen around Prescott. When I inhaled the fragrant air, my loneliness disappeared. We passed through the saguaro cactus forest, a squadron of green soldiers that protected the desert and all its animals. They were different from other cacti . . . different, like me.

My Lithuanian grandparents were always called Grandmother and Grandfather. Grandmother always wore a simple house dress; today it was with tiny blue flowers. She took care of everything and everybody, even me when we visited. Mama wasn't like her at all. But Grandfather was a different story. He always smelled nasty and had a beer or some other drink in a tall glass near him. None of us went near him when he was watching fights on TV, not even Grandmother.

We all of us sat together for breakfast the next morning, even Mama's quiet, scowling father.

With a big smile, Daddy made an announcement.

"Janet's reading now," he said proudly, giving me a wink.

"And Connor's sitting up now," Mama added, bouncing my brother on her knee.

"I think we should go to Baskin-Robbins to celebrate!" Daddy added. "And also to celebrate our new plans. We're moving to Eugene, Oregon next summer."

I almost spit out my orange juice. My stomach turned into a knot and my head started to pound. I stared at Daddy and watched him give

Mama a big smile and a "there, I said it" look. I barely even registered the shock on my grandparents' faces.

"I can't leave here, Daddy!" I burst out. "Uncle Ted is buying me a horse!"

"Oh, I talked with Ted, Tiger," he said dismissively. "He's going to let you ride his horses when we come back here for visits." Daddy gave me the "no arguing" look.

"This is about your father, Missy," Mama chimed in sharply, "not you."

"I've been accepted into the doctoral program at the University of Oregon," Daddy continued.

I jumped up from the table and practically knocked my chair over. Without looking back, I ran out to the date tree in the backyard and stood against it. Eyes closed, my heart beat wildly and my breath came in short gasps.

I'm too different to fit into a new place. Eugene, where is that? How far is it from Grandy? What will I do without her? Mama sure doesn't want me around. Life will be terrible.

Just like he said, Daddy moved us to Eugene the summer of 1961. The house on Clubhouse Drive was sold and we left everything I'd known for my first ten years of life. The drive there was long and boring. I rode with Daddy, his Jeep pulling a trailer with all our belongings. Connor sat in his baby seat on the passenger side of the DKW with Mama.

Blinding sun bounced off the truck's hood as we drove north with every window rolled down in both vehicles. Only hot air blew in and out from a weird desert that looked like something out of a nightmare, nothing like the one I loved. This one was all yellow-brown and dried up with dehydrated, gray-green bushes. I wanted the saguaro, the turquoise sky, and the fragrant desert breezes from between Prescott and Phoenix.

Instead, we journeyed through the dry hot ground of Highway 93 north. By evening, the landscape had become small hills. As the sun set, the landscape turned purple with twisted pink shadows. Hills shifted to mountains of dynamite-blasted granite walls that loomed over our truck. We motored through the towering rock formations and down into a ravine, snaking around in a figure eight, down to the Hoover Dam. The monstrous structure took my breath away. I gawked watching out the window, trying to take it all in. We inched along behind other traffic as we crossed over the dam. Off to our right, we passed the intake towers, giant sentinels that rose up from Lake Mead.

After a night in a KOA, we passed on through Nevada into California, stopping in San Francisco for a brief visit with an aunt. I looked around at the houses all crowded together up the hill above Fisherman's Wharf and the never-ending ocean. I was born there, but it might as well have been a foreign country. I'd always known I was adopted, but my brain held no memories of this city or the people who brought me into the world. Still, I was awed despite feeling, like I always did, that I just didn't belong.

Aunt Zella lived in one of the narrow three-story houses up a distant San Francisco hill. Her place had that familiar smell of coffee and cigarettes . . . and something else, something like moldy bread. She was a slender woman with a bounty of gray hair brushed back from her face. Daddy said she'd been quite a beauty in her high school days in the early 1900s. Now she sat quietly and listened, nodding and sipping coffee as Daddy told her about our plans.

After an hour he said, "We'd better get back on the road. It's good to see you, Zella."

"Oh! Wait a minute, please," Aunt Zella replied, as we got up to leave. She left the room, then returned quickly with a porcelain doll. She placed it in my arms and whispered, "This is for you, sweetheart. I want you to have it. She has real hair."

About a foot tall, the doll's hair was yellow and matched the little yellow flowers on her cotton dress. *A gift for me?* I looked at her in wonder. "Remember me," Aunt Zella whispered.

Who is this woman? I thought as I nodded at her. *It isn't even Christmas or a birthday.*

Joy ran through me down to my toes. No one had ever given me a spur-of-the-moment gift before.

Taking my hand, she walked with me to the front door to join the rest of the family. She gave Daddy a slight hug, nodded good-bye to Mama, then closed the door behind us.

We left the city and drove up the coast, past the ocean that never ended. Daddy looked far away as he drove in eerie silence. It was odd to be so still; the radio wasn't even playing. The doll sat on my lap all the way to Oregon. I had other dolls, but nothing like this with her shiny glass-like head, hands, and feet. Right then, I loved her best.

After two days, we reached Eugene. It was more green than anything I'd ever seen. Trees, flowers, and plant life were everywhere. I shook my head with astonishment. I knew we'd lived in a desert area, but I hadn't understood what that meant 'til now. I couldn't count all the different colors of green. And neighbor's driveways were right up next to each other, only separated by hedges.

We stopped and entered the house, crossing the lush grass that bounced back with every step. There were two bedrooms separated by a bathroom with black and white tile. Connor's crib was set up on one side of our bedroom and my bed was across from him. A dresser was in between, high enough for my record player and to keep away toddler hands.

In September I started at Willagillespie grade school. I was the nervous kid in a strange place with a weird name. Worst of all, it was raining. It seemed to rain all the time.

We're not in Arizona anymore, Toto.

Saturday, October 21 was just another drippy Oregon day, but today there was a knock on the front door. I opened it to find Grandy and Gramps standing on the doorstep. Grandy wrapped her arms around me. Her warm embrace made me gush big drizzly wet tears.

"Oh, sweetheart, I missed you!" she announced, kissing the top of my head.

She missed me? I was sure it wasn't as much as I missed her!

In the late afternoon, Grandy and I wrapped up in our coats and went out to the backyard. A sliver of sun cautiously peeked out through gray clouds as we sat on the cold steps. Grandy pulled out a piece of light blue writing paper from her pocket and handed it to me. Two vertical wavy lines traveled the length of the paper with a crude drawing of a creature crawling up between them.

"I saw that lizard climbing up my drapes last week," Grandy shared. "I got him off the drapes and put him outside under a pine tree. He actually had some turquoise color on his belly. Pretty little thing. It's not a very good drawing, but I want you to have it."

"Oh, thank you, Grandy! I'll put it up on my bedroom wall."

"There's something else . . . we've talked about Jesus before, but I want you to know He will be with you anytime you need Him. You can ask Him to help or comfort you. He's a friend you can count on. I do. Let me show you how to talk to Him."

Grandy took my two hands in hers and pressed them together. "Jesus," she prayed, "Janet's here in a new place without friends. So please let her know you're her friend, like you're mine, and that You love her. She's special, Jesus. Watch over and protect her. Amen."

When we waved good-bye a week later, I still hadn't put the drawing on my wall. Instead, I kept it in my pocket where I could wrap my fingers around it. It comforted me. I had a secret with Grandy.

With Daddy's school year already at a full sprint, he was gone most of the time up to the university. And, when he *was* home, his books covered the kitchen table where he sat reading and writing. Head down, face serious, he was too busy for good night kisses or hugs.

I missed him with a physical ache I'd never had before. But I had no idea how to tell him that. Wasn't I worthy of his time anymore because he was doing more important things? I was getting older too, and, even though we'd moved out here together, he was leaving me behind.

One November Saturday, Daddy finally took a break and came to sit with me and watched *Tarzan* movies. I could have jumped up and down but just smiled with my whole face instead. We laughed about Johnny Weissmuller swinging through the jungle in his loincloth, giving his Tarzan yell that made the monkeys run all over in the trees.

"Now that's a guy with great muscles, see? He was an Olympic swimmer before he started swinging around on a vine," Daddy chuckled.

"That's what I'm studying about, muscles and what they can do."

"Joe, the phone!" Mama called from the kitchen.

"Keep watchin'," he told me. "I'll be right back."

A few minutes later, Daddy rushed through to his bedroom, his face white, his eyes startled. Mama was right behind him.

"We have the money, Joe, don't worry," Mama's voice sounded from the bedroom. "What do you want to take? I'll help you pack."

Now even faster, Daddy rushed through the living room again and directly out to a waiting cab.

"What's happening, Mama?" I asked, no longer watching the TV.

"Daddy's mother's in the hospital," she explained quickly. "Uncle Ted wants Joe back in Prescott. Nothing to worry about; he'll be back here to take a final in a few days."

Mama brushed past me and into the kitchen.

Grandy's in the hospital? I stifled a feeling of panic. *Well, people get sick and go to the hospital all the time, don't they?* I glanced at the TV where Tarzan was still running about in the jungle. *Then they get better and go home.*

The next Thursday, Mama packed Connor and me into the car and we drove to the airport. As usual, it was raining and I hated it. I felt cold right to my bones, even in a warm car. Why did it feel like a heavy weight of falling water came from more than just the weather?

We parked where we could see the runway and watched for Daddy's plane to taxi in. A fog crept in and dropped the temperature even more, so Mama turned on the engine and cranked up the heater. The thick gray drifted over everything and made us invisible. After twenty minutes, I opened my eyes real wide and I saw a ghost of a man approaching the car.

Daddy suddenly walked out of the fog and came around to the driver's side as Mama slid into the passenger seat. His face a blank mask, he got in behind the steering wheel, turned on the headlights and windshield wipers, and we took off through a steady downpour.

No one spoke and my nerves began to twitch with the quiet. My breath came in rapid puffs as I worked up my courage to speak. I looked at the back of Daddy's head; his hair was damp from his walk through the mist and dripped onto the collar of his coat. I looked at Mama staring out the window, a hand over her mouth, her eyes dull and heavy.

Why doesn't someone say something? Anything?

My face felt hot and I clamped my hands together between my legs and stared at the floorboards.

"Did . . . did Grandy die?" I squeaked.

"Yes, she did. She was sick," Mama said, staring sharply back at me. "But that's all that needs to be said about it, Miss. We are *not* going to upset your father."

A huge rock formed in my stomach and I started to sweat. Nasty-tasting juices bubbled up into my throat and mouth, and I thought I might be sick all over the back seat.

Daddy parked in the driveway. I clamped my hand over my mouth and I ran to my bedroom. Crossing my arms tight against my chest, I swallowed hard.

STOP! STOP THIS!

I turned on the record player and cranked the music up as loud as I could. *The Lonely Bull* roared against the bedroom walls. I let music smother my spasms and stop me from reeling.

I fell on the bed and closed my eyes as the trumpets serenaded me. Then, as hard as I could, I slammed my face into the pillow . . . and screamed and screamed and screamed.

CHAPTER 4

FIRST AND SECOND LOVE

*D*o *people who die stay near the people they love? Can they talk to you from where they've gone? Can I smell them, maybe even see them? I can't lose Grandy. I just can't.*

After that rainy November, no one said another word about Grandy, at least not to me. From then on, there were no more Daddy smiles and no more *Tarzan* movies. 1962 was a clammy, cold winter and the '63 spring was just as soggy. I could hear the old Underwood typewriter hitting the paper as Daddy typed sequestered in his bedroom.

He might as well be a hundred miles away.

Mama brought him coffee, homemade cinnamon rolls, or Daddy's favorite, Hershey bars with almonds. She even took in his dinner.

Will I ever see him again? Why can't we just hug each other like we did after the fire?

Nervous and a little afraid, I made myself invisible at school by disappearing behind the library stacks whenever I could. Ray Bradbury helped. I wanted to fly in his story with the teen girl named Cyndi, the spirit teen who hovered around a live girl her same age named Molly.

How would it be to fly and be free . . . free of people who hurt you?

The story said on a summer afternoon Molly was walking home, then suddenly stopped and held her breath. There was something unseen nearby, she knew it. She had a special sensory gift and she was never wrong. She sniffed the air . . . lilacs, but there were no bushes nearby.

An unworldly presence? she wondered to herself. She knew about this kind of thing, and it wasn't always nice, something not to be trifled with.

Spirit Cyndi called out, "I'm here, Molly. I'm your friend, I really am." A warm breeze softly fluttered Molly's hair and tickled her chin, but that was all. Molly didn't hear Cyndi at all. *Maybe the "something" is an angel.*

In my hidden school niche, I sat up very straight with my back against the wall. I whispered to myself, "Grandy, are you there? Can you see me? Can I talk to you? Can I feel what you feel?" *Is this right to hope for, Jesus? My heart hurts all the time.*

But there was no warm breeze or perfumed air. I scrunched up my face in disappointment. Maybe it wasn't the right time, maybe it was too soon . . . *or maybe it's just Bradbury's imagination.*

One Friday in May, Daddy's friends from his University of Arizona days came to visit. It was the most color and joy I'd seen in his face for months. Roy and Margie Callahan joined Daddy and Mama in the kitchen and left me to visit their son Johnny in the living room. I was an inch taller than Johnny even though I was eleven and he was twelve, awkward. He had black hair and glasses and was a smaller version of his father, except for his brown, mischievous eyes. At 9:00 p.m., we bedded down in our separate sleeping bags on the living room floor, since Johnny's parents slept in my bedroom. I drifted into sleep as the adults talked and laughed around the dining room table.

Deep into my dreams, I was once again with the burned girl on the Jensen's couch. Her blue eyes flashed with pain, her white face streaked with soot. "Can I help you?" I asked. A hollow loneliness engulfed me. But she said nothing, leaving me frustrated and helpless. I couldn't help her and I couldn't help Daddy.

Grandy's gone too, what can I do for anyone anymore?

Suddenly, with a body shudder, I was awake.

Johnny's sharp elbow had nudged me and he was propped up on his hand staring at me, a nasty grin on his face.

I looked around, opening my eyes wider to focus in the dark. A dim light from the streetlights filtered in through the living room window and I made out the shadows of furniture and the steam radiator against the far wall.

"Let's get something to eat," he insisted.

"It's the middle of the night," I grumbled. "What time is it? I'm not hungry." I closed my eyes, rolled over, and pretended to go back to sleep.

"It's three. Come on! Let's sneak around and see what we can find."

"I don't want to. If Mama finds us, we'll be in a lot of trouble!" A familiar knot in my stomach began twisting up.

"I'm not afraid of your mama; besides they had some wine tonight and they'll all be zonked out in their bedrooms. Come on, scaredy cat. I dare you!"

I gave him a dark scowl, but he was already unzipping his bag and slithering out.

All right already . . . let's go look for something, you rattlesnake.

Johnny tiptoed into the kitchen, right up to the refrigerator, and opened the door. The blazing inside light bounced off the tile floor. I swiftly dashed to the entry and closed the door.

"What, are you, crazy?" I whispered.

"Nothing in there anyway," Johnny muttered, wandering around, opening and closing cupboards. "Okay, now *here's* something!" he declared in a loud whisper. Excitement filled his face as he took a bright yellow box out of the cupboard.

I rushed to where he was standing and saw the dark brown words: "Hershey's. Twenty-four bars. Milk chocolate with almonds."

"There's so many in here. We could take a bunch and they'd never notice!" Johnny chuckled, his eyes full of deviltry. He turned the box this way and that until he found a way to pry the end up. He grabbed six full-sized bars and handed them to me. I stared at the contraband, hoping they wouldn't melt in my hot hand and from the heat I was sure was coming off my face. Johnny took six for himself and put the box back. We raced to our sleeping bags, got in, and zipped up.

My heart was pounding so loud I was sure my parents would hear it, but so far so good.

I'd never had food in the middle of the night before, especially not chocolate! I unwrapped a corner, took a bite, and let the chocolate melt, warm and sweet on my tongue, exposing a bit of almond that I crunched and swallowed. Bliss! I gobbled down the first bar as fast as I could. Five more to go, all of it mouthwatering and delicious!

"We can stash our wrappers in our pillowcases and put them outside in the trash can in the morning," Johnny shared, revealing his plan. He'd obviously done this before. Chocolate? Oh yeah, I could get with that, but I wasn't going to admit it, especially not to *this* guy. But this was love! I couldn't swallow the chocolate and nuts fast enough.

The tight knot in my tummy eased up, relaxing a little more with every bite. It was fun—eating something forbidden in the middle of the night—and now it was curing my tummy problem that never seemed to go away since Daddy got that awful phone call. It even chased away the lasting images of that poor burned child from my nightmares.

Johnny watched me with a wicked grin. "I knew you'd dig this . . . it's a blast doing what we want, especially if we're not supposed to do it."

He was right. Eating forbidden chocolate brought back my "different not wrong" feeling . . . it also deadened the hope that I'd see Grandy's spirit.

I need to remember this fix.

That summer, we moved again. Daddy didn't like Oregon any more than I did.

The constant rain and overcast skies drove us back to the southwest. Daddy had secured a job teaching at Otero Junior College in La Junta, Colorado. He planned to return to Eugene in the summer to finish the doctorate requirements. Anything was better than muddy ground to walk home from school in and muddy shoes to clean in the damp cold on the back porch.

Like before, Mama drove with Connor and I went with Daddy in the truck he'd traded the Jeep for. Even though I was more grown up at twelve, my heart pumped fast and I could hardly sit still from being alone with the dad who had disappeared for months.

"How far are we traveling, Daddy?" I asked as we bumped along US 20.

"It's a long drive, Tiger. It'll take us two days to get to Colorado, so be patient."

A long drive meant I could sit closer to him and listen to my dad sing along with the radio. When *Wolverton Mountain* played, his voice rose up in a squeak with the yodeling soprano. I laughed as he screeched along, looking very serious. He jumped in with the lyrics:

Her tender lips are sweeter than honey
And Wolverton Mountain protects her there
The bears and the birds tell Clifton Clowers
If a stranger should enter there

"I like that story," Daddy commented with a chuckle. "Going up Wolverton Mountain to take Clifton Clower's daughter for a wife. Honey sweet lips . . .I can just imagine." Daddy got that faraway look in his eyes, like he did when we'd left San Francisco.

"Did you go up a mountain to get Mama?" I asked, wondering what he was thinking.

"Oh no," Daddy replied. "Your mother and I, well, that's a different kind of love, Sug. An everyday—you change the diapers, I'll take out the trash—kind of love . . . solid, dependable."

"I didn't know there were different kinds of love, Daddy."

"Many different kinds of love, different kinds of folks. Ah, let's stop for gas," he said, changing the subject, as we pulled into a gas station. I didn't like stopping because now I had to leave him and go sit in the DKW.

Mama played easy listening music on *her* radio as we pulled out on the road. I knew not to share about Daddy and girls with lips sweeter than honey or Mama's change-the-diapers kind of love. I was learning more and more the things that set her off. But she still took me by surprise sometimes with her temper.

Connor slept with his head against the passenger door, and I read my *Tom Sawyer*:

"Huck Finn and Tom Sawyer swears they will keep mum about this . . ."

There wasn't much scenery to distract me from my book, so I read on as we crossed the plains of Idaho, Utah, and Wyoming. When we crossed into Colorado, I remembered Daddy had told me, "Sixty miles from Denver to Colorado Springs; sixty miles from Colorado Springs to Pueblo, and sixty miles from Pueblo to La Junta." I did the math, even though it made my head spin. One hundred and eighty miles! No wonder the trip was long and boring.

As we pulled into the driveway of a yellow house, I read the last page of Mark Twain's book: *"So endeth this chronicle; it being strictly a history of a boy, it must stop here."*

Another new place, another new school. Dried out and dusty, like that nightmare desert we crossed by the Hoover dam. What is Daddy thinking? This is more disgusting than Eugene.

September came fast and fifth grade attendance at La Junta grade school. Another place where I was the new awkward kid. The school building had been army barracks during the Second World War and they looked like it; plain brown paint in the classrooms with squeaky linoleum.

Connor had morning kindergarten. Then he was home with Mama in the afternoons, and Daddy taught at the college weekdays. We had a routine . . . and it was miserable. I didn't fit in at this school and now, I *really* didn't fit in at home either. Mama was annoyed with me at every turn, so I tried to stay away from her every chance I could.

Things were also changing in my body . . . and boys noticed. The second week of the school year, I walked down the hall past three boys who huddled in the corner, looking at me and snickering. Now even more self-conscious, I pulled down the edge of my sweater and clasped my books tight against my chest. Now their chatter was louder. With no other way to get out of the building, I tried to hurry by.

TWANG! I felt the unmistakable slipping of my bra straps as my bra was completely unsnapped against my back. Everything was loose and I ran, clutching the unhooked bra as tight as I could with my books against my body, trying not to cry.

Laughter followed me, as I heard the boys congratulate each with words like "ta-tas" and "grapefruits." I raced to the house, my breasts completely sagging now in spite of holding everything in place with my books. I banged open the front door and let it slam shut behind me. I ran into my room, my face red and blotchy from embarrassment.

"Don't slam that door, Janet!" Mama yelled from the kitchen. "I don't know how many times I have to tell you!"

Books scattered across the floor as I fell face down on the bed and squeezed hot tears into my pillow, my sweater and bra all bunched up near my shoulders.

After the tears finally stopped, I turned over and stared at the ceiling and made a decision. I would be a straight *A* student for Daddy. He loved education and physical fitness, so I would too. From then on, I left out the backdoor of the school, unseen. I kept my head down, my chest hidden behind my books, and went in and out of the classroom as fast as I could to keep away from everybody, especially boys. Being a teenager was awful and there was no one to talk to about it.

That evening the dreaded gooey, gloppy canned asparagus lay slumped on my plate next to the fried hamburger and tossed salad with iceberg lettuce. I didn't feel like eating at all, but there would be consequences if food wasn't consumed to Mama's satisfaction. She always reminded me how she didn't even *have* canned vegetables when *she* was growing up. "So you'd better appreciate every forkful."

But that asparagus was still slimy and I couldn't choke the stuff down. The next morning, I faced the consequences: there it was again, cold green slop for breakfast. I didn't bother trying to chew it. I just swallowed back big hunks of it with a glass of half powdered/half real milk, then I ran out the door to school before Mama could make me scrape the plate clean.

Why do I have to be punished because Mama didn't have vegetables? I'm never eating that crap again!

Two months later on a blustery November day, Daddy came home with a mysterious smile.

"Mildred, *Lawrence* is finally playing downtown."

Even though he was talking to Mama, I still asked, "What is *Lawrence*, Daddy?"

"*Lawrence of Arabia*, a movie I've been waiting for, for months. I thought I'd have to travel to Denver to see it, but it's here in La Junta . . . finally! I'll go see it Saturday."

"Can I go, Daddy?"

"Well, Tiger, it's no movie for a little girl. It's a serious history film about T.E. Lawrence from World War I. I studied him and his time in Arabia. I've heard the film is good too."

"Daddy, look, I'm *not* a *little* girl now, see? I *like* history. Can't I go with you . . . please?"

Daddy looked at me with a straight face, as if he was seeing me for the first time. Then he looked at Mama. She rolled her eyes, shook her head, and walked away.

"Okay, Tiger, okay . . ."

I grinned at him, then left the room. I didn't want the adrenaline pumping through me to get out of control and make me jump up and down. I was going to be alone with my daddy, just like when we watched *Tarzan* movies.

That Saturday, I sat in the middle of the middle row at seven in the La Junta Fox movie theater next to Daddy. No one could spoil our special time, now that we were really here.

"This is a long movie, Janet, so if you want, you can put your head down and close your eyes if you get tired."

"Okay, Daddy."

Slowly the house lights came down and darkness surrounded us. I heard the projector start to whir. With the screen still black, drums started to boom, low at first then louder, more insistent, demanding. They reached a crescendo and a full orchestra blended in. Cymbals crashed with exotic rhythm.

I shivered with excitement. I strained my eyes open as large as I could, watching for color or movement on the huge black screen in front of us, but I saw nothing. When the drums died down, violins came up. An intense thrill coursed through me as the movie's haunting theme filled the theater.

What would I see when the film actually started? Arabia? What did *I* know? Camels, sand, men in long flowing robes, mummies? The drums were low now, a quiet foundation for the continuing violins and orchestra.

In the coming hour, Peter O'Toole as Lawrence filled the screen with his brilliant blue eyes and almost white blonde hair. His gifted Arab robes seemed to glow, a silver and gold curled dagger was at his waist. The sun was blinding and the heat was so hot you could see the waves of it in the distance. Armies of Arabs followed Lawrence to fight the Turks across breathtaking vistas of Arabian desert. I didn't understand the story, but I couldn't look away. And I had never seen anyone as handsome and charismatic as Peter O'Toole. I was mesmerized.

"What did you think?" Daddy asked as we drove home.

"I didn't know movies could be like that!" I replied, still in awe, having only seen movies on TV in black and white.

We walked into the house and I went right to my room. I lay down and closed my eyes, envisioning the actor I'd just watched for four hours, a quirk of a smile on my lips. I had a very serious second love crush.

"How was Janet at the movie?" Mama asked as she and Daddy walked down the hall. "That has to be the longest movie of all time."

"You know, she did fine," Daddy replied. I could hear a surprised smile in his voice. "She stayed awake the whole time, seemed to be caught up in the story like I was. I guess she really isn't a little girl anymore."

A different kind of warm pleasure welled up inside me. I'd made Daddy happy.

Maybe now *my parents will treat me differently. Maybe now I can truly be a member of the family and feel like I belong.*

CHAPTER 5

EVERYTHING HAS TO CHANGE

Back in Eugene for the summer, I could only do one thing right: getting everything wrong. When Connor got yellow jacket stings while picking berries, I tried to help, but Mama pushed me out of the way so *she* could take care of him. I still tried to cut veggies for Daddy's dinner, but nothing I did met her standards. I couldn't even vacuum properly.

We stayed in a fraternity house that summer, as caretakers, free of charge. There was a beautiful reception room with soft turquoise carpet and a baby grand I could lie under and read. There was a main floor, a second floor with twenty, single small rooms, and a huge communal bathroom. Mama made sure we used only one stall and one sink to make clean up quick and fast.

Being fourteen was hard enough, but it got even worse when I found out from a *Playboy* magazine in the basement that my body wasn't the right shape or size. Apparently, women were supposed to be curvy, tanned, and effortlessly confident. My chest was starting to get curvy, but I had short, dumpy legs and, according to Mama, a "broad backside." I wasn't even *close* to looking like the magazine pictures and I was definitely not what Mama wanted either. She was a slender size 10. I either had a lot of growing taller or exercising to do to reduce from a size 14.

I went to the local pool every weekday, but I still didn't win her approval. I just got exasperated eye-rolling from her when the scale numbers didn't move. At least my skin began to develop a golden glow. I looked forward to being leaner and more tanned when I went back to school next fall, and maybe a size 12.

Then, disaster! The grand finale to the summer was isolation for six weeks from chicken pox that I *did* manage to bring home from the pool. Confined in my room, I could hear Daddy typing in the fraternity library room down the hall.

Please come check on me, Daddy. It's hot, I'm so miserable . . .

But he never came.

I went back to school in La Junta, with a polka-dotted tan where the chicken pox had been. I covered up with long sleeves all year long. At least my *A-* average on my report card got me the, "Keep up the good work, Tiger" that I desperately wanted from Daddy. The grins and winks he gave me when he saw those letters helped me feel worthy of his love.

That was also the year two deaths hit our household: one was Sam, our old dog. Daddy had to have the vet put him down. No more Sam's eager face to greet Daddy when he came home. His passing hit my father so hard that he came home and went to bed for the rest of the day.

The second death sent the entire nation into a deep spiral.

On Friday, November 22nd, the school principal rushed into my classroom, his face white, his hands shaking. "Class, someone shot at our president," he said, struggling to get the words out.

What did he just say?

"The president of the United States, President Kennedy has been assassinated in Texas," he said, louder this time, his voice quivering. "Class dismissed . . . go home! Quickly now, get your coats."

We grabbed our coats, hats, gloves, and lunch boxes and hurried out the door. After the last student, the principal closed and locked the school, then charged out to his car.

I walked home, clutching my lunchbox under my coat to keep it out of the falling snow. I didn't like to walk and moved as fast as I could. My shoes and socks got wet from the snow that was coming down in a slant that was more like sleet. As I reached the front door, Daddy's truck pulled into the driveway. It was close to noon and Daddy was home for lunch.

"What are you doing home, Janet?" he asked as he met me at the front door.

"President Kennedy's been shot."

"WHA-?! That's not very funny, young lady!"

"I'm not kidding, Daddy. Someone's tried to kill President Kennedy."

Daddy rushed in and snapped on the TV as Mama and I joined him. CBS NEWS BULLETIN flashed across the black screen in large white letters. Then Walter Cronkite shared the shocking, unthinkable news.

Mama and Daddy stared at each other, their eyes huge, their mouths open. Then Daddy stumbled to the dining table, sat down, took off his glasses, and put his head in his hands. Mama gave his shoulder a quick pat, then went into the kitchen. I scooted into a chair next to my father and took his hand.

"What in the world? This can't be happening in the United States," he spit out. "I didn't vote for the man, but he's our president . . . this just can't be. We're not a banana republic."

Mama brought in sandwiches and sat down with us. I had my sandwich from my lunchbox and we all ate quietly. After the food, we returned to the TV and watched, sitting in complete silence. Mr. Cronkite was front and center. He put on his glasses and spoke to the camera: "From Dallas, Texas, the flash apparently official, President Kennedy died, at 1:00 p.m., Central standard time." He removed his glasses and looked up at a nearby wall clock, "Two o'clock Eastern standard time, some thirty-eight minutes ago."

Cronkite replaced his glasses, caught his breath, and tried to say something about Lyndon Johnson. He tried to get his composure back, but he was too choked up.

My father switched off the TV and stood up, his now pale cheeks damp. He walked down the hall to his bedroom and shut the door. I had never seen Daddy cry before—not when Sam died, not even when Grandy died. It made me want to cry too. I longed to go after him and put my arms around him, to help him feel better, like I did after the house fire when I was little. I looked at Mama who shook her head, then traipsed off to the kitchen without a word or tear.

I bowed my head, clasped my hands behind me, and shut my eyes tight. *What do we do now that the president is dead? What's going to happen to our country?* A spark of fear traveled up my spine as heartache settled in my throat. I picked up my school stuff, went to my room, and sat on the bed. I could hear Daddy softly weeping in the next room.

The TV was on all day Saturday. Long news reports flashed on all channels. All entertainment broadcasting was suspended until after the president's funeral on Sunday. Daddy watched with me as long as he could, then disappeared to the garage for the rest of the day.

Connor played quietly with his toys in his room and I went to mine to read. I escaped to Maycomb, Alabama reading *To Kill a Mockingbird*, the muffled TV broadcasting in the background. At least there was some morality in the fictional Alabama story. It softened my sorrow for the president's family, but especially for Daddy.

I came away from those terrible days realizing my father wasn't immune to grief, no matter how stalwart he always appeared. Two deaths within weeks of each other put him in an anguish I thought would never end. But I loved him more than ever for his emotional honesty. We were more alike in that way than I'd known.

For the next two years, we traipsed back and forth between La Junta and Eugene. Summers were full of hot, scratchy blackberry-picking, Daddy banging away on his typewriter, sequestered from the rest of us, and me exploring the empty frat house. In 1966, it was finished; Daddy was awarded a PhD in Physical Education. Mama made sure everyone called him *Dr.* Joe Ingalls now. She was prouder of his accomplishment than he was.

That last week in the frat house was also the week the foreign film theater across the street ran *Juliet of the Spirits,* by Federico Fellini. I sat by an open window on a hot summer night and watched the crowd line up to buy tickets under the flashing neon lights.

The U of O student newspaper described the film like this:

Juliet lives in a beautiful house by the ocean. Her sisters, and especially her mother, overshadow her with their beauty. She is spiritual, superstitious, and naive. [Later] she visits a psychic seer who tells her that she must follow the sex trade in order to be happy and she becomes intrigued by her sexy neighbor, Suzy.

Daddy laughed about that write-up early the next morning. "Only in Italy would they make *that* kind of film."

Mama tightened her jaw and red started to creep across her face. "Why would any woman want to do a filthy thing like that?" she hissed.

"Oh, Mildred, it's a foreign film. You know how they are. Not our kind of story. But those Italians . . . might be interesting to see the film, though."

I knew better than to ask to go along. Mama glared at Daddy from behind her glasses, then got up fast from the breakfast table pushing her chair three feet away. She snatched up the breakfast things and moved to the sink. I tried not to stare. *Something must be wrong with sex.*

"Oops," Daddy whispered, giving me a smile and wink as he pushed away from the table. He headed for the door with Connor in tow. *Or maybe something's not wrong with sex, but with some people's ideas about it? I sure wish someone would explain it to me.*

"Come on, Connor. Time to go with Ralph to catch some fish . . . see you later this evening, honey," he said as he looked at Mama. "You be good for your mama, Janet."

Mama didn't turn from the sink to say good-bye. With rigid shoulders, she slammed dishes around in the stainless-steel sink. I was glad I didn't have to go fishing, but in my heart I was sorry I never had time alone with Daddy since I was now a teenager.

Getting up from the table I thought about that foreign movie. Coupled with the *Playboy* women, sex and the symbols of sex seemed to be everywhere . . . and I knew nothing about it.

"Mama, can I ask you something?"

She nodded as water splashed into the sink to rinse the dishes. "Make it quick," she said brusquely, rinsing and tossing silverware into the dish drainer.

"I need to ask you about sex."

She shut off the water with a sharp twist and turned to face me with her arms crossed, wiping her wet hands on a dishtowel.

"What do you want to know?" she questioned, with an "I dare you to ask" glare.

I swallowed and blinked. "Umm, well, anything . . ."

Mama's lips curved into a mocking smile and her face relaxed. "Well, when you figure out what you want to know, come back and ask me." She turned away.

I stood there, staring at her, then I walked away. *How can I know what to ask when I know nothing except half-naked beautiful women are in men's magazines and something called "the sex trade" makes Mama mad at Daddy? Brain cramp!*

The University of Oregon was *the* place for all things track and field, Daddy said. It was the reason he wanted to earn his doctorate there. Toward the end of summer, his black friend, Perry, came by to talk about his training for the Olympic tryouts. Daddy hadn't brought any of his friends home before and it was exciting. Perry had beautiful brown eyes, an athletic physique, and golden-brown skin. His ready smile and happy persona made me like him instantly . . . and also because he tenderly held his wife's hand.

That's what handsome means. . . happy, healthy, and obviously in love. I really like the way he looks at his wife, Patty. Why doesn't Daddy look at Mama like that?

Patty was just as white as me, with blonde hair that softly fell in a pageboy cut to her shoulders. Her two young daughters were light brown, their hair in braids. Shy, they stayed behind their parents, peeking out only to get a glimpse of us.

Daddy shook Perry's hand and ushered us into the fraternity's reception room with the special plush carpet and tufted, rolled-arm tweed sofa.

"Joe, look at these shoes Bowerman asked me to try out. I really like how they grip the track surface. They have some kind of wafflely sole, Nike something."

Perry handed Daddy the shoes and they looked them over together. The U of O was all about improvements to track, helping runners run faster and win more races. Perry and Daddy bent over the shoes, turning them over, talking intently, totally oblivious to the rest of us.

Mama slipped away to make ice tea while Patty, me, and her girls pretended to listen. I smiled at the cute little girls who were holding hands and cuddled up next to their mother. The mom put an arm around the nearest girl and patted the shoulder of the other one as she leaned over and whispered to them.

That was how Grandy was with me . . . I like this mama.

It gave me a rush down to my fingertips and a little longing for someone gone.

Mama served ice tea to the grown-ups and lemonade to me and the girls. When glasses were empty, and there was no more to say about track and field, Daddy's friend got up to leave.

"Be sure to let me know how your trials go," Daddy said to Perry as they walked toward the front door. "I'm curious if those shoes will make a difference for you."

The men shook hands and Mama said, "Thanks for coming by, Patty. Maybe we could have you over for dinner sometime."

"I'd like that," Patty replied. "That would be nice, wouldn't it, girls?"

The girls nodded and then all of Daddy's friends shuffled out the door.

I watched Mama and Dad walk down the hall, chatting, knowing from my mother's demeanor that the family would never be invited again, much less for dinner. "I feel so sorry for those little girls," Mama stated. "They'll *never* be accepted by either race, you know. Their lives are going to be pretty tough."

I walked up the stairs away from my parents, bewildered.

That woman sure has weird ideas about people she doesn't even know.

In the middle of August '66, the frat house was put to order and the truck and DKW packed up for our last family journey, 180 miles south to Ashland, Oregon. Daddy was the new assistant professor of physical education and women's track coach at Southern Oregon College. We were finally going to stay in one place.

We got settled, then drove around the town. Ashland's Main Street descended to Lithia Plaza with its bubbling fountain of Lithia water that tasted like liquid iron. We drove through Lithia park with its canopy of trees, passing walking trails and small man-made ponds where ducks and swans slowly paddled around. The road traveled into a residential neighborhood with a smattering of houses. That was where our home was: a two-story house, bluebird blue with white trim.

"This is a much better place than Prescott," Mama declared, "a much better climate."

The town *was* beautiful, but it wasn't Arizona. I missed the fragrant pine trees with chattering squirrels, the saguaros, and the safe refuge with my grandparents. I even missed Uncle Ted.

My upstairs bedroom had two large screened windows that looked out across the lawn. A rocky wooded area was across the street where Lithia Creek burbled down the hill into the park. Swelling as it moved downhill, the creek fed the man-made ponds in the park. At night, the gurgling waters soothed my Arizona blues and helped me drift into sleep.

We were here for good. I stood at the window and watched the moonlight weave in and out of the foliage across the way and listened to the short screech of a nighthawk as he surfed the gentle breeze. It *was* all lush and green, even in October, just like the rest of Oregon.

Gazing at the landscape, my thoughts tormented me. What was my grown-up life going to be? One thing was sure, I didn't want to be like Mama with her nasty, controlling moods. I *did* love learning and education like Daddy, but I wasn't athletic or driven toward a career. I'd always thought I'd be with Grandy longer so I could become more like her. Always kind, she even brought in the mail for her bedridden neighbor and made her soup. She told me once that Jesus informed her life. Her convictions to be like Him were the center of her world.

I wanted to be that kind of grown-up. But how could I? Maybe if I went back to church. But my parents wouldn't let me because they didn't believe in the same kind of God, Catholic versus Protestant. Daddy also didn't like putting money in a collection plate.

My thoughts drifted in and out. I couldn't shut my brain off as time ticked by and the bright moon moved across the sky.

What is this life thing all about? Why are any of us here? Where did we come from? Where do we go after we die? And where's Grandy?

Will I ever see her again or is she just gone and there's no heaven, like John Lennon said? Does anybody know the answers? Not in my world.

I looked at the clock: 3:15 a.m.

I glanced up at the now darkened sky as tears welled up and fell. But what I saw, all the beauty of nature, had to be of God, had to be *His* creation. I closed my eyes and committed the view to memory, then laid down in bed. Determined to quiet my thoughts, I rolled away from the windows and willed the merry-go-round of emotions to stop.

I knew one undeniable fact: it was time to grow up and find answers to those questions that plagued my spirit. There had to be a place where I could be completely accepted, where I wouldn't be judged or abandoned . . . and I'd have to find it on my own.

CHAPTER 6

LET THE GAMES BEGIN

Prescott was five years gone and I missed it terribly, but there was no returning. I had to make the best of living in Ashland now. After all, it was home to the Oregon Shakespearean Theater, a replica of the original at Stratford-on-Avon. Theater existed long before movies or TV and it would be exciting to be a part of it.

In June, I got hired to work there, referred through the high school job program. I earned $1.50 an hour for three hours of work, five nights a week in the summer. I had some money for the first time in my teenage life. Thirty-eight dollars every two weeks was a lot in 1967.

The first of June, I tied on the apron with the theater logo, a huge smile on my face. Being in that atmosphere was thrilling. I had to be careful not to talk too fast to customers from sheer elation as I sold mini pecan pies and programs from the tray hung around my neck. And the best part was I got to sit anywhere there was an empty seat, twenty minutes after the play began, if there were no latecomers. For two blissful hours I got to disappear into Elizabethan England. Shakespeare opened my eyes about life, love, trickery, and revenge. Life in the 1960s felt the same on many levels.

An added benefit? I was away from Mama's glares and sarcasm. Everything I did was wrong and she was irritated anytime we were together. The hurtful truth I'd resigned myself to was that there was nothing I could do to please her and I had no power in her home. Trying to discuss school or life was excruciating and turned into heated arguments that ended with Mother saying, "Don't you forget, we *chose* you!"

I hated it when she threw adoption in my face.

But why did you choose me? You sure as hell don't want me. You should have left me where I was.

I *did* find bliss that 1967 summer in the afternoon watching rehearsals at the Shakespearean Theater. Adrenaline-fueled butterflies vibrated through me as professional actors from all over the U.S. pro-jected their voices to the farthest rows of the seats from the semi-round stage below me. They practiced swordplay and rehearsed lines with scripts in hand. Players embraced or kissed for *Romeo and Juliet*, and blocked choreography for a duel to the death for *Hamlet*. How did they do it? It all looked so real; their skills fascinated me.

I sat completely focused on the stage for four hours, oblivious of the hot sun. By the time I got home, I was sunburned on my head right down to my scalp. It was as beet red as my sunburned face. Mama doused my head with vinegar to stop the burning sting and plastered my face with a baking soda paste.

"P-U, what a stink!" Mama remarked sarcastically as I wrapped a towel around my head. Disgusted myself, I ran up the stairs as Connor was coming down.

"What's that smell?" Connor asked, wrinkling his nose. "Eww, it's you! I've never smelled a sunburn like that before," he chuckled.

I hunkered down in my room for the rest of the day, embarrassed. But it was finally quiet; the peace was nice.

Please God, make this smell disappear fast so I can return to the theater!

I had some money now, but it wasn't long before I learned I had no control over my small earnings. Mama made me put half of my check away in a savings account where she was a co-signer.

"Oh, come on, Mildred. Everyone needs a little jingle in their pocket," Daddy proposed one evening. "Don't be so hard on the girl. This is her first job! Let her spend her money as she wants."

Mama nodded in agreement, but when he wasn't looking, shot me an evil eye. Still, I was determined to use what I had as I wanted. It was a small taste of freedom and I relished in it. I bought Clearasil, which Mama refused to buy, and pantyhose for school since we were required to still wear dresses with stockings. At five-foot-five, I had curves now, though I still hid them as much as I could in shapeless shifts without a belt. However, I rebelled and let my always short hair grow out. Wavy and unmanageable, I slept in empty frozen orange juice cans to straighten it. It was my hair and Mama had no control. I loved knowing she was mad about it but wouldn't do anything to stop me.

It was July and my chore was to clean the bathroom before I left to watch rehearsals.

"See if you can do something right for a change," Mama sneered. "Flush the toilet first and push the water down so the bowl will be exposed. Then wash it all down with a wet rag and Comet. Be sure you use a dry rag to make the fixtures shine. And no cleanser grime anywhere. Finish before I run to the store, so I can check your work. Get your lazy butt moving!"

I tried to follow her instructions, moving as fast as I could. Putting my hand in the toilet was disgusting!

Why can't she just use a toilet bowl cleaner and brush like everybody else? Cheap, cheap, cheap!

I shined up the faucets and spigots with a dry towel, then splashed water and cleanser on the sides of the tub, trying to remember what it looked like when Mama did it. Suddenly, shivers began to run down my neck. I turned. There was Mama, watching, hands on her hips.

"What's taking you so long?" she huffed. She examined the toilet and gave it a shrug of acceptance, then looked at the tub. "I gave you specific directions and if you'd followed them, you'd have been done ten minutes ago. You're using too much scouring powder!"

She wrenched the wash rag from me and pushed me away. "Why do I trust you to do anything? I don't have time for this! Go to your room, no rehearsal watching for you today, Missy! You're pathetic!"

The tight knot in my stomach returned as I slumped onto the floor in my room. I heard water running in the tub as Mama grumbled about one more stupid task she had to do because "Janet was an idiot and couldn't do what she was told."

Maybe I am stupid, but I've gotta get away from all this!

It was no surprise that dinner three hours later was a misery. Mama ignored me while Daddy droned on about Lions Club, oblivious to the electric tension between his wife and me.

"I heard the best blessing on the food this afternoon, Mildred," he said, chuckling. "We had the pastor in from the Methodist church. He said, 'Let us all bow our heads.' We did that, then he said, 'Thanks, Lord . . . let's eat!'" I watched Daddy burst into laughter and I couldn't help but laugh with him.

Thank you, God, for Daddy's ever-present sense of humor.

If I was stupid, what was more stupid was having to find a way to survive one's own mother. I wanted to run out of the room whenever she entered and avoid speaking to her. Some girls went shopping with their moms, talked about boys and makeup, some even shared clothes . . . they actually *liked* each other. Being a teenage girl who could think for herself, I was as disappointed in *her* as she was in me.

We argued about everything, especially my need for money. With half of mine in an untouchable savings account, I was always broke. Daddy insisted I get a small allowance now that the theater was closed, but any mistake in Mama's eyes forfeited my money. A dirty dish or dried milk in the bottom of a glass when I washed dishes? Twenty-five cents each. If I forgot to take the sheets off my bed on sheet-washing day, it was a full dollar fine followed by, "You're worthless, Janet, I can always depend on you to be a screw-up."

I had an outlet from the insults: sneak eating. It helped when Grandy died and everyone went silent in '62 and it still relieved my misery. I was a size fourteen from the milkshakes I gulped down on my way home from school, but it cooled my temper.

"When are you going to learn that no one wants a fat teenage girl to work in their store?" Mama said that fall, after another job application was rejected. "If you'd quit eating greasy food, your face wouldn't *be* greasy and you wouldn't have all that acne," Mama said, giving my face a once over. "I know you pick at those things at night. Connor told me," she added with disgust. "Your face will be scarred and no man will marry you. It's bad enough you wear glasses and shoes meant for a cripple." She went back to stirring her spaghetti sauce.

Are glasses and clunky shoes my fault? Is this why Mama hates me so much, because boys don't make passes at girls who wear glasses? My future is about marriage?

"I wouldn't have such bad acne if you'd let me see a doctor. You'd take Connor to the doctor if he had a sniffle," I shot back, my anger rising.

"*What* did you say?" Mama replied furiously. She turned and stepped close to my face, her spoon dripping spaghetti sauce on the floor. "I take care of *all* my children as needed and don't you forget it! There isn't a doctor in this town who can fix that face of yours, miss. The mess in your mirror is your own fault. I know you're eating things at school you shouldn't be. That's why your pores are all clogged up. You don't deserve to have money spent on you when you're making your acne worse."

"Oh, what the hell!" I shouted.

CRACK! Mama's hand hit my face with a fierceness I didn't know was possible. I covered the slapped cheek with the palm of my hand.

"Don't you use that language in this house, young lady! Wait 'til your father hears."

"Mama, really, I—"

My mother looked down at the puddle of sauce on the floor. "Now look at what you made me do! I'm sick and tired of you and your attitude. Get away from me!"

I rushed up the stairs to my room, shame a hot throb pulsing in my neck. I looked in the mirror, saw the red welt plus all my pimply skin, and scabbed over sores.

She's right. I am horrible to look at . . . and I can't do anything right. I hate myself.

I sat on the floor with my face in my hands. After twenty minutes, a slow burn started to smolder.

"Mama" is a term of endearment for someone who loves and is beloved. No more of that! It's "Mother" from now on.

The following Friday rolled around and a call came for me from the neighbors. Brian and Karen were a young couple with an eight-month-old baby, Sara, whom I adored.

"Janet, it would be great if you could babysit for us on Saturday and Sundays 'til the end of September. I can lay out everything you'll need and have Sara's formula and baby food ready. Would twenty-five dollars a day be all right? Sara naps every day too, so you'd have time to do homework. Can you do eight-to-four?"

Twenty-five dollars a day was a fortune with the added benefit of not being home on the weekends. I agreed, hoping they'd pay in cash so I could keep my money to myself.

When I told Mother about the job, all she could say was, "Breakfast dishes have to be done before you leave, no exceptions."

Of course. I could do that.

The first Saturday morning in September, I woke up at six. I could almost taste the excitement of having money of my own. Breakfast came at seven, all the dishes got washed, and I arrived early for my first day on the job. "I'm so glad you're here," Karen said, smiling. "I can tell you're going to be dependable."

It was a peaceful day. I hadn't had one since the theater closed for the season. I loved little Sara. With her laughing blue eyes and her tuft of white blonde hair, she was easy to take care of and fun to play with.

On the second weekend, breakfast didn't finish until 7:45 a.m. I gathered up the dishes, then rinsed and stacked them on the sink, promising Mother I'd take care of them when I returned. But when I came in at 4:45 p.m., all the dishes had been washed and stacked in the dish drainer. I looked at Mother, but she didn't say a word. In fact, she didn't even look at me.

This could be good or *bad.* A nerve started to twitch in my face.

The next day, Sunday, breakfast finished at 7:50 a.m. I put the dishes in the sink and ran out the back door. *Why is breakfast so late now? Doesn't Mother realize I have to be on time?* When I returned, once again the dishes were washed and Mother was preparing dinner.

"Um, I'm sorry about the dishes. I wanted to get them done before I left, but there wasn't enough time. I have to be next door to watch Sara so her parents can leave for work. You understand, don't you? I would have washed them when I got home."

I watched Mother cut up vegetables, then add them to the roasting pan. She opened the oven door and shoved the pan in. Heat rushed out and encased me as my stomach ignited and pushed acid up to burn my throat.

She gave Daddy the silent treatment once, and it was horrible. Something terrible's coming.

I stayed upstairs 'til five and came down for dinner with every hair in place and clean hands. I sat at my place and waited with Daddy and Connor for food to be served.

"Mr. Wilson likes to start the mower for me, Dad." Connor shared about his job with the elderly neighbors. "It's kind of funny. I can start it by myself, but I think he gets a kick out of being able to still yank the cord."

"When you get older, you *do* lose muscle tone, so just let him do it, son. You're doing him a favor. It makes him happy, and that's always good; gives him a little exercise too."

Mother brought plates of food to the table for Daddy, Connor, and herself. I looked at Mother, stunned, an unspoken question on my face. She didn't look back. I looked quickly at Daddy. He was cutting his chicken and didn't look up either.

Here it is, the terrible thing. Will I get yelled at if I go get my own food?

I got up from the table, walked to the kitchen, filled a plate, and returned to my chair. No one looked at me, not even Connor. I ate as quietly as I could as conversation crossed back and forth between the parents. When dinner was done, Mother took everyone's plate and cutlery to the kitchen except for mine.

I'm invisible. Okay, maybe this will turn out to be a good thing. I can eavesdrop.

I snuck away to my room, then crept down the stairs as far as I could without being seen. I listened for the conversation between my parents, but they were too far away in the living room with the TV on. I tiptoed down the stairs, took my dishes off the table, and washed them.

Mother's "silent treatment" gave me an empty feeling, like a hole was drilled through my middle. It was more demoralizing than being yelled at. Day in, day out, no one looked at me, talked to me, or acknowledged my presence. A dark gloom hung over me I couldn't shake.

Will that witch ever stop punishing me? For what, dishes? She's enjoying this.

On Monday, the last week of September, Daddy drove me to school. A gentle breeze came through the half-open windows, bringing with it the musky, sweet scent of fallen leaves.

"Why is Mother doing this, Daddy? Why won't she talk to me or even yell at me?"

"You'll have to take that up with her, Janet."

A flash of anger rose up. It was with me almost all the time now.

"I think she hates me, Daddy. Can't you see what she's doing?"

Daddy didn't say anything. He just watched the road and drove.

"Please talk to her, Daddy. Get her to stop."

"Here we are at your school. Pay attention to your teachers," he said dismissively.

I turned to give him a kiss, but he was staring out his window, waiting for me to get out.

I watched as he drove away, totally dumbfounded.

What is the matter with him?

I stopped going down to dinner. Instead, I waited until everyone was in bed, then stole into the kitchen, made myself a sandwich, and drank some of the pretend half and half milk. I never felt like I fit in and now, here was proof that I was right.

The last Sunday in September was also the last day of work. The Harrisons paid me my last fifty dollars and we said our good-byes. I already missed them and especially little Sara. I walked sullenly back to our property and right out to the garage. I couldn't face going in the house. Not right now. I climbed the ladder to the stuffy loft and sat down. The sun was going down and shadows slinked across the dirty floor. Alone, I was just dead weight on the planet.

I wrapped my arms around my knees. Tears fell, unending and heated, like my stomach that was always on fire now. I was one immense ache from my toes to the top of my head. A black impenetrable misery covered me and seeped in, smothering any desire to do right.

I swayed back and forth, my eyes clenched tight, biting my lips. I rocked against the hard wooden floor until my tailbone ached. When I stopped, it was dark outside.

"AAHHH!" My anguished cry shocked me out of lamenting.

"Enough of this!" I spat out in anger. *I hate her! She chose me? I don't choose her! Who does she think she is? No real mother would do this to their child. But I'm not her child, am I? Why doesn't Daddy do something? He's afraid of her, too, I'll bet. I'll burn the house down with them in it.* I shook my head. *No, I can't do that to Connor.*

An hour later, pitch dark and chilly, I climbed carefully down the loft ladder and walked across the cold grass to the house. The living room lights were on and Mother sat on the couch knitting. Daddy was in his maroon, overstuffed chair reading the paper. Connor must have gone to bed, because his room was dark.

I cracked open the front door and stepped into the foyer, ready to cross through the dining room and go up the stairs.

"Is that you, Janet?" Daddy called. "We were worried."

"I just wanted to think."

"I left some food for you in the kitchen," Mother said absently, "It's in the oven. Be sure to turn it off when you take the food out."

I stood there, dumbfounded. *It's like nothing's happened. What if I never speak to her again? She can control a lot, but she can't control my thoughts.*

From that day on, I kept my mouth shut and stayed away from Mother whenever I could.

Eavesdrop whenever you get the chance and stay invisible. There's one more year of high school. You'll survive if you're careful. To hell with her—to hell with all of them!

CHAPTER 7

LET'S BE DISOBEDIENT

I loved biology class, especially because in October '67 I met Kip Jensen. He was no Peter O'Toole, but he was tall and broad-shouldered with a shock of reddish-gold hair. His smile could warm any mother's heart, except probably mine.

Kip had a reptile collection in the back of the biology building that included a python about five feet long that swallowed baby mammals whole. Shades of Uncle Ted!

"I'm a herpetologist," he told me one morning, his brown eyes gleaming. "Here, wanna hold a snake? Isn't she amazing?"

I was glad we were alone so no one could see my face go white. I stared at the massive snake and gulped back my repulsion.

"Yeah, well, I'm not fond of snakes," I confessed as I slowly backed away. Kip didn't notice my jitters. He just walked over and wrapped the huge thing around both of my arms. My mouth gaped open and I sucked in my breath. The "she" was tan with large dark brown spots, smooth and shiny, with strong muscles that rippled against my arms.

Not slimy, but still disgusting. This boy better think I'm amazing for just being here!

"Isn't she beautiful?" Kip gushed, his face full of excitement. "She'll get to be sixteen feet by the end of the year. Look at you, holding Bella! No other girl has done that!" He flashed me a proud smile.

"She's big, all right . . . heavy too," I replied, as a rat-sized knot formed in my stomach. I gritted my teeth and tried not to wretch.

I'll put up with this because Kip is just weird enough to be interesting.

"Hey, Dean said your church is having a dance. I wonder if you would take me," I offered casually as Kip began to unwind his pet from my arms. There was a tense quiet as he walked back to the twenty-gallon tank sitting on the floor. He gently dropped the reptile in and closed the wire screen over the top. He picked up his books, and when he looked at me, his face started to flush.

"Ah, I'll see if Dean has room in the car; there's a bunch of us going," Kip replied hurriedly, walking to the door. "I gotta go to class."

I hope he won't forget to ask Dean; I don't want to spend another Saturday night at home. Besides, I thought as I quickly raced down the hall, *he's cute and it might be a first date!*

Two weeks later, when the Ingalls held a BBQ, I escaped to a church dance with Kip the snake boy, his friend Dean, and two other girls. *I'm leaving the house on a Saturday night, just like other teenagers. Hurray!* I practically oozed elation, my smile taking up my whole face.

"The dance is at the stake center," Dean offered as he drove toward Clay Street.

"Oh, is it a restaurant of some kind?" I asked innocently.

My four new friends burst into laughter. Embarrassment colored my face as I looked at Kip. He hunched up his shoulders, grinned a little, and patted my hand, then quickly pulled away. I wondered if this was *his* first date, too. He was shy . . . and then he wasn't.

"No, Janet," Dean explained kindly. "It's just what we call the bigger church building where we have activities." He paused. "It confuses a lot of folks. We'll have refreshments but definitely not steak." He turned and gave me a quick smile and I breathed a sigh of relief.

We walked into a large gym-like room with shiny wood floors, a basketball hoop at one end, and a stage where someone was manning the recorded music equipment. People of all ages were on the dance floor: older men with plaid shirts and khakis and, what I assumed, were their wives in dresses and pumps. Teen girls were on the floor or standing in groups dressed in jeans, white frilly blouses, and cowboy boots. I hadn't seen outfits like that since we'd left Prescott.

I was out of place in my homemade skirt and matching blouse. Maybe I could hide in the car. Then a nicely groomed forty-something man asked me to dance and we waltzed around the floor. When finished, he bowed and walked away as Dean approached and offered his hand for a dance. I went from one dance into another. I was actually enjoying myself!

We drove home at eleven, my heart still beating rapidly, my senses exhilarated. I couldn't stop smiling. There was no sign of Kip, but I didn't care. I felt wonderful.

"Is it always like that? Everyone dancing with everyone else? What a ball!"

"Oh, we Latter-Day Saint types know how to have a good time," Dean grinned. "If you'd like to come to another activity, I'll give you a call."

Wow, Dean's really cute. Maybe this will turn into something since Kip's not here.

To spend an evening where I wasn't being ridiculed? Hanging out with people who accepted me? Of *course*, I'd love to go again!

The next Monday, the phone rang and Daddy answered. "No, but thanks for calling." He hung up and turned to me. "Janet, come join me in the living room."

I sat on the ottoman near him, delighted to be alone with my dad after such a long time. It was like old times before the PhD, before chicken pox, before becoming a teenager.

"I have to explain about Mormons," Daddy said in a no-nonsense voice.

My mouth gaped open, realizing he was talking about the "LDS" kids I'd gone to the dance with. *What?*

"They're good people, like Baptists or Methodists or anybody else, but they believe in this nut named Joseph Smith who claimed to see some kind of gold book with magic glasses that an angel gave him. How can you believe a cockamamie story like that?" he stated in a rush.

"Wow. Right, Daddy." I was stunned, my eyes wide open.

Are my new friends all cuckoo? Daddy has a PhD, so he must *be right.*

"Some of their missionaries just called," Daddy added. "They wanted to come teach you about their church, but now you know the truth."

"Yes . . . but I *did* have a good time Saturday. I'd like to go out with them again."

"Well, let's jump off that bridge when we come to it," he said, smiling. He tousled my hair, gave me a quick hug, then left me to ponder his words. Watching him go, loneliness for Daddy fell over me like a heavy blanket.

The next Saturday I had the dreaded bathroom chore again. After the last fiasco, I hoped Mother would be disgusted enough to release me from the responsibility, but no. She stood in the bathroom doorway with the cleaning stuff, her face unreadable.

I took the cleaning things, waited 'til she was gone, then started in. I was careful to follow her directions exactly. I even cranked open the old-style window to let in the fragrant autumn breeze. Before ten minutes had passed, she was standing behind me once again.

"Are you *ever* going to be finished in here?" Mother spit out. "I see you're doing your half-baked job again. Can't you ever do anything right?"

Rage coursed through me, a fire ignited in my stomach. I stood and faced the woman.

"I *am* doing it right, just like you taught me!" I said hotly. "Maybe I'm not as fast as you, but at least you're getting free labor!" I said, my voice rising.

"Are you talking back to me? Who do you think *you* are? Who pays the bills around here, keeps you clothed, puts a roof over your head?"

"Uh . . . Daddy?"

Her arm pulled back, then her open palm slammed into my face. *CRACK!*

The slap burned. She knew how to deliver pain.

As if I were on autopilot, *my* arm shot back too and then *SMACK!* My hand slammed into her cheekbone.

We stared at each other for a split second, then Mother burst into laughter.

"Do you feel better now? Want to hit me again?" she snarled.

Defending myself hadn't done any good . . . how disappointing! Nausea rose up in my throat as I took off running. I dashed down the stairs and out the front door, letting it slam behind me.

"Where are you going?" Mother screamed, chasing me. "Come back here!"

I ran past the elderly neighbor's house. I heard her behind me, still yelling and calling me names.

Why is she chasing me? She's making a fool of herself right out in the open!

It was disorienting, a teenage daughter being chased by her mother. And she was closing in. All those morning runs to please Daddy were paying off for her while I was panting, breathing hard.

"You, stop . . . come BACK here!"

I didn't. . . I couldn't. I ran down the street, crossed the street, then turned and started up the hill above Lithia Creek. I scrambled in a panic state, shaking, breathing in quick gasps.

She's mad! What if she catches me?

Adrenaline pushed me as sweat drenched my shirt. I grabbed at weeds to pull myself higher up the hill, but I finally had to stop to catch my breath. I looked down and saw Mother standing on the road thirty feet below, her hands on her hips.

"What a brainless idiot you are. You'll be sorry for this, Janet!"

I was already sorry, sorry I hadn't escaped that demented woman sooner.

I hope the neighbors see this maniac with her wild hair chasing her daughter down the street!

I turned back to the hill and continued climbing. I pushed past pine trees and scrambled around bushes 'till I reached the top after a twenty-minute ascent. I sat down on a boulder with my eyes closed tight against the pounding in my temples. I was tired of being hit, sick of her tirades, her sarcasm, her name-calling. I was nauseous from hearing what a disappointment I was.

Do I have to go back? Is there foster care, even though I'm only a year away from graduation?

My breathing slowed to normal and I opened my eyes. A paved road meandered into a neighborhood just below me, and I suddenly realized where I'd climbed to: the neighborhood of high school's brainy Valerie.

Thank you, God!

I ran down the hill, into her yard, and knocked on the back door.

Valerie opened it and gave me a stare. "Janet! What happened? You're a mess, you've got leaves in your hair. You better come in."

How could I explain that I was running away from a psycho mother? I brushed the leaves out and straightened my clothes.

I'd only been in Valerie's home for a few minutes, but I already felt safe. In the sitting room, her father looked up from his paper as I came in, then stood up to greet me. With salt and pepper hair and rimless glasses, he had a kind face like the Daddy I used to know.

"Good to meet you, Janet. You're just in time for dinner."

"Um, thank you? " I stuttered.

I show up out of nowhere and they invite me to dinner? I like this place!

I sat next to Valerie as a woman in a white apron placed food on our plates. Before me were grilled steak, au gratin potatoes, and a side of fresh green beans. I was grateful my nerves were calming down and the fiery tummy was just a smolder now. Grateful, too, that neither Valerie or her father asked questions.

I dug my fork into my food, realizing I'd built up quite an appetite. Listening to Valerie and her father talk, I nodded my head as I ate. She asked about his stockbroker work . . . and he responded! My fork stopped halfway to my mouth in awe.

"It's a bull market right now, so when your mother gets home, she'll be glad we moved our investments," her father shared between fork-fuls of potato.

"But Dad, didn't the S&P fall off 9 percent? You should tell your clients to stay put."

Father and daughter talking like two equals? My mind is blown.

After dinner, Valerie, her father, and I returned to his sitting room. He gave me an encouraging friendly smile.

"I don't know what's happening in your life," he said, pausing, "and you don't have to tell me, but I wouldn't let your fears control you. Fear's like a red light. You get to stop and think for a few minutes about what action to take next."

I smirked and rolled my eyes. *If he only knew.*

"No, don't roll your eyes," he continued, with a slight chuckle. "You can't outrun fear; I know from where I speak, believe me. It's better to turn and face it. You'll be stronger for it."

"Yeah, well, facing fear can be dangerous too," I said politely, rubbing my hand on my sore cheek.

"Maybe," he said quickly, "but just know you're not alone; everybody's dealing with something."

Valerie and I looked at each other and snickered.

"I know you've left something behind, so go forward and face whatever *this* is."

"Thank you. I'll give it some thought," I said as Valerie and I got up to leave. We climbed the stairs to her bedroom, a room so clean you could eat off the polished wood floors! I envied her matching Bassett dresser, nightstand, and queen-sized bed. It looked brand new, unlike my twin hand-me-down bed I'd had since I was ten.

The next morning, I timidly told Valerie everything, leaving out the part where I slapped Mother. I'd have to come to terms with that later.

"I thought it was something like that," Valerie said gently. "I didn't want to ask since I could see how upset you were. I wish you could stay here, but I don't think that'd work out for either of us. But maybe you can stay 'til we go to school Monday."

A good thirty-six hours away . . . yes, that will work. I'll think of something by then. Maybe I can talk to the school counselor.

Monday morning, Valerie loaned me a dress and her dad drove us to school. He parked the car, then turned to me.

"You're a smart girl," he said with compassion. "Val doesn't have stupid friends so I know you can manage whatever it is that brought you here."

"Thanks," I replied. I wasn't convinced, but I had come up with a plan.

Around noon, I walked to Mrs. Wick's office and knocked on her closed door. When she said, "Come in," I did. She looked up at me with a smile, then became serious.

"Hello, Janet, have a seat. I can see you have a problem. School, home, boyfriend?"

"Home, Mrs. Wick. My mother, well my *adopted mother*, hates me," I began. Once I started talking, I couldn't stop. I'd never told the truth about home to anyone, especially not to an adult. The telling lifted an emotional weight off of me I didn't realize I had. I even *felt* lighter.

The counselor quietly took notes. Then, when I took a breath, she replied, "I'm glad you came to see me. Let me see what I can do. I'll be back in a few minutes," she offered as she left the office.

Is she going for the principal? Maybe I'll get some help now that someone on the outside knows my secrets. Maybe she's calling foster care. I've heard things about those places, but it can't be any worse than where I am.

After ten minutes, Mrs. Wick returned and sat down across from me. "I think it will be good to discuss all this further when your mother arrives. She's on her way."

The color drained from my face and I began to shake.

"Here, let me get you some water!" the counselor gasped. She went out and came back with a paper cup filled to the brim. I gulped it down, then looked at the floor.

There's no way out. I'm lost. I'll be locked in my room or beaten black and blue.

Within fifteen minutes, Mother knocked on Mrs. Wick's door and was ushered in. She shook hands with the counselor and smiled like she had just come to a tea party with friends. The two women exchanged a few words about me, like I wasn't there: the troubled girl with acne going through her teenage angst, feeling unloved, and picked on.

"I'm sure we can resolve this problem at home, Mrs. Wick. But thank you for giving so much of your time to my daughter."

The two women shook hands again. Mrs. Wick gave me a kind nod and I followed Mother to the car. It was deadly silent as we drove home.

I walked into the house and turned to go up the stairs, but Mother grabbed my arm and pulled me back. With a look of disgust in her eyes, her lips thin, she stepped back a little and clenched her fist. *Is she going to punch me?*

I could hear Daddy running the lawn mower out back, and I said a silent prayer that Connor was out there with him.

Please God, help me. Don't let me do something I'll regret.

I yanked my arm away and stood stock still. I crossed my arms and starred back at the woman, my chin up.

"Don't you ever do that again!" Mother shouted, as if I was across the room. "We do *NOT* air our family laundry to strangers. Capisce . . . understand? And next time you run away, make sure it's for good." She turned on her heel and stalked off to the living room.

I went to school the next day as if nothing had changed, but everything *had* changed. I wasn't sure if Valerie's family was the norm, but after yesterday, I was sure my family was off the freaking deep end. Why was I treated like a tramp off the street just because I was adopted? Why was I adopted at all? I never cared much about it before, but every day I was becoming more disconnected from the Ingalls. All the secrets about my past had to be uncovered. I needed answers now like never before.

"Remember, we chose you . . ." What a load of crap.

June 1970 finally came and high school was done.

On my graduation evening, I was called into the living room.

Smiling, Daddy said, "I'm proud of you, Janet, but I knew you could do it. Now I'll enroll you at Southern Oregon College. As a professor I can get you in with a small cost, so let's start you this summer and see how you do."

"Oh Daddy, I love it! Thank you! I *do* love to learn," I replied as I moved in to give him a hug. There was hope for the future.

Suddenly Mother stopped knitting and looked up. "Wait a minute, Miss. Aren't you a little too old for hugging?"

CHAPTER 8

COME WHAT MAY

*Y*ou *have real freedom now, Janet . . . let that sink in. No more being gaslighted, no more unfair punishment. No more skulking around, trying to stay invisible to keep out of trouble.*

I breathed in a long, deep breath and let it out in a burst. Summer was here! The months moved fast as I continued to work at the Shakespearean Theater in the evenings, staying for plays when I could. During the days, I worked in the dorm cafeteria, a job Daddy had arranged. The rest of the time I was in class. And I didn't have to deal with Mother.

I got $2.50 an hour at the dorm job, and I went right to human resources to pick up my check and cash it at the school credit union. The first time I put that money in my pocket, a thrill of power ran through me. Cold, hard cash coupled with freedom to come and go as I wanted, total bliss! I did miss Connor, but I liked being alone more. I was finding my own way into a life *I* was choosing, whatever that turned out to be.

With the fall came more serious classes, including biology, this time with Latin terms and long reading assignments. One Friday, the third class of the week, a man with a fierce, bronzed face showed up and sat down at the desk to my left. He had short brown hair, tanned arms, and a slim, muscular physique. I gave him a welcoming smile, but he never looked up. With polished black boots, olive-green pants, and a cotton plaid shirt, I liked him instantly. I wasn't sure why, but I wanted to get to know him. Finally, he met my gaze.

What a sober face.

"Hi, I'm Janet," I offered.

"Dave . . . uh, hello."

He gave me a cautious smile, then looked back at the instructor. His demeanor was different, no teenage goofiness, not even a sense of insecurity.

Serious intensity . . . and something else too. What am *I feeling?*

Class ended and we walked to the door at the same time. He gave me a quick look, then a little smile. "Uh, can I give you a ride somewhere?" he asked. As we exited the building, he lit up a hand-rolled cigarette. "I don't have much studying, so I could drop you somewhere."

"Yes, that would be nice, thanks," I replied, feeling a little nervous but also hopeful for this new beginning. "I'm just going to the other side of campus for my job."

We walked to his red Dodge Dart and he opened the door for me. Five-foot-seven, a couple of inches taller than me, he had muscular arms, and a solid chest to match.

"Are you from around here? I don't remember seeing you, not that I get around much anyway," I offered, settling in on the bench seat.

"No, I'm from a small town about two hours from here," Dave explained. "My dad has a ranch. I just got back from military duty."

"Ah, that explains your green pants," I said with a big smile, hoping he'd open up a little. "Can I ask where you served? You don't have to say; I'm just curious."

"Yeah, it's okay. I was a Marine in Vietnam," he said quietly, looking straight at the road. "You know people spit on me when I was at the airport in Portland. I don't get it. I served in that hellhole for two years and they spit on me."

He flicked his cigarette out the window. His face was intense and flushed, his lips tight.

"I'm so sorry! I didn't know about the—well, that's not right. Ah, stop here. This is good. Thanks for the ride. I hope things go better for you now."

"Okay. See you next class, I guess," he said, his brow still scrunched in a scowl. He pulled the passenger door closed and drove off in a hurry.

A Vietnam veteran. No wonder he's so intense. I can't even imagine . . .

That was our first meeting and I *did* get to know Dave little by little after each class. He liked Led Zeppelin, Carlos Santana, and, especially, a band called Jethro Tull where the main singer played a flute while standing on one leg.

The study of life in biology class was nothing compared to the study of life with my new male friend. Dave's stories fascinated me way beyond the evolution of biological organisms. *Do I call him a boyfriend?* He definitely wasn't a boy.

We rode to class together three days a week, when we *actually* went to class. Sometimes we just went back to his place and played cards. He was more at ease there and looked every bit the rancher's son now in jeans and T-shirts, even though the shirts were still a military-issued, olive green. He talked nonstop when we were alone and I listened and tried to visualize.

By the end of October, we were spending time alone every spare moment in the small, one-room trailer his dad had given him. A miniscule bathroom the size of a closet, one built-in single bed, a card table, and a tiny used sofa was what he called home.

"Would you like something to drink? I have orange juice, I think," Dave asked one afternoon, staring into his tiny fridge. "Have you ever had a screwdriver?"

"No, what's that?"

"Oh, it's orange juice . . . with a special ingredient. I'll make you one. Deal the cards."

I picked up the deck we'd been playing with, shuffled awkwardly, and dealt a game of gin rummy. Dave poured a clear liquid from a stubby, flat-looking glass bottle into our glasses, then topped it with orange juice.

"Just sip it," Dave said with a suspicious grin. "It's an acquired taste."

I sipped, then gasped . . . and coughed, which brought on a sneeze. Nasty stuff! It tasted like wet paint smelled.

"Here, you can have it," I said, my eyes watering. "What *is* that crap?"

Dave chuckled, the first real laugh I'd heard since we'd met two short months ago. His laugh was a revelation.

"'Crap'? Where'd you learn that word? There are more descriptive words than that," he instructed with a grin. "I'll teach you. . . a screwdriver is orange juice and vodka. I told you it's an acquired taste. Here, give it back. I've got some ginger ale, I think."

For Dave, profanity and booze was just every day. Cursing wasn't for me and neither was alcohol. I was tempted though 'cuz I wanted him to like me, accept me.

He intrigued me. His conversations were honest and sometimes a little scary. I'd never experienced anyone like this guy and I liked learning about a life I'd never imagined.

With November, the weather turned nippy. Fallen leaves turned crunchy from overnight frost. That was the month Dave took me to meet his folks. We left Friday after class.

I told my parents I was going on a weekend biology trip. There were no questions or concerns. More proof I was totally off their radar.

Excited to get deeper into Dave's life, I drove with him out of Ashland as the sun disappeared behind the mountains. Ten miles out, we turned onto a windy two-lane country road.

"I love this wild country, man," Dave said eagerly, a distant look in his eyes. "More peaceful than 'Nam. The closest comparison would be the wild jungles over there; that's *their* wild country."

He turned on the headlights as we drove along quietly. If Dave was thinking about his time in the service, I hoped he'd share; I knew so little about the military *or* Vietnam. We rounded a bend as the darkness closed in around us with only a sliver of road visible ahead.

"The jungle was so thick you could sit against it," he began. "We did that: we sat *against* the jungle, got loaded, and after enough time passed, like we'd been on a reconnaissance, we returned to camp. We could never find the Vietcong, anyway, so why get ourselves killed in an ambush? They'd spray us with bullets, then disappear. There weren't even any footprints."

Man, what kind of soldier was this guy? Was that normal behavior over there?

I didn't know *what* to think; a queasy feeling began in my stomach.

He took a long breath, lost in his memory. "The jungle was a good place to get stoned. I always had my Thai milk laced with—"

Suddenly he stopped and glanced at me. My eyes widened with every word.

"Well, you don't want to hear about that stuff. But there was all kinds of stuff you could get loaded on over there; most of us did, too; it was survival. Vietnam is a screwed-up mess, it's the government's war. EMs, enlisted men, are just sitting ducks and most of the brass could care less. I love my country, but I *hate* this government!" he said, spitting out each word.

Dave kept talking, getting more intense as he went. Part of me didn't want him to go on, but it was all fascinating in a sick sort of way, like a car accident you couldn't look away from.

"We weren't just fighting the Vietcong. You never knew who the enemy was or where they'd show up. We let the village Vietnamese women clean our barracks, the showers, even the latrines. They got U.S. dollars for it and that was a big deal. But one of my buddies was killed there. Some female gook put a bomb behind the toilet. He never knew what hit him."

I looked out the window, now really nauseated and lightheaded. I was sure my face had turned green.

Try to focus on the scenery, Janet, on anything else... but I couldn't see a thing. *Stupid of me to want him to share his war experiences.*

Dave glanced at me again. "I'm making this quite the road trip for you ... sorry. You shouldn't let me go on like that!" he said, bowing his head a little with embarrassment. His cynical smile now a frown, he watched the road.

We didn't say another word the rest of the ten miles. Dark silhouettes of pine trees flashed by, the Cascade Mountains outlined behind them.

It must be beautiful country in the daytime. Right, think about beautiful things.

Dave steered the car left onto a dirt road that led to a modest house, nestled under more pines. A shed stood behind the house and a large barn was across from it. We passed fenced-in pastures and grazing animals.

"Are there horses too?" I asked, trying to return my senses to normal. "I grew up in Arizona around them; I'd love to see some."

"Yeah, but they're work horses, not for Sunday-style riding. They're in the barn. We have pigs, too, chickens, and a garden; we hardly ever go to the market in town."

His parents came to the door as we drove up. We got out of the car and a pungent thick aroma assaulted my nostrils . . . pigs! What a stink!

"It's about time," his mother said, running to Dave and wrapping her arms around him.

"You must be Janet," his dad said, extending a rough rancher's hand. Tall, with a sunburned face, a crew cut, and wrinkled eyes behind bifocal glasses, he gave me a cautious smile. "I'm James. Glad to finally meet you. Dave's told us a lot about you."

He did? What about? Should I worry?

"Ah, hello," I said shyly.

"You're as pretty as he said, but why you're with my knucklehead son, I can't imagine."

I froze for a moment. *Pretty?*

Dave's mother, a chubby, short woman with a fast walk, barely reached up to her husband's chest when she stood on her tippy-toes. Her short-bobbed hair fell just below her chin and there was a no-nonsense air about her. She nodded slightly at me, then walked into the house holding Dave's hand, dragging him along with her.

"Don't mind them. She thinks he's a mama's boy," James said with a short laugh. "Come on in. Do you want something to drink? With this cool night, we thought we'd have something special, hot buttered rum. We like to have it when there's a guest."

I followed mother and son into the small living room and James turned into the kitchen. The house was barely warm, so I kept my jacket on. Their ranch used gas-driven heat from a generator James cranked up at night, but only for the two rooms downstairs, and only in the evening. That meant upstairs would be even colder.

Imbibing hot-buttered rum was a much better alcohol experience than Dave's screwdriver. I couldn't turn it down since it was made

especially for me. Besides, it was delicious—spicy with a buttery rich-
ness. I watched the others sip theirs, and I did the same. Between
Dave's Vietnam horror stories and traveling through unfamiliar country, I relished the fuzzy warmth coursing through me. The rum mellowed my senses and relaxed my body.

At eleven, we said our goodnights. Dave and I walked through the
kitchen and took the stairs to the upper dorm room.

"Ah, I forgot to mention, there's only one double bed. It's more of a
loft than a real normal-sized bedroom. I hope that's okay."

As we climbed the stairs, my mind raced. *We're going to share a
bed? Do his parents know?*

In the loft, moonlight trickled in through a single window. Dave
found a lantern, took off the globe, and turned the knob to let gas
escape. There was a hiss and a rotten-egg smell that made me plug my
nose. With his lighter, Dave lit the gas, then adjusted the wick, and put
the globe back on. I looked around the room and saw the double bed
with handmade quilts.

Hot buttered rum made my brain foggy, but I backed slowly toward
the stairs anyway.

Dave gave me a weary look, then turned and looked at the bed.
"Um, I'm used to sleeping on hard ground, so toss me a quilt and a
pillow and I'll just sleep right here," he offered, tapping the floor with
his boot.

Dave looked at me with his blurry eyes and I squinted a fuzzy look
back. Then we burst into laughter, both of us zonkered. I lay my head
on his hard chest and let him wrap his arms around me. "We better lie
down before we fall down," he said, holding me at arm's length.

And I did fall on the bed and into a deep sleep immediately. A
dream of flames and burning and a scorched child wandered through
my oblivion.

CHAPTER 9

US VERSUS THEM

The weekend visit with Dave's parents wasn't what I imagined. The horrible Vietnam descriptions still echoed in my mind. The hot buttered rum had turned my joints to jelly, and now I had slept in a room with a man I barely knew.

The late November evening was freezing in Butte Falls, so Dave and I had ended up in the bed together fully clothed. I woke up early the next morning snuggled up close to Dave.

"It got kinda cold on the floor," he whispered. "I hope you don't mind cuddling."

Pressed against Dave's chest, no, I didn't mind at all. It gave me an unfamiliar sense of belonging. Someone genuinely cared about how I felt. Quilts were good, but I decided then and there that a man's arms around me were even better.

New undefined emotions pumped insistently through my bloodstream; I was sure my feelings for Dave were real. Even before being close like this, I'd felt something. Empathy? Maybe. We both knew misery and heartache–his, certainly much worse so than mine.

Okay, calm down, Janet. It's only been a couple of months–too soon to say this is love.

That Saturday, Dave showed me all around the property. We made an attempt to go in the hay loft, but climbing up only pulled more hay down. We picked the stuff out of each other's hair, laughing, and shook the wisps out of our clothes. Outside, we petted the horses who came up to the fence. Big brown eyes looked me over as I patted the velvet brown nose. No wonder Uncle Ted loved these animals. They radiated pure love.

Hand in hand, I walked with Dave back to the house for dinner as the sun was setting. We had homemade stew, homemade bread, and ranch talk with Dave's dad.

"I'll miss you shooting the pigs this year," James said to his son as he ladled a spoonful of stew into his mouth. "I've had to do it the last two years with you overseas. But getting an education's important, too, so I guess it's still up to me. I hope you appreciate it, wandering the campus with your long hair and beard," James remarked with a rueful smile. "I guess you look like everybody else," he continued. His jaw tightened as he brushed his hand over his crew cut. "I'm glad you've got the GI Bill. I never got past the eighth grade myself."

Dave gave me a look and we both dipped our chins to hide our reactions. Honestly, I liked Dave's hair. It looked better than the military cut he had two months ago.

"Yeah, just wish I knew what direction to go," Dave replied, ignoring his dad's dig about his appearance. He wiped up stew with his bread. "Janet and I are trying to figure that out."

We really *weren't* trying to figure out anything except how to spend more time together, but no one needed to know that. I was obsessed and spent time with Dave every chance I got, in spite of my college grades plummeting. I snuck around, too, to keep my parents out of the loop; it took a lot of energy.

Sunday morning, we had coffee and hot, homemade wheat cereal before taking off for Ashland. We said good-bye as we went out the back door, although I felt a little sad to leave.

"I hope you'll come back up here soon," James said earnestly. "Looks like Dave's finally done something right."

"Oh now, James, Dave always does things right!" Dave's mother threw in, slightly scolding. "You just never notice."

Dave hugged his mother and she hugged back with all her might. She had no affection to give me so I gave his dad a tentative hug. Dave pulled himself away, gave his mother a kiss, and shook his dad's hand. As we took off down the dirt road, Dave heaved a big sigh, then looked at me. We broke out in a laugh, both of us relieved to have the first visit done.

I was nervous, but Dave seemed even more nervous. Was it his dad or was it bringing me to meet the folks? Dave looked more at peace now, as he drove. His face was calm, the grim intensity of the earlier drive just a memory. I sank back against the seat, relaxed.

I watched the scenery pass and thought about the differences in families I had seen. Dave's parents accepted him. They might have even been proud. There was definitely some tension among the three of them, but they spoke civilly to each other anyway.

We arrived at the foot of my driveway and stopped just behind the hedges to keep hidden. Dave gave me a quick kiss good-bye, did a U-turn, and left me to walk up to the house with my small suitcase.

When I got into the house, Daddy asked, "How was the biology trip?"

I dropped my stuff by the front door and joined him in the living room, the paper in front of his face. "The mountains were beautiful, but it's really cold up there."

"No doubt, mountains are that way, even in Arizona," he said absently. "I hope you learned something new." He turned to a different newspaper page.

"Uh, yeah," I replied, plucking up my courage, "I learned that I could do all right in new situations . . . and I've made friends with a guy named Dave."

He turned the page once more. "That's nice, Janet. Good for you."

Dismissed, I picked up my stuff and walked towards the stairs. I had stuck my toe in possibly rough water with Daddy but it wasn't too choppy. I walked through the dining area and saw Mother in the kitchen, her stiff back to me. She poured herself some coffee, then turned to me.

"I hope you're keeping your mind on your studies and not on getting a boyfriend," she stated, her expression hard. "We're paying for your education and your father will be very disappointed if it all turns out to be a waste."

Money, education, and physical fitness: the pillars of success in the Ingalls' household. Save your money, get a degree, stay physically fit . . . and, whatever you do, *don't* talk about real life, politics, or how whacked out your family is. I didn't want to disappoint Daddy, but I would make my own decisions and create my own life.

I guess I have to start keeping my own secrets.

The rest of autumn zipped by with Dave in my life. I stopped going to class and spent every spare minute with him instead. I still worked at the cafeteria to earn a little bit of money, and felt free doing what I wanted. Being naughty felt good, too, at least with the rules of a critical mother and a dismissive father.

One late Saturday evening, Dave drove us through the street-lit Lithia Park and stopped in a dark parking lot. He turned off the motor and scooted across the bench seat next to me. Without hesitation, he suddenly wrapped his strong arms around me, bent my head back, and kissed me hard, his tongue in my mouth, rubbing against my teeth. I did my best to kiss him back in the same way, but had no idea what the heck I was doing!

"Oh man, I'm really sorry. I got carried away," he quickly said as he pushed himself back to the driver's side. "It's been a long time since I've been with an American girl. I just, well, after being up at the ranch, being in bed together, it seemed okay, ya know?"

"I didn't mind, Dave," I said shyly, "I'm just not sure how to kiss like that."

"Really? It's a French kiss," he said with a playful tone. "You haven't been kissed like that before? I find that hard to believe, as pretty as you are."

I was glad we were in the dark so he couldn't see my pink-tinged cheeks. *Pretty* wasn't a description I'd ever heard, except once from his dad. And what did pretty have to do with kissing, anyway? Still, it made my nerves flutter.

"Now you're going to tell me you've never had sex, er, made love . . . Just how old are you, anyway?"

He'd never asked my age and I didn't know his either, but I didn't pause. I trusted him.

"Yes, it's true, I'm a virgin, okay? And I'm eighteen. How old are you?"

"Ah, I didn't think there *were* any eighteen-year-old virgins in this flower-power generation. And I'm twenty-four going on fifty-two.

Vietnam and the Marine Corps will do that to you," he replied with a low growl.

"You've had a rough time, babe," I said compassionately, snuggling closer. "We ought to just tie the knot. We've known each for a few months and we're both adults," I added cautiously, taking his hand. His arm tensed and he pulled his hand away. "I mean, it might be good for both of us, besides . . . I think I'm falling in love with you," I admitted.

Where did that *come from Janet?*

"Man, slow down, sister," he said. "There are other things we need to do first. Although I'll admit . . . I've thought about getting hitched, but I don't think I'm ready yet."

I took in a sharp breath. *He's thought about it; I'm not too out of line then.*

"One step at a time, okay? Maybe I can meet your parents later tonight when I take you home."

"Oh, no! You really don't want to do that," I stated emphatically, squirming back to my side of the car. Even though Daddy *had* given me a little hope recently, Dave had been dropping me off for months where no one could see us. Somehow, I'd have to make all this "acceptable" to them before Dave showed his face in the Ingall's living room.

"Why not?" Dave asked, trying to catch my eye as we sat in the dark. "What, are they some kind of nightmare?"

How can I tell him what an understatement that *is?*

"Not exactly, they're . . . well, they're different."

"Oh, come on. How bad can it be?" he replied, chuckling and starting the car.

I wasn't sure I liked this particular step toward adulthood. Still, Dave had to meet my parents sometime. As we drove toward the house, my romantic feelings became a sour lump in my stomach.

Dave pulled into the driveway, turned off the car, then came around and opened the door for me. Mother stood in the living room window watching, her face contorted. I knew that look; it was the storm clouds before the volcanic eruption. Hopefully she would wait until Dave was gone before she slammed me.

We walked in the front door, hand in hand. Daddy put down his newspaper and came over to greet us, extending his hand for Dave to shake. They clasped hands in a strong grip.

"Hi, I'm Dave Jenkins," Dave said, dropping Daddy's hand. "Janet and I have been seeing each other since school started, but you probably know that," he said with a meek smile.

"Ah, yes, something like that. She hasn't been home much these days. I told Mildred it was probably more than work and school," he replied in a professor-like voice. "Have a seat."

We sat down on the loveseat close to Daddy's chair, still holding hands. Mother took her usual place on the sofa and began knitting intensely.

"Tell me about yourself," Daddy invited. From the corner of my eye, I saw Mother looking at us both, with a "this better not be anything serious" face.

Can't you just back off for once?

Dave told my parents about his plans to finish a degree at SOC, then rambled on, clearly trying to share what *he* thought they wanted to hear. Everyone played nice for half an hour, which felt like an eternity. It made my underarms damp in spite of the autumn temperatures. After twenty more minutes, we said our good-byes and I walked Dave to the door. He stepped out and I closed the door just enough to hide our kiss before he took off.

I ran up the stairs to my room before there were any parting shots. I fell back on my bed and smiled at the ceiling. That definitely could have been worse.

Maybe Dave will take me out of here, after all.

Nothing was said until Sunday. Just before dinner, Mother insisted I meet her in the living room for a "talk."

"I hope you're not serious about that young man, Janet. He looks like a hippy and he smells like cigarettes. Your father and I are disgusted."

Really? You're disgusted? Good! What a hypocrite; you both used to smoke all the time!

"Okay," I said shortly, then got up to leave.

"I mean it, Janet! If you marry this man, you'll never be welcome in this house again. You have no idea how this will hurt your father."

I stared at the woman who had made my life a living hell since I was ten.

Hurt Daddy? Then why isn't he here talking to me instead of you? No one talks about anything that matters anyway, especially not where I'm concerned. Why didn't we talk about Grandy when she passed and where she is now? No, this wasn't about Daddy. This was about controlling me and how she'd lose it if I left.

When I saw Dave the next day, I told him about Mother's warning. "It's her normal thing with me," I said. "She's just nuts."

"Well, I should make more of an effort to get to know them," Dave replied. "They don't know me and it can't be easy, you being their only daughter. My father freaked out when my sister Dina married Mark. They're okay now, though, especially since there's a grandchild."

A grandchild! That gave me a spark of hope.

A baby, yes, that might melt Mother's heart. I loved babysitting and I was good at it, I'd love having my own baby!

"I guess, but they haven't shown any interest in me for some time, really. It's just like Mother to make a big stink now though. I'd love to just leave– but I'd miss Connor."

Daddy, too, but I've been missing him for years.

"Can they bully us like that?" Dave said, determined. "I should talk to your father alone."

Dave came to the house the following Saturday and I let him in. I was told to leave, so I went up the stairs and stopped just past the retaining wall where I couldn't be seen, but I could hear. I pressed my head close to the banister and strained to make out words, but it was just a bunch of mumbling, with Mother dominating the conversation.

Suddenly she raised her voice. "Over my dead body! You don't come into *my* house and tell us what *we* can do with our daughter!"

The front door slammed and I ran to the window at the bottom of the stairs. I watched Dave back out of the driveway and race down the road, burning rubber. I was proud of him for standing up to the old crow, but nervous about what might come next for me.

I met Dave the next Wednesday at Omar's for shrimp cocktails and beer.

"The semester's almost over. I want to pack up your stuff and get you out of there," Dave announced, staring into his mug.

Oh! He still wants me, despite my parents not accepting him.

I warmth rushed through me. Despite whatever harsh things they'd said to him, Dave might still be the place where I was wanted, a real first for me since Grandy died.

He took a breath then, and gave me an intent look. "By the way, your dad tried to warn me off by saying how mentally ill you are, schizo. Your mother agreed, of course."

My mouth flew open and I stared at the man, shocked.

What? My daddy, who helped me learn to walk, sang Wolverton Mountain on our trip together, took me to see Peter O'Toole . . . he thinks I'm schizophrenic?

The warmth I'd felt only a minute ago turned into a wincing, biting cold. *I'll never forgive him.* The pain over Daddy's words hurt worse than anything I'd ever heard or experienced with Mother. My face, contorted with indignation, I clenched my jaw, my mouth a hard line. I glowered back at Dave. It was all I could do to stop angry tears from falling. If the only man I knew as a father *really* thought I was sick in the head, then Dave was right: it was time to get out forever.

December came and the fall semester ended. That was when I learned that Daddy could track anything about me at the college. He was furious about my *D* in biology.

"This is because of that Dave, isn't it? You're smarter than this, Janet!" Dad bellowed. "Don't you *ever* bring home a grade like this again, do you hear me?"

My eyes rolled as my shoulders shrugged up defensively. "Yes, Daddy, you're yelling, so yes, I hear you."

I looked at the floor. I'd never disappointed him before, but he thought I was mentally ill, so what difference did it make? A huge abyss had opened up between us. I looked up at him with defiance. I wanted to shout the truth to this educated professor, that he'd married a mad woman who went out of her way to make sure I was unloved, ignored, and punished for not being her biological child. She was the crazy one in the house, not me.

Daddy looked at Mother and she nodded. "You need to get your head on straight, young lady." He paused, then said something that floored me. "Maybe it's time you were more on your own and not so dependent on us. I'm going to arrange for you to move into the dorms."

I kept my face blank. Not arguing with my parents over who knew what, or worrying about their reactions to what I did or didn't do? Yes! Maybe us vs. them was finally finished. Move me out? Groovy!

January of 1971, I packed up as much of my personal stuff as I could fit into Dave's car and we piled it into the back seat. Before we took off, I looked around for the parents, but they were nowhere to be found. *They must be in their bedroom, no man's land.*

I was off the hook. What could I have said, anyway? And where was Connor? I wondered how he felt about all this, but I hardly ever saw him anymore.

Excited to be free, I buried my disappointment at leaving Connor behind, and drove off with Dave.

CHAPTER 10

OUT OF THE FRYING PAN

When Dave and I finally pulled away from my parents' house, it was after ten and the dorms were closed, so we drove to Dave's trailer instead. We left my stuff locked up in his car that sat in the carport next to his mobile home.

We sat on the sofa together, holding hands, trying to calm our breath and our thoughts. Then, without a word, Dave pulled me to my feet and we went to his single bed and lay down together. His strong arms around me melted my heart. No wonder many women thought being close to a man was breathtaking. I hoped this was a jump into life with Dave, filled with love. My heart opened; I was free. We loved.

Now Dave has to marry me! All 1971 young women know the rules—if you're a "good" girl and you make love with a guy he has to marry you.

The next two weeks, Dave and I played cards when he wasn't working at the gas station. He never went back to school. Neither did I, and we didn't discuss it. He still dropped me off at my cafeteria job, but I knew when we married, I'd have to quit. At least I still had some money in a savings account. Mother would *have* to let me take it out if I was leaving for good. Keeping someone else's money was dishonest, even for her.

We kissed a lot, drank Boone's Farm apple wine, and talked about our future. "Let's go over the border to California and get hitched," Dave offered as he laid down his gin rummy hand. "There's no waiting period and no blood tests."

I loved the idea; it was right in line with the rules I believed. I hugged my soon-to-be husband and whispered, "Oh yes!"

The phone rang and brought me out of my fantasy. Dave answered, then handed me the receiver. "It's your dad," he said, grinning.

"Not funny," I muttered, my cheeks flushing pink.

"Not kidding," Dave said, holding out the receiver, more insistent. "Here, you better talk to him."

I held my breath as we looked at each other. Dave shrugged and gave me a sympathetic look as I took the phone. "Hello?" I said, panic rising up in my throat.

"Are you pregnant?" Daddy questioned. His anger crawled through the phone wires and slapped me.

Not 'Hello'?

"No," I said timidly. "But we're getting married, Daddy."

It was obvious Daddy knew where I was staying, not in the dorms. The receiver still at my ear, my head began to throb.

"Thanks for letting us know."

CLICK.

My cheeks flamed with embarrassment. I didn't want to cry, but I did. *Who is that guy? He's not the daddy I used to know. He didn't even let me say how happy I am.*

Dave put out his cigarette, then put his arm around me. "No dad likes to see their daughter grow up and leave home. It's like Neil Diamond says, 'Girl, you'll be a woman soon, soon you'll need a man.' So here I am, right?" he offered with a chuckle.

I wiped my tears and leaned against him. I didn't know if I could transfer my affections from my daddy to Dave, but I sure wanted to, especially now. Soon everything would change and I might not even see my father again.

"Well, I hope you really want me," I began with the best joking tone I could manage, "because my dad thinks I'm probably pregnant and I've crossed over into hell."

Dave looked at me with compassion, then grabbed a beer from the fridge. "It'll all turn out okay, babe. Let's not worry about it now."

I wiped my hand across my eyes and Dave called his parents. He gave them the news and got a much better reception. Surprisingly, his mother was disappointed that we hadn't let them know sooner so they could give us a wedding shower. How wonderful to be welcomed into the family with enthusiasm.

With our upcoming nuptials, his dad generously switched out our trailer for a bigger one. It had a separate bedroom, with drawers built into one of its walls and the living room was big enough for Dave's stereo and some furniture. The only problem was the trailer was Pepto-Bismol pink, our first unforgettable home.

We had days of work and evenings of rock and roll with Dave's friend, Larry. I worked at the cafeteria right up to January 20 and Dave worked at the nearby gas station pumping gas, washing windows, and checking tires and fluid levels.

Larry probably weighed all of a hundred pounds, had a mop of blond hair, and a pockmarked face. Outgoing, he laughed easily at anything. When we met, he shook my hand and said, "So, you're the lucky lady, HA!" He was friendly . . . too friendly. I finally made him let go of my hand.

"Yes, I *feel* very lucky—er, blessed."

"We're all blessed, right, Larry?" Dave said, beckoning Larry to join him. "Come over here and help me clean the twigs out of this stuff."

The guys sat together, poured the contents of a baggie out on the coffee table, and began separating leaves from little twigs. Then they tightly rolled the cleaned leaves into thin paper and pinched the ends closed. They laughed and joked, eagerness on their faces. The pungent smell of marijuana soon permeated the trailer atmosphere.

I was stunned. Oblivious of my presence, I backed into the bedroom and closed the door.

Well, they can go on with their "activities" without me. I guess pot is okay, but wow . . .

Jimi Hendrix's distinct guitar music filled the air along with smoke from their joints. I opened a romance novel Dave's mother had given me and tried to read in spite of the loud laughter from the other room.

After an hour, the door slammed open, and Dave stood there, roach clip in hand.

"Why don't you come join us? You don't have to smoke weed. Just come out and be with us, babe," Dave said, a dazed grin on his face. "Man, I'm feeling no pain . . . I want you near me, hon, so come on." He offered his hand and I let him pull me up and into his arms.

What would it hurt? It's warmer in the front room anyway.

It wasn't long before I felt relaxed and a little sleepy.

"Oh here, take a puff," Dave said, handing me the roach clip. "It'll make you feel good. Here, watch."

Dave sucked in the smoke and his cheeks as he inhaled. He closed his lips tight and held in the vapor for several seconds before slowly blowing it out.

Okay, that doesn't look too hard. Maybe just one puff.

Feeling good was something I needed, I'd stop thinking about Daddy. I took the doobie, inhaled, and tried to hold the smoke in like Dave did, but the intense smoke irritated my throat. I coughed in long spasms as my eyes watered and my face got hot. Dave and Larry roared, the sound grating on my ears as I continued to hack.

"Glad you find me so funny," I choked out.

"I'm sorry, babe. I just haven't seen a first timer since high school," Dave remarked with a laugh. He wrapped an arm around my shoulder. "You'll be good at this in no time, but I'll admit it's fun to watch you."

I made a face at Dave and tried to stay annoyed, but with his arm around me, I relaxed. Before I knew it, my sadness had drifted away with the smoke. I closed my eyes and let peace surround me. Dave was right; I liked this escape and it wasn't long before I was hanging out with them regularly. Weekends, and sometimes midweek, we drank and got high, then ate bowls of Ralston hot cereal with lots of butter and syrup.

Wednesday, January 21 came fast with snow falling steady and wet. Larry and Dave sat together in the front seat of the Dodge, studying the road map for directions to Yreka, California. We were going over the California border to "get hitched. " Once the route was determined, we motored up I-5 and over the Siskiyou Pass.

Butterflies flew wildly through my bloodstream as I snuggled down in the backseat to keep warm. Snow came down thick and white in the Siskiyou Mountains, so the Highway Patrol slammed orange poles in place alongside the road to track snow depth. I was glad to leave my parents' town, but I'd be even more glad when we were back in the trailer, married.

It was a simple wedding in front of the justice of the peace. No dress-up for us since most money went to cigarettes, beer, and "incidentals." Besides, we were hippies and I wore a dark pink sweater, a matching, long flowered skirt over my snow boots, and a floppy hat over my hair. Dave wore his only white shirt, jeans, and his ever-present plaid coat that smelled like everything he smoked.

Not too romantic, but I'd soon be someone's wife. I blurted out an adrenaline-fueled, "I do," after Dave said his, we had a quick kiss, and got back on the road in less than an hour. I was now Mrs. David Jenkins and had the legal paper to prove it. There was no ring for either of us, although Dave promised to get me one once he'd saved up some money.

God must have had pity on us because the snow had stopped. Still, I prayed. *I know I don't have a right to ask right now, but please, God, don't let us slide off the road into a snowbank and get buried. Help us get back to Ashland safely!*

It was still tricky going back to Ashland on the pass. We moved slowly, with Larry and Dave passing whisky between them. I was grateful traffic was light on that Thursday. As we approached the summit, Dave pulled over and stopped. He and Larry stumbled out and yanked an orange marker pole out of a snow drift and tied it to the roof of the Dodge. Safely back at the trailer, the pole was wiped dry and positioned across the front room near the ceiling, balanced on top of window casings.

In a haze of marijuana smoke and laughter, the two men used black light paint and decorated the pole with weird imaginings and peace signs. With the black light on, the ceiling reflected all the neon weirdness. That was the start of my married life. Freakin' groovy and I liked it.

"Dave, I need to go get the rest of my stuff from my parent's house," I told him a week later. "You'll be working, so can Larry take me? I'll call the parents. Maybe I can see Connor too."

Dave decided *he'd* better call the house since he was now my husband. Arrangements were made and Larry and I drove up while Dave went on to work. The bluebird blue house hadn't felt like home for a long time, but I still opened the front door without knocking. Daddy was standing there, his angry eyes glaring at me as if they could melt me into the floor. I quickly looked away, searching for Connor, but he was nowhere to be found.

Two boxes of belongings were already packed and sat near the door. I had a hard lump of fear in my chest, so I didn't dare ask to go search my room. I looked at Dad, wanting to say something, hoping *he'd* say something, but his furious expression wouldn't let me. What little courage I had disappeared.

I picked up a box and handed it out to Larry waiting on the porch. I grabbed the second box and turned to leave when suddenly Daddy gave me a push out the door and a kick in my fanny. Then he slammed the door. My face turned beet red clear up to my hair roots.

I stashed the final box in the back seat and got in. Larry looked at me in the rearview mirror, then let out an uncomfortable laugh. I tried to chuckle, but I choked as hot tears burned behind my eyes. The only father I'd ever known had literally kicked me out of his life. Humiliation and agony I could taste.

We drove on to the gas station to meet Dave. But before we even got out of the car, Mother drove in behind us, snow flying off her car tires. She pulled up short in front of the gas station office, flung open her car door, and rushed in, yelling at Dave. She screamed in outrage —*stupid, ignorant, how dare you invade my family!*

I stare at the witch, horrified. But Dave grinned and just watched the crazy woman, his arms casually crossed over his chest.

Without a word, he exited the office and her screaming and went to pump gas for the customer who had pulled in. Mother wasn't about to stop. She followed him out, still screeching.

Dave didn't turn around. He just shrugged his shoulders, smiled at the man in the car, and kept working as if Mother wasn't there.

Finally, he stopped and looked at her. "Listen, lady, I'm working here! Take your nasty temper back to your nasty house!"

Dave went around to the front of the car, opened the hood and began checking fluid levels. I stayed low in the back seat of the car with Larry, hoping I wasn't seen. Larry watched amazed, his head moving from Mother to Dave as he followed the fight. "I'll bet it's a long time before *that* guy comes back here for gas, " he declared with a chuckle.

A truck rolled in and stopped near the station: it was Daddy's. He turned off the engine, got out, and walked calmly over to his shrieking wife. "Mildred, get in the car and go home. Right now! Leave the man alone."

With hatred spilling from her eyes, Mother stomped over to her car and roared out as fast as she had roared in. The car fishtailed and jumped back onto the main road, then moved out of sight.

Daddy shook my husband's hand and said, "No hard feelings. I wish you well." He calmly got back in his truck and drove away.

I guess glaring at me and kicking me out the door was all he needed to show his outrage. I wish I'd punched him or better yet, punched her! They are not my parents!

I let my tears fall in a cascade. When Larry dropped me off at the trailer, I was still bawling. I grabbed a paper towel and wiped the snot dripping from my nose. I couldn't stop sobbing and I didn't want to. I lay down on the couch and cried until my tear ducts were dried out and sore. Then I passed out from exhaustion.

CHAPTER 11

YOU'VE MADE YOUR BED

When Dave came home at nine-thirty, he smelled like gasoline and his hands were grimy from cleaning a lot of windows and checking tires. Snow and cold weather brought in lots of customers to the gas station. He looked as bad as he smelled. He gave me a grin, then went and showered. As we lay in bed, I shared about my savings account with Mother.

"How much is in there? I've been thinking we need to move to Portland so I can make better money. I can probably get a job with Western Electric. I was trained for that work in the Marines, so yeah, any extra moola would really help."

Portland?

"I honestly don't know," I replied, thinking about a new place in a new town. "Mother took my checks and stashed half of them in that account. I didn't get paid much, but I worked at Shakespeare for three summers, so it might be a nice chunk. Problem is, she has to sign with me to take out money. It really burns my biscuits. I didn't know a parent could do that to a child."

"I'll call your dad. He might help," Dave offered, kissing me on the cheek. With that, he put his arms around me, cuddled close, and passed out. Dave's idea was good, as long as Mother didn't get to Daddy first.

He reached out the next day, but Daddy passed him on to Mother. I hung my head when Dave told me it was a lost cause. I could imagine Mother's sarcastic smile as she told Dave the money belonged to *them*. I'd stopped going to school after they'd paid my tuition, so they were keeping my savings money as pay back. Intense disappointment gave me a headache, but Dave got irritated.

"That's it," he said. "We're done with them for good."

But we still needed money to move. Dave's dad came through at the last minute. He'd sold our pink trailer and offered us the sale money.

"Wedding present," he stated. "Sorry I didn't get a very good price, but it's better than nothing. I just wish you had let us know you were getting married so fast! We'd have thrown you a nice wedding."

Thank you, God, for the extra funds, I know that was You!

"It really was a last moment decision," Dave lied. "Sorry, Dad. We have to get up to Portland real soon for a potential job. But we're very grateful for the funds."

"Yes, thank you," I said. I gave James a hug and whispered, "Kindness is the real gift."

The car was already packed up and we waved good-bye to Dave's dad as we pulled out. I almost cried as I watched the old man disappear from view. He really had a good heart even though he was a tough rancher and didn't want anyone to know it.

With five hundred more dollars, we were both high with anticipation. It was 1971 and we left Ashland for good. We agreed to be careful with what money we had and that meant no more "extracurricular" activities. We'd have to be real grownups, at least for a while.

"We're making good decisions, Mr. Jenkins," I said to my husband with a smile, hoping to start a conversation. But there was no response, and Dave's face was a mask. He focused on driving, his thoughts taking him hundreds of miles away. Ashland to Portland was a five-hour trip at sixty-five miles an hour. It was only when we stopped for gas and lunch that Dave realized I was there.

He has a lot to do, I told myself. *Finding us a place and getting a job. I'm sure that's what he's thinking about.*

We ate bologna and American cheese sandwiches with lots of Miracle Whip on Wonder bread; it was cheap. Santana, CCR, and Jethro Tull blasted from our eight-track tapes as we drove. The weather was clear and cold, but the car was warm. I cuddled close to my quiet husband, happiness in my heart for the first time in years. I'd finally have the home life I craved.

We arrived in Portland and took the Burnside Bridge to the west side of town. The buildings towered over us on both sides as we drove up the street; Eugene wasn't near this size. Overwhelmed with the immensity, a nervousness crawled through me.

Dave got us a room in a rundown hotel and left early the next morning to find work. There was one bathroom with a toilet on our floor, down the hall, and a sink in our room for water. How did people live like this? I was all alone in a strange place. I sat on the bed and looked around the room with wide eyes, my cold hands clasped together.

What have I gotten myself into? Daddy would never leave me in a dangerous place.

I couldn't go crying back to my parents now. Mother would say, "Too bad, you've made your bed so lie in it." I was stuck.

Abandoned, I remembered Grandy and I tried to pray.

Dear God, I'm married and away from everything I grew up with and that's good. Dave seems to be a nice guy with courage, at least I think so. But have I made a big mistake? What if Dave doesn't come back? What will I do? This is a terrible place. But You're in charge, so please, God, watch over me. And help Dave too. Amen.

I didn't hear a voice or see an angel, but a warm feeling passed through me. Finally, the last week of February, things *did* change for the better. We left Portland's rundown section of town and moved to the middle-class East side. Dave rented an apartment in the back of an older three-story building up three flights of stairs. There was no elevator, but there was a coin-operated washer and dryer on the main floor that would make life easier.

We had a refrigerator, electric stove, and a good-sized kitchen sink with green laminated counter space. The living room was as big as the room we had stayed in at the rundown hotel. A Murphy bed at one end twisted open to reveal built-in closets and a vanity with a mirror. Our bedroom was at the other end of the living room separated by curtains that hung from a taut rope. I had to crawl across the bed to get to my side as there was only an inch between the bed and the wall.

Old-fashioned steam heat kept us warm and the only utility we paid was electricity. The best part of the place was the bathroom—it had a door that locked. Dave had come through. I gave my new husband a big smile, hug, and a kiss.

The first week in our new digs we were up early so Dave could go do contract work in a warehouse. Home by four, he went to the corner payphone and called human resources at Western Electric. While he was gone, I daydreamed about our future. Dave worked hard and I believed he'd make our future happiness come true . . . maybe that little house with a picket fence and two kids, a boy and a girl.

I read *The Hobbit* in the morning, then decided to weed through Dave's Marine duffle bag in the afternoon. I washed clothes worth keeping and threw out the rest. I *tried* to cook, but we mainly ate sandwiches, chili, or soup heated in a used saucepan we'd grabbed with other kitchen things from the local thrift store. At least we could cook and had our own rented space.

I made boxed macaroni and cheese with powdered cheese one night with canned green beans on the side, not as bad as the asparagus glop from my mother, but close. It was awful. Dave just ate quietly and never said a word about my awful meal prep. I loved him for that.

With his Friday pay, he brought home hamburger, potatoes, and fresh tomatoes.

"Can you make fried potatoes? You can fry them up first and then add in the hamburger to make a hash. I bought some basic stuff—Crisco, salt and pepper, catsup, that kind of thing."

"Sure, I can do that," I replied, turning away quickly so he wouldn't see my panic. I had no *idea* how to fry potatoes, but I was determined to figure it out. I turned on the biggest burner and set our beat-up frying pan on top. I dropped in some Crisco and, when it sizzled, I put in slices of cut potato, some thick, some see-through thin. I still was no good with a knife.

"What's all this?" Dave asked with surprise, looking over my shoulder. "You've never fried potatoes, have you?"

"No," I said, looking at the floor. "My mother wouldn't let me cook. No matter what I did, she just got mad. I'm sorry, I really do want to cook for you."

How could I tell him I wasn't allowed in the kitchen because I was left-handed and my mother hated me?

Dave just smiled, took the potato remains from me, and tossed them in the trash. He scooped the sliced potatoes out of the pan and tossed them in the garbage as well. Mother would have hated that, so wasteful.

"We'll put the meat in first," he stated. He took the meat out of its package, crumbled it up with his hands, and dropped it in the hot pan. Then Dave picked up another potato and started to peel it using an actual paring knife. I'd only seen potatoes peeled with a peeler. Impressive!

"I peeled a lot of spuds in 'Nam," he shared with a chuckle.

He stood over the trash can and used his thumb to slide the knife along the potato under the skin. Turning the spud, he sliced off the skin and dropped the peels in the trash. Once done, he held the naked potato end up in the palm of his hand and made cuts down its length, stopping short of cutting all the way through. I knew nothing about how to dice a potato either. It was Dave's potato school! My heart beat a little faster. I was riveted!

Dave pushed the cooked meat to one side of the pan, then cut the potato into half-inch cubes and dropped them in the meat grease. He cooked them 'til they were tender, then pushed the meat in with the cubes and stirred it together into a hash. Hot, steamy starch and cooked meat; the slightly iron smell made my mouth water.

"Thanks, sweetheart. It smells delicious! I've never had potatoes cooked like that. I'll try to learn how to cook that for you," I said, eyeing my plate hungrily. We sat together and gobbled down the concoction with catsup and slices of tomato. Real food, what an improvement! I knew how to clean, but not how to cook. I'd better learn how real fast.

April '71 came and Dave was finally hired by Western Electric. More progress! Delighted, I knew we'd soon have our own house. Getting real work also meant better food, beer to go with Dave's cigarettes, and new sheets and blankets.

My new husband worked regular hours and I stayed home. I cleaned floors with a broom, washed them on my knees with Spic and Span, and learned how to cook using a new Betty Crocker cookbook. We gathered dishes, silverware, and other cooking utensils from Goodwill. Now I regretted not having that wedding shower. A toaster oven would have been really handy. Still, it really didn't matter how we got household necessities. I put my hands on my face and smiled as I looked around.

I got a bit better with the cooking and kept our little place clean. In spite of it being Mother's hobby, I bought yarn and knitting needles and tried to learn simple stitches to make a scarf. It was really just something to do while I listened to Janis Joplin on Dave's stereo. Everything she sang was so intense, felt so deeply, with every word clear. My soul soared with every high note she hit. I wished she would have lived longer and made more music.

In May, Dave came home one Friday and announced we were going to go enjoy the park and go out to dinner. We hadn't gone anywhere except for shopping since we'd arrived. Excitement tingled through me and I almost jumped up and down. Dave laughed seeing my eyes light up. Making me happy seemed to please him.

"I want you to meet this guy I know from work, so wear something cute, okay? And don't forget your coat. It's a bit chilly, especially when the sun goes down."

I changed into a straight Levi skirt that hugged my body and made me look curvy. With a dark red sweater and peace sign earrings, I was hip. I'd had some women's flats from Goodwill. Not fancy, but at least they weren't clunky like my high school shoes. Dave gave me a smile of approval when I came out of our little bedroom. Here we were, a real married couple, going out together.

As we drove to the park, I saw excited anticipation in Dave's eyes. He puffed fast on his cigarette, tapping the ashes haphazardly in the ashtray and on to the floor of the car. I'd only seen him this excited one other time and that was when he came back to the trailer with Larry and their baggie of pot. But no, surely not . . .

CHAPTER 12

YOU CAN'T ALWAYS GET
WHAT YOU WANT

*O*ur first married evening out! It was like a first date. I wanted to feel as excited as Dave, but the tiny drops of sweat trickling down the side of his face told me otherwise.

We drove across the Burnside Bridge and traveled twenty minutes to Washington Park. It was dark by the time we got there with lights only in the parking lot. Weren't there parks near where we lived? Why had we crossed over the Willamette and driven back to the less-desirable side of town?

What is he thinking? Dave, really disappointing, man.

We exited the car and stood on the sidewalk as Dave gazed into the dark expanse of the park. I followed his gaze, but I couldn't make out a thing. Raindrops fell sporadically now, promising a real Oregon downpour. I wanted to get back in the car.

"Ah, here it comes. People in Oregon don't tan, they rust," Dave said with a loud chuckle. "Hey, there's my friend."

I didn't like what I was guessing as I watched Dave walk over to a dark-skinned guy standing under a tree. I made out the guy's bell bottoms and a high school team jacket closed all the way up the front, his face hidden under an oversized ball cap. I pulled down on my skirt and pulled my coat closed tighter, and crossed my arms. My eyebrows pushed into a frown and I clenched my lips closed tight. I knew this scenario. I ran for the car and slammed the door shut.

We're back full circle; I could spit nails!

The rain was falling steadily now and fell down the back of Dave's jacket as he handed the man some money and came back to the car with a baggie. We were right back to the Ashland days. I thought we'd moved away from all of that. Dave took off his jacket, shook the rain off, then got in the car and started the engine. We drove in silence as I watched the rain stream down the passenger window.

Dinner was at a bar where I sat with a cold sandwich and greasy fries and watched Dave play pool, joking with the other pool players and taking their money. After each game, he came over and checked on me, his beer breath warm on my face as he kissed me. By the end of game three I was so ticked off I couldn't even look at him.

"Do you need anything, babe? Let me get you a Coke refill. Listen, one more game and we can go home. I'm cleaning up here! You're a good sport, hon. Let me get you some more fries," he insisted. I watched him walk to the bar and tell the bartender to take care of me.

He was totally caught up with winning, probably like his bachelor days. Couldn't he see I was POed? No, he didn't know I was there.

My arms crossed tight across my chest, I glared silently at the man with the dirtiest look I could muster. I tried to burn a hole in his head with my stare, but Dave didn't even look over.

Isn't that what wives do when they're mad? You let the man know you're furious by not speaking and give them the "drop dead" stink eye. If the husband doesn't get the message? I guess the silent treatment goes on 'til he does. That's what Mother did.

Dave finished his last game, collected his winnings, and came to take me home. As we walked to the car, he hustled us a little faster with every step. He opened the door for me to get in, then looked back at the bar. Light streamed out of the open door onto the pavement. Two men with pool cues stood in the doorway but now started walking toward us at a rapid clip. Dave jumped into the car and we peeled out.

A few miles away from the bar, Dave's breathing finally slowed as he wiped his hand across his face. He gave me a side glance. "I guess that wasn't much fun for you. Listen, let's pick up some ice cream on the way home. That'll make you feel better."

"No thanks!"

We entered the apartment and I threw my coat on a chair and stomped into the bedroom. I wanted to slap Dave, but all I could muster was keeping my mouth shut.

Coward!

I didn't know *what* to do with the pent-up rage that was building in my chest, but I sure wasn't going to put up with any more nights like the one we'd just had.

"Ah, come on, honey," Dave said, sitting close on the bed and wrapping an arm around my shoulders. "Don't be mad! We can go to the ocean and eat crab and walk on the beach with our bare feet. Wouldn't that be nice? Let me make it up to you. I've got money now."

His acrid breath almost made me wretch. I turned my back to him.

Later, my husband snored and I stared at the ceiling, thinking. It was too cold to go to the coast, but maybe it wasn't *that* big of a deal to let him have some fun. If we did other activities, maybe we'd stay out of bars. He had worked hard to get a real job and found us a place to live in a better part of town. With a knot of disappointment in my stomach over our first married date, I rolled over and forced myself to fall asleep.

The next weekend we did indeed stay home. I let Dave kiss my neck and move his hands over me passionately. "Wait a minute, let's make this better," he said, walking into the kitchen. He returned with a lit joint, a capsule and glass of water, then switched off the lights.

"Here, take this. It'll make you feel better."

"What is it?" I said nervously.

"Oh, something to relax you. Don't worry, it's all natural, comes from a cactus. Here, I'll take one too."

Being one with Dave always made me feel wanted, loved. As I entered some kind of altered state, I felt those feelings more intensely. I *did* feel relaxed, even peaceful, but Dave became more energetic. He started talking in long, long spurts, most of which I couldn't understand. My mind was full of floating colors, my thoughts scattered, so I didn't care *what* he was saying.

The next morning, I woke up with a terrible feeling. Things happened the night before that I couldn't remember–things we did with our bodies I was sure I didn't want to do, but I couldn't get my mouth to work last night to tell him no. That I *did* remember.

Besides, women did what their husbands wanted, didn't they? In a high school class, the woman teacher passed around *A Good Wife's Guide* and then read from it with her sugar-sweet voice: "A good wife knows her place. Try to make sure your home is a place of peace, order, and tranquility for his return . . . make the evening his. Never complain. After all, he works hard to support you and provide a roof over your head."

In other words, marriage was about pleasing your husband, *no matter what.* I was being a good wife, wasn't I? I did what Dave wanted. But I felt bad, inside my heart and my body, humiliated, even dirty. It was Dave's behavior that made my eyes burn. My spirit was crushed, burned-out coals in the bottom of a grate.

We were both of us high . . . but what do I do with what I'm beginning to remember?

I'd have to work hard to make the memory disappear and the revulsion towards Dave.

When the Fourth of July weekend came, Dave drove us to the Oregon coast on Saturday with sleeping bags, food, and beer in a cooler. Even in July the Oregon coast was cool, so we slept in the car, sleeping bags zipped together.

Sunday, we held hands and walked along the smooth, brown sand at Seaside. The seagulls flew around us and the large rock cropping of Tillamook Head, dipping down to the ocean, always screeching. Salty, crisp air and the possibility of finding a whole shell or sand dollar renewed my soul. I was beginning to feel better, even like Dave again.

We ate sandwiches with crab meat bought at Bell Buoy of Seaside and dug our toes into the sand as we sat on our rough Marine Corp blanket. Dave wiped his hands on a paper towel then ran toward the surf. He was like a small boy racing in and out of the waves, daring them to catch him. He was so complex. I really didn't know him, maybe I never would.

At least here he was free of his dark memories for a while. The crash of the Pacific Ocean against the rocks, all the surrounding outdoor sound and color, disconnected me from life too. Dave was enjoying this time at the shore, something I'd only seen him experience when he was stoned or drunk. He still drank his beer that evening, but

YOU CAN'T ALWAYS GET WHAT YOU WANT

cigarettes were all he smoked. That night we sat on the beach, wrapped together in the blanket and did what most people did: we watched the sky change color: light blue to dark orange, pink then a light yellow as the sun fell behind the horizon.

Getting away from the city was restful and even fun. But when we returned, we were back in our hippy life with Dave going to work, me staying at home. And the partying began again in earnest. We had the black light from our trailer days, and hippy posters Dave bought, along with other paraphernalia just for pot-smoking hippies. We had a large multi-colored peace sign, an actual photograph of a couple in coitus with gas masks. Dave's special find was an actual black and white photo of Frank Zappa on a toilet with the caption, "Frank Zappa Crappa."

"Perfect for our weekend guests," Dave said with a laugh, confessing he hoped the posters would make people gasp. Counter-culture, he loved to shock. I was secretly horrified with the graphic detail, but I stayed quiet so Dave wouldn't see how "unhip" I was and remember what a "good wife" I was. Besides, as he reminded me often, he was paying the bills.

In our new digs, the party weekends included lots more people who showed up unannounced, from who knew where. We hosted potheads, junkies, drug dealers, and a young couple who lived in our building on the first floor. Linda and Casey had met in foster care and ran away to be together. They'd been in the building six months before we came. Casey worked downtown near Dave in a corner grocery store and regularly rode to work with him.

Linda was truly a Godsend for me with all the weirdos who showed up on weekends. She was expecting and I was intrigued. Her moods changed as the baby developed and her tummy expanded. We shared like long lost girlfriends; I hoped I was a Godsend for her too.

On Fridays, with money burning a hole in their britches, Dave and Casey went on the hunt for other "necessaries." LSD, speed, and pot had to be purchased to fuel the weekend party. I suspected there were other substances, too, but I didn't want to know. I'd already had an awful experience with Dave and drugs on a night I was still trying to forget.

Since we spent our money first on drugs and booze, we only had cash leftover for cheaper junk food. Linda and I ate as much hot Ralston cereal or Captain Crunch as we could. Smoking pot was the main thing I had in common with Linda along with the sugary crunchiness that was delicious and satisfied our marijuana munchies. It mellowed us, too, but I wished she was more concerned about its effect on her baby. Linda couldn't have been more than seventeen. Her auburn hair curled under her chin and made her look like a baby herself. Thin with an oval face, her beautiful brown eyes were a little bloodshot as we sat together gobbling.

Laughter and muffled talk floated in from the living room. People I didn't know took turns with the water pipe, drank beer, and passed around the roach clip. The air was permeated with the recognizable burnt rope smell. I really didn't have to smoke the stuff; I only had to breathe. Masses of people filed in and out and, by evening's end, three or four couples, who we didn't know, had passed out on the multi-colored carpet that ran the length of our living room. Casey and Linda had went down to their apartment so Dave and I disappeared to our own bed behind the flowered curtains.

At noon the next day, Dave woke up in a terrible state. He put his hands on his stomach, closed his eyes, and rocked back and forth. "Acid indigestion, and my head is exploding."

He stomped out to the living room and stared at the sleeping couples.

"You guys get the hell out of here!" he screeched, then grabbed his temples.

His long hair was a rat's nest, his beard scruffy, but at least he'd pulled on a pair of boxers. He was coming off the LSD, speed, or whatevert else, a total crash. I was glad to see the crowd go, chillingly aware that we could have been killed in our sleep by those unknowns.

How did all these freaks end up in our place?

Dave wandered into the kitchen. I loved that he forced people out, but I was sorry to see him sick.

"Do you want anything? I need the hair of a dog," he muttered.

"No thanks, hon. I'm just going to lay here for a while," I mumbled, glad not to have to move. My head was pounding too. I needed aspirin, but the bathroom seemed so far away.

That was the month I let Dave talk me into dropping acid for my August birthday. I'd just turned nineteen and wanted to be a part of things, even though I was surrounded by weirdos. I swallowed the powdered milk tablet, then sat on the tweedy couch and stared into space. I loved Santana; his unique guitar rhythms and gentle African melodies pierced my heart and made me floaty. It didn't take long for the LSD to flow through me. I could *see* the music, cartoon notes that floated up and burst against the ceiling. I got up and danced, twirling as the music flowed in and over me.

I wanted to stay awake forever and watch the fantasies in the air. Someone in the room said, "You're peaking, man, you're at the heights!" I laughed and looked around for the guy; it was some stoner with dreadlocks sitting on the floor with the hookah pipe. I sat back down on the couch and closed my eyes. I loved everyone everywhere with an intensity I'd never known.

A woman next to me said, "You're experienced now. Hendrix ain't got nothin' on you!"

Her words made me open my eyes wide . . . and there before me, in mid-air, spread clear up to the ceiling was a giant, transparent American flag. It waved gently in an unseen breeze, undulating slowly and silently across the room. "Hey, you guys, do you see that?"

"What is it, honey?" Dave asked, looking where I was looking. "I don't see nothin'."

"You can't see that giant American flag?" I looked at him with surprise and I pointed to my beautiful banner of colors. I stared at the people all turned toward me, then we all laughed. Dave chuckled along with this but then quickly turned away, a sadness in his eyes.

I was lost in my own paintings of light and color, vivid happiness. The room was warm and conversations buzzed around me. Relaxed, mellowed, sheer contentment flowed through me, alone in my imagination that had come to life.

It had been eight months since we'd moved from Ashland and we were right back in the drug world.

The Monday after my birthday shindig, I woke up with a sour stomach. Dave called it "acid indigestion" because LSD was cut with arsenic. I looked over the living room—empty beer bottles, overflowing ashtrays, and empty carryout boxes. The air was stale with the stench of cigarettes and weed. Dishes were piled up in the sink and dirty pans sat on the stove with dried-up hot cereal.

Dave had long since gone to work and I was in charge of cleanup, but I felt so sick. I laid back down. I could stay under the covers until one o'clock, then I'd have to hustle to get things picked up before Dave arrived home at four. *What kind of a life is this?*

CHAPTER 13

DRUGS, BABIES, AND GOING TO CHURCH

My dream of a happy marriage with kids was gone. It wasn't the life I wanted and I hated not knowing where we were heading.

Where is the brave guy who stood up to Mother? Does he even love me? Drugs, sex, and rock 'n' roll was fun for a while. But now?

I was bored with all the partying, but Dave wanted it to go on. He was just fine with our life as long as he could get stoned on the weekends.

The last day of September, we drove with Casey and Linda to a city park. The sky was dark blue and starstruck. We lay on our blankets in the grass laughing, drinking, and getting high. By 1:00 a.m., the Indian summer had turned to prewinter cold. I pulled my sweater tight and snuggled closer to Dave. All at once bright car lights scanned over us.

"Fuzz," Dave muttered. "We should blow."

Once the lights had faded away, we scooted into the car and headed back to the main road. My eyes closed in a hazy tranquility; I was glad Dave could drive in spite of his own hazy condition. He didn't speed or weave but was focused on the road, his large glassy stare aimed ahead.

"Look! All the signs are backwards," Casey announced with a laugh, pointing at the overhead highway signs. I looked through the windshield and, surprise, he was right: everything was reversed.

Suddenly a car's horn screamed as its bright headlights nearly blinded Dave and me in the front seat. Dave *did* weave sharply to the right and onto the shoulder just as the car whooshed passed us going the other way, car horn still blaring.

Dave rolled down his window and stuck his head out. The brisk cold air blew in, blasting us starkly awake. Then he sat back and cracked up.

"We've been going the wrong way on a one-way road," he laughed, shaking his head. Casey and Linda broke into laughter with him, but it wasn't funny to me. I stared at all of them, wide-eyed and jaw-dropped.

"It's good it's one-thirty in the morning and there's no traffic," I spit out.

"I'll give you that, babe," Dave replied as he whipped the car around.

The three of them continued to jabber and laugh as we found our way to the right highway. I held onto the door handle so tightly my knuckles were white. A chilled sweat dampened my shirt right through to my sweater, my lips tight with worry.

This time, I made sure I could read every road sign that whizzed by us. When Dave parked, I couldn't get up the stairs fast enough to our third-floor apartment. Steam heat helped me defrost as I fell on the sofa, letting out the breath I'd been holding in.

"Hey, you two," Dave said to me and Linda as she plopped down on the couch next to me. "We're gonna go find some speed so we can go to work Monday." He handed me a tab. "Mellow out, babe. We'll be back as soon as we can." He gave me a big stoned grin, kissed the top of my forehead, then went out the door with Casey.

I locked the door behind them and sat down in the overstuffed armchair. Linda had laid down on the sofa and wrapped a blanket around her. She was out. Her baby was due next month and sleep was what she needed, not fear from going the wrong way down a one-way road.

I gazed around the room, enjoying the beginning haze from the LSD tab. Even though I wanted drugs out of my life, I welcomed the high. The anxiety of almost dying in a head-on collision finally began to subside.

The black light was the only light in the room and it made our hippy posters glow. Streetlights cast shadows on the walls and made my hallucinations more vibrant. Ribbons of purple, pink, and orange looped above me. At least my escape from reality was colorful. I stared across the living room, trying to squint my dilated eyes. The Murphy bed wall across from me was partly open, a thick darkness behind it.

I should push that wall closed. Who left it open? Or am I imagining that it's open?

I stared at the opening, fixated. I was sure I saw something moving. With that thought, the darkness took on a life of its own and weaved like a living fog into the room. I watched with terror as the gloom separated into twenty ugly, flying creatures.

I hunkered down against the back of the chair, keeping a terrified eye on the demons. There was no sound as they flew around the ceiling, their glistening wings a purple phosphorescence in the black light's glow. Sharp teeth gleamed and their red, beady eyes sought me out. They circled back and forth from the ceiling to the half-closed area behind the Murphy bed, their secret cave.

I opened my mouth to scream, but nothing came out. Panic tightened my stomach and pushed its contents into my throat.

Linda was still asleep, curled under the blanket. I crept off the chair and slowly backed into the curtained-off bedroom, pressing my hands against my stomach to stop it from roiling. The winged creatures didn't notice and didn't follow. I pulled the bedroom curtains closed fast and pushed my eyelids shut. Still no sound from the other room.

Safe, I am safe . . . I am. They aren't real, they aren't real. I'm stoned, that's what this is. I'm hallucinating! Get a grip, Janet. They're just creatures from your warped mind.

I sat on the edge of the bed with my eyes closed, then scooted back against the pillows as scrambled thoughts and colors raced through my mind. Opening my eyes, I scooted up to the curtains and peeked through. Only my friend was there, asleep in the shadows of the street lights. The partially opened Murphy bed wall still had a deep chasm of dark behind it, but no creatures. With a deep sigh, I closed the curtains and lay down. Flickering light from the stars outside the bedroom windows assured me that the world was still the same.

I placed my hands on my heart, willing it to slow down.

I'm done! No more of any of this!

I must have drifted off because when I opened my eyes, Dave was asleep next to me and the windows around us were heating up from the morning sun.

Adrenaline pumped through me and I felt weird. I crawled over my sleeping husband, went to the kitchen, and gulped down a large glass of water. I filled the glass again and walked into the living room. Linda was gone and all was quiet except for Dave's snoring. I sat on the couch and thought of my night terrors. An immense wave of guilt and self-loathing washed over me. I sat in my self-pity for half an hour, trying to figure out how to get out of the mess I was in.

Then, ever so gently, a different sensation surrounded me with warmth. *Is something or someone here? Molly felt a warmth in Bradbury's story. Is there an angel with me?*

No, no angel; I wasn't pure enough for that, but a soothing peace quieted my heartache.

What would Grandy think if she saw the way I'm living now? I gulped and closed my eyes shut tight. *She'd be so disappointed in me!*

I hadn't thought of Grandy in years and terrible remorse grabbed me. In my mind's eye, I saw her watching me, smiling her compassionate smile, her arms open as if to embrace me. It made me remember cuddling with Grandy in her Prescott house. Now here I was, living a life with a husband whom I didn't really know and doing things I didn't like. I was sure my unseen grandmother saw everything . . . and she still loved me. My heart cracked wide open.

A gassy churning started in my tummy. Acid indigestion . . . or was it something else?

Pregnant? Would Dave even want a baby? Would I?

The thought of what I'd done the previous night and its effects on an unborn child briefly flitted through my mind. I pushed it away fast.

The following week I took the city bus to a clinic and got the truth. I was three months along, due April 1972. Thank you, God, that we had health insurance. *Groovy! I'm going to have a baby!*

I couldn't wait to tell Dave. Would he *ever* get home? At 1:00 p.m. I sat down to read, but it made me sleepy.

I was startled awake by the rattle of a key in the front door lock. It was 4:30 and Dave was home. I ran to him as he came in the door and wrapped my arms around him.

"Well, that's the way to be welcomed home," he laughed, hugging me back.

"There's some news," I gushed. I took his hand and led him to the overstuffed chair.

He stared at me with expectation, impatient. "Come on, spit it out!"

"We're going to have a baby!" I blurted out in one breath.

Dave's face went white and he was silent. I stared anxiously at him.

Finally, a smile broke out across his face, making his beard poke out in every direction. "Really?! Far out!" Then, "I made that happen! Wow! My parents will be thrilled!"

Parents! Will mine be thrilled? I'd been told a grandchild could change things.

That weekend, Linda and Casey came by and we partied as usual, but it was 7-Up for me and staying away from the living room smoke.

"Now we'll both have hippy babies together!" Linda burst out. "What a gas!"

A hippy baby . . . I hadn't thought of that and I didn't like the sound of it. Good decisions had to be made with a clear mind. I'd decided long ago *not* to be like my mother, no matter what, and now, I made another decision. This baby would have a normal, drug-free upbringing.

"I don't want our baby around drugs and partying and weird people," I told Dave later. "Someone could steal our baby to sell for drug money or worse."

"Oh, come on, you're overreacting, Janet! Those weirdos were fine when you were partying with them. I'm not going to change my life just because we're having a baby," he pronounced. "I'm happy the way things are. Hippies have babies all the time and live the way they want. We will too."

My face turned red with anger.

Dave laughed and lit up a cigarette. "What're you going to do about it anyway? Your parents don't want you, you have no money, and you have nowhere to go."

It was true, but he'd never thrown all that in my face before. I went into the bathroom, locked the door, sat down on the toilet, and cried. I was pregnant, helpless, and obviously alone.

You big crybaby. Stop it!

BAM!

The door slammed open with Dave's foot right in the middle of it, a hinge hanging from the frame.

"Don't you ever f*ing lock that door on me again!" Dave screamed. He grabbed my upper arm, dragged me out of the bathroom, and shoved me into the living room. I yanked free and ran to the bedroom, getting as far away from him as I could.

SLAM!

Dave was gone and I breathed a sigh of relief. I went to the phone and called Casey.

"I'm leaving Dave," I told him when he answered. "I know he's your friend, but I need some help to get to the bus station and buy a ticket. Can you get me a ride?"

Casey hesitated. "Uh, okay, I guess I can do that. But really, you should think about what this will do to Dave. He's way excited about the baby."

"Of course he is. I bet he said, 'look what I did!'"

Now I'd have to go home with my tail between my legs . . . or maybe I could call Dave's parents. I didn't know *what* to do, but I sure wasn't going to stay here. Smoking a doobie didn't make someone violent, but Dave's drug use did.

I sat down suddenly, my burst of energy depleted.

Well, Janet, you're really in a mess this time. Now *what? Mother won't take you back, but maybe Daddy will, especially knowing he's going to be a grandfather. But if Mother gets a hold of him . . .*

I waited to hear from Casey. *I hate depending on other people.* I rested my head against the back of the chair and closed my eyes.

When I opened my eyes, it was totally dark. Dave switched on a light, then gave me a sheepish look. "I'm sorry, babe. I really am."

Should I give him a slap in the mouth or call Daddy?

"Okay, well," I took a breath, "something's gotta change for this baby, Dave. I mean it. Us two being hippies is one thing, but I won't raise a child this way."

Dave sat down on the couch. He pulled a reefer from his pocket, lit it, and sucked in the smoke. "What do you want anyway?" he said heatedly. "You have me, you'll have a baby, so what else do you need?"

When he blatantly asked me that, I knew what the solution to my problem could be. "I want to go to church. I used to go to church all the time with Grandy, and I miss it. I miss having God in my life."

Where did that come from? I was bewildered, but it was true.

"The only church I'll ever go to is the Mormon Church. I used to go with my parents when I was a kid," Dave responded. He closed his eyes and smiled as the weed took effect.

WHAT?

I couldn't believe what I'd just heard. Dave's past was a shocker. *I guess going to a Mormon Church would be okay. My friends from high school were Mormons and they were real nice to me, even if Daddy thought they were "nuts."*

"I guess I could try it," I said. "Are they Christians?"

"Of course they're Christians," Dave sneered. "It's The Church of Jesus Christ of Latter-day Saints. That's the real name, see? It's *all* about Jesus."

"I didn't know that. Don't get irritated," I shot back. "All I know about Mormons is that they don't drink coffee and they worship Joseph Smith."

"They do *not* worship Joseph Smith; he was just a prophet. He returned the church to how it was in Jesus' day. Where'd you learn *that* crap?" He rolled his eyes.

"My father said some angel gave him a gold book and that Smith was a nut."

"Well, your father's wrong. You find a ward and we'll go."

The following Sunday we got in the Dodge and headed out on the freeway. The trees were full of color. Fall was beautiful in the Pacific Northwest and I felt a little giddy. We were actually going to church and a new person was growing inside me.

We pulled open the doors of the church and walked in on a soft turquoise-colored carpet. The first thing I saw was a painting of Jesus sitting by a well, a halo of light around his head, and a woman sat near him, listening. It was like a painting I'd seen in Grandy's Bible.

We took a seat on the back row in the chapel. Neither one of us had any church-going clothes and Dave's wool plaid jacket smelled like cigarettes and other things we'd smoked. Some people turned around and gave us a quick once over. Their looks were *not* friendly.

When the meeting dispersed, we couldn't get out of there fast enough. I didn't remember a thing that was preached, but I did notice we weren't welcome and there was an empty path for us to leave. It was definitely *not* like church with Grandy.

Dave lit up a cigarette as he got in. "That's the coldest, nastiest group of people I've ever been around. I mean, come on! Even when I wasn't behaving right as a kid, our family church was still nice to me. Just more proof you got us to the wrong place. You can't do anything right without me showing you, I guess." The irritated tone was all too familiar.

My shoulders and neck tensed and a headache began to tap the back of my head. I inched closer to the window, my breath coming in fast puffs. Tears filled my eyes, but I was *not* going to give into crying. I watched the passing scenery and tried to think about what to say.

"Ah, forget those people back there. That's why I'm a hippy, ya know?" Dave stated. "Love and peace, accepting people, no matter what they look like, no matter where they come from. No one has the right to judge anybody else, especially not church-going people."

"I agree," I chimed in, as my shoulders and neck began to relax.

For the next two weeks, I had constant headaches and threw up everything. Jell-O to crackers, nothing stayed down. Dave took part of a day off to drive me to a woman doctor he'd found. She shooed Dave out of the room so she could examine me. I liked her immediately.

"First babies can be a bit tricky," she said, pulling the light closer as I lay on the table, my feet in the stirrups. "But you're built like a horse so you won't have any trouble."

Built like a horse? Is that a good thing? I hope she doesn't think I look like a horse.

The last week of October Dave agreed to give church one more try. As we drove, he laid down the rules. "Listen, LDS people like to stand around after church and talk a lot. We're not going to do that. And we're not meeting the missionaries."

I nodded. *Why would I want to meet missionaries? Didn't missionaries go to Africa or China?*

The meeting began with a prayer, some announcements followed then a prayer was said by two teenagers over the communion. Other young men passed the bread and water to the congregation after the "amen." The boys were so young and didn't even wear altar boy robes. Everyone was real quiet, even the kids. Dave waved the bread and water away.

"Don't we get communion?" I whispered.

"You're not baptized. And it's called sacrament," he whispered back.

I only took communion at Christmas with Grandy, so I didn't miss it, but *had* I been baptized? I frowned and looked at the floor. I hoped the rest of the meeting would be better. I wanted to feel like I did when I went to church with Grandy. I wanted to feel like I belonged.

After the sacrament was passed, a woman approached the pulpit and began to preach.

They let women preach here? Groovy!

A man got up next and talked about Jesus and how he had ministered to society's outcasts. Dave and I were hippies, outcasts too. I liked that.

With a final prayer, we all got up to leave, but Dave was stopped in the foyer by a mustached man. He began chatting with Dave—and Dave was smiling! *Huh?* I hurried over.

"I'm glad you came," the man said. "I'm Gary Henshaw. Are you a member?"

"I am," Dave answered, "But my wife isn't."

Gary's face was friendly; there was no hint of judging us like before. He didn't even wrinkle up his nose from the smell of Dave's coat. Gary offered me his hand. "Welcome." He turned back to Dave and said, "Do you think your wife would like to meet the missionaries?"

Okay, here it comes, He's going to lose it and the church guy will see the real Dave.

"What would that mean?" he asked hesitantly.

"When you're home with your wife, two missionaries would come teach her about the gospel. Then she could decide whether or not to be baptized."

There it was again, baptism.

Dave was quiet and looked at the floor. Then he said, "Okay, I guess we'll try it."

What? What happened to "we're hippies"? Peace, love, and rock 'n' roll?

"What do you think, Janet? Do you want to give this a try?" Dave questioned.

If it meant we'd come to church regularly, then yes.

The following Monday evening, with missionaries scheduled, I watched Dave smoke some weed and down a beer. Old habits die hard. I just hoped he'd behave during the lesson.

At 6:00 p.m. sharp, there was a knock at the door and I opened it for two young men in suits, ties, and name badges. They entered the living room and saw our obscene posters, but quickly looked away. Dave gave them a wicked grin and offered them each a chair.

Marijuana and cigarette aroma filled the air. Embarrassed, I waited for some judgmental remarks, but they didn't say a thing. *Thank you, God!*

"Thank you for letting us teach you. I'm Elder Clark, this is Elder Benson."

Elder Benson was tall with shoulders that looked like they'd poke out of his suit. I loved his carrot top hair and wire-rimmed glasses. Elder Clark barely reached Elder Benson's shoulders, but his smile was genuine and his blond hair was neatly parted and combed. Dave was every bit a hippy with his long unkept hair. I wasn't much better with my blonde hair a frizzy mass.

All of us seated now, we looked at each other awkwardly.

What do you say to missionaries? Do you offer them something to drink?

"We have an inspirational message to share with you," Elder Clark began, "but first we'd like to start with a prayer and invite the Holy Spirit to be with us."

To me, spirits were the night of *unholy* flying terrors. But there was Grandy's spirit the morning after, so maybe . . .

I hope they can answer some of my life questions. I'll need it for our baby. What can I teach my child? I know so little about anything.

CHAPTER 14

PEACE, LOVE, AND PRIESTHOOD?

"Sister Jenkins, please notice what you're feeling as we pray."
I feel nervous and insecure. Does that count?

I clasped my hands together, as I'd been taught to do and watched the Elders cross their arms over their chests. Was that a Mormon thing? Were they protecting their insides from bad juju? I wanted to do what was right so I crossed my arms while the Elder prayed for guidance, a blessing on our home, and, "please bless Sister Jenkins. Amen."

I looked up at the young men, my eyes wide open. No one had ever asked for me to be blessed, ever, not even Grandy. I felt important. My adrenaline changed to flying butterflies.

"I hope you had a warm feeling just now," Elder Benson said.

A warm feeling? No, but I'm curious and excited to get my life questions answered.

"I'm feeling okay," I offered. I looked at Dave. He just shrugged his shoulders.

"I want to ask you guys some questions before you start teaching though." I gulped and rushed on. "I wonder why there isn't a large cross up behind your preachers in the church."

"We have deep respect for other Christians who use the crucifix as a sign of love for Jesus," Elder Clark explained, "but we choose to focus on what Jesus *did* rather than how he died. He loved each of us so much He allowed himself to go through that horrible death to pay for our sins. We try to follow his example, think more about what He did when He was here."

I liked cross jewelry. But thinking about how Jesus lived instead of how he died was much better, made more sense.

"Do you guys believe in angels?"

"Absolutely!" Elder Benson assured me. "You can read Mark 16 for a beautiful description. Angels are very real and holy. Each of us also has guardian angels who watch over us or bring us comfort. Sometimes an angel can be an ancestor, someone you might have been close to in life who loves you dearly and watches out for you."

I caught my breath and blinked. *That was no accident that I'd felt Grandy's presence two months ago. Wonderful! She really is near me.* I felt my tears well up.

I asked a few more questions and shared what Daddy had told me. But soon I was overloaded with so much information from the two young men I could hardly think. I was just glad they weren't pushy; it was a lot to take in. And it *did* feel comfortable, like church with Grandy in Arizona.

After an hour, the missionaries left and Dave put the chairs back in the kitchen. "Well, none of what they said was news to me. Kind of boring, really. But it was fun seeing their reaction to my posters. Did you notice they sat with their backs to them?" He gave a hearty laugh, then went to lie down.

Annoyed, I mashed my lips together. Those were nice kids. I didn't like the posters myself, but it was Dave's house—he paid for everything, as he pointed out. Right now, thinking about Jesus as more real was a curiosity in my brain. I'd have to try to imagine Him listening when I prayed.

After that first lesson, we went to church every Sunday. I wasn't sure how long it would last, but the people were nice and it gave me a reason to get maternity clothes. Dave still smoked both kinds of plants and drank when he felt like it, but he seemed a lot less stressed. When he *did* get upset, I worried. It was like he'd never kicked in the bathroom door. The subject was never discussed so I tried to forget it.

Another secret to keep. I shook my head. I didn't want to raise my children with secrets and self-esteem crushers. It might be something to pray about. If God really had all that power, couldn't he take bad memories away? Like Mr. Spock in *Star Trek*, with his Vulcan mind-meld. I'd have to try . . . a good reason to stop putting off saying prayers on my own.

That Sunday, while Dave napped, I sat on the couch, bowed my head, and crossed my arms like I'd seen the missionaries do. "Hi, God, it's me," I whispered gingerly. "Um, I have some bad memories and awful feelings about Dave. You know all, so I know you know. It's not good to have anger and resentment in a marriage. So please take these feelings away, God. In Jesus' name, amen."

Two months into my lessons, I met Gwen Foster from Church. With auburn hair and gold-rimmed glasses, she was a mother to three teen girls. Gwen was kind enough to pick me up for a Church women's meeting on Wednesday. Leaves flew off maple trees as we drove along. The sky was silvery gray and the clouds looked ready to burst.

"We have one of those big maples in our backyard," Gwen shared as she drove. "I sure love those big crimson leaves, but it's also quite a mess to rake up."

"We had pine trees growing up in Arizona, Oregon too. I like the way they smell," was all I could think to say.

The meeting was called Relief Society. When it was founded in the nineteenth century, women were focused on giving relief. Today there would be a lesson and a chance to visit.

We went upstairs above the sacrament room. It was comfortably warm after running in from the rain that was coming down hard now. Gwen and I sat down just as a woman stood and walked to the front of the room.

Gosh, I hope there'll be snacks; I'm always hungry these days.

"That's Sister Gardner," Gwen whispered to me. "She works for an insurance company but always takes her lunch break to come here."

"I've always had trouble fasting," Sister Gardner began. "I like the idea that our fast offerings are used to help people. It's a privilege. But I always get sick and have terrible headaches when I try to fast. This past Sunday I was determined to try one more time. I asked God to please help my body manage the lack of food; please allow me to show my faith. I wanted missing meals to mean something on a deeper level, not just going hungry."

Her eyes started to glisten and she gulped, holding back her tears.

"I love the fact that we can approach the most powerful Being in the universe. I testify that God heard me and I was able to fast without any physical problems. God *does* hear our prayers, sisters, and I'm so grateful."

Sister Gardner sat down as emotion built inside me, a fire beginning to spark. I'd never felt this way before. I didn't feel like shouting hallelujah, but it was an intensity mixed with a feeling of peace. There were so many things to think about with this church. I liked the people. The women were friendly, not gossipy or critical. More like Grandy and not at all like Mother.

The next time we met with missionaries, the young men shifted their attention to Dave.

"Brother Jenkins, we have an important question for you," Elder Benson began.

"Okay . . ." Dave replied hesitantly.

"If you can give up your smoking and, ah, other Word of Wisdom practices, you can be ordained as a priest and baptize your wife."

My jaw dropped. My husband a priest? The thought stunned me! He *was* back to treating me nicer these days, like when we first met. He stayed home more on the weekends and helped with things around the house. A real husband, like I'd dreamed he would be. Maybe it was the church thing, or maybe it was just because I was pregnant. I cuddled closer to him and he took my hand. Dave looked at the floor, his brows pushed down.

"I'll see if I can manage that," Dave quietly offered. "I'll need some help, though. I've tried to quit smoking before and it's harder n' hell. Uh, sorry, Elders."

I'd never seen Dave without a cigarette. And drugs seemed to help him manage the things he wouldn't discuss. My heart filled with tenderness.

"We can give you a blessing, Brother Jenkins," Elder Clark said, ignoring his word choice.

"Okay, you guys. What's with the brother and sister thing?" I asked with a small giggle. "Sisters are nuns, right? So what gives?"

"Well, it's not too different from what hippies believe," Elder Benson smiled. "We're literally brothers and sisters, Heavenly Father's spirit children. A lot of faiths believe that."

"I see," I replied, feeling a little silly.

Dave received a blessing the following Sunday. But on Monday morning, he started off to work with a pack of cigarettes in his pocket.

"This is my last pack, see?" Dave showed me. "I only have three ciggies left. When I get home, I'll be done smoking for good." We hugged each other and I thought he'd never let go. He began to tremble as what he'd just admitted sank in.

"I'll have to give up the booze, too, I guess. I really *would* like to baptize you, honey," Dave shared with me, his eyes a little moist. "I hope I can get through this." He gave me a peck on my cheek and left, closing the door fast behind him.

I *was* really pleased he was going to try. Whatever dragon he had by the tail I hoped would soon be behind us.

Mother's accusing face and words flashed through my mind: *"If you marry that man, you'll never be welcome in this house again."* Well, *Mother can go to hell! Sorry, God.*

Dave came home from work that same, cold November day and slammed the front door. He stalked into the living room and glared at me. He looked like a train wreck.

"Wha- what's the matter? Are you okay?"

Did he lose his job? My nerves were instantly on edge as I wondered what had happened to the loving husband who had left for work that morning.

"I'm fine," he growled as he stomped into the kitchen. I heard the hiss of a beer can opening.

Drink in hand, Dave threw himself into the overstuffed chair. He knocked back more brew, then looked at me again. His blue eyes were hard, his face intense with anger.

Will he put his fist through a wall or come after me even though I'm pregnant?

I scooted a little ways away from him on the couch, clutching my napping blanket up under my chin. Fear choked my thoughts.

Finally, Dave blurted out, "I gave my last three cigarettes to Casey this morning because he was broke. So, I haven't had a smoke all day!

Dammit!" He finished his beer, crushed the can, then bent over to untie his boots.

"Quitting smoking is harder than I thought it would be . . . and it's barely been a full day." He took a breath. "I don't know how long it'll take to get this poison out of my system. It's been years since I started," he admitted. "And the cravings, smoking whenever I wanted was how I got through the day, ya know?"

I snuck food when things were bad, but it was nothing compared to smoking. Nervously, I moved a little closer to Dave and took his hand. I was trembling, but I felt sorry for him. I hoped he saw my support for him on my face.

"I'll stick it out if you can. You've been through worse, right?" I asked gently. Dave pulled his hand away and covered his face with both of them.

"Yeah, but who wants to remember? My memories are movies in my head," he said haltingly. "I can stop drugs–pot–anytime, but kicking cigarettes? It's hell." His forehead wrinkled up tight and he clamped his lips shut. His misery flooded the room.

"How about some dinner?" I offered. "We could go to that little hole–in–the–wall place."

Dave nodded. We headed down the street to the little pizzeria, a favorite, owned by a real Italian family. It was a dive, really, with four small tables, checkered tablecloths, and low lighting, but we loved supporting the locals.

The authentic pizza tasted real good going down, but the moment we got home, Dave rushed to the bathroom and threw it all up. A few minutes later, he came and sat next to me on the couch, his face pale, his eyes glazed over. We sat in silence holding hands, the only light around us coming from the kitchen.

Please, God, if you're real, if you hear me, please help my husband.

"I haven't thrown up like that in years. I think I'd better lie down," he said as he headed to our curtained-off bedroom.

It would be three more miserable days for Dave. When he came home from work on day two, his face wasn't all scrunched up with irritation. I had food waiting for him and the house was clean and peaceful. I tried to be the "good wife," like I'd seen on TV.

After eating, we sat in our separate spaces. With him in the overstuffed chair and me on the couch, we read through our individual blue copies of the Book of Mormon, like the missionaries asked us to do. We were supposed to pray about the Book, too: was it true scripture? An angel telling me would be groovy . . . or even some kind of warm feeling, but I didn't feel much of anything. I *did* like reading with Dave; it was one more thing we could do together. And it took his focus off his nicotine cravings.

At the end of day three, he came home and gave me a kiss as he sat down to eat. "Hi ya, wife," he said with a wink.

Relief! Maybe we're over the hump. Time will tell. I still better be cautious though.

Dave's appetite increased, just like mine. Four months pregnant and I realized the cliché was true: I was eating for two. I couldn't down enough chocolate ice cream, spaghetti, and red licorice.

"It's good to have an income to let us both eat like pigs," Dave said, laughing.

With the next missionary visit, we were ready to become part of the ward. Dave was finally without any kind of smoking odor around him, and he said he was even done with beer, although it had only been a few days since he'd thrown one back.

I cautiously looked forward to the new kind of life we were trying to create. We had a decent income and, after the baby was born, maybe there could even be a house. We'd be settled in as another normal, American family.

"Are you ready to be baptized?" Elder Clark asked.

I nodded and felt that warm pressure build again in my chest. "Okay," I said abruptly. "Let's do the baptism!"

I was going to be a Latter-day Saint like Dave, who was now drug and cigarette-free. Maybe this would make my parents happy too.

I need to share my news with Daddy.

One Friday afternoon, I placed a call to Daddy's college office. No

SO MANY FREAKIN' SECRETS

need to get my husband, or especially my mother, involved. I heard my father pick up the receiver and say hello.

I couldn't speak. It had been a while since I'd heard his voice and the last time I saw him . . . I didn't want to think about it.

"Okay, who is this? I don't have time for any student pranks now, so you'd better–"

"Daddy, it's me, Janet," I said quickly, my breath coming in short, shallow spurts. "I . . . I wanted to say hello."

There was a long pause, then Daddy said, "Ah, Janet . . . good to hear your voice. You're in Portland now, I believe. I hope your husband is taking good care of you."

Wow, he still doesn't believe I married the right guy.

"Yes, Daddy, he is. Turns out he's a good guy. And . . . and, we're expecting our first baby." I paused and then blurted out, "I'm happy, Daddy."

"Good for you," he said, now sounding distant and preoccupied.

"Um, I wanted to share some other news with you too," I said in a rush. "I'm getting baptized into the Mormon Church. They really believe in Jesus, Daddy, and I have met some nice people. We're building a good life for our baby by attending church now."

The next pause was so long I wondered if he had hung up on me.

"Dad?"

"I never said Latter-day Saints weren't good people, Janet, but why'd you go and commit to something stupid like baptism? I guess you finally got yourself into a church, didn't you?" he said cynically.

Sadness poured through me. I held the receiver closer to my ear and dropped my chin.

How can I make him realize I'm happy? I'll never please him.

"Okay," he sighed with finality. "It is your own life now. You're a grown woman, so you can do what you want. I hope you're happy."

"I am, Daddy."

"Well, I have a lot of work to get back to. Thanks for letting me know how you're doing; I've been wondering," he said quietly. "Call again sometime."

Click!

The attempt to draw my father into my life ended abruptly.

He thought I was doing something stupid. I disappointed him . . . again. I didn't care about Mother's opinion, but I wanted Daddy to understand me. Maybe once the baby was born and my parents were grandparents . . . I'd heard attitudes toward forbidden marriages changed.

I was baptized on a Saturday with only a few people in attendance, including Gwen, her three daughters, the bishop, and his wife. After I'd been immersed in the water and confirmed with hands on my head, I saw myself with new eyes. Was I different now?

How do you feel, Janet? Do you feel free of bad things? It sure was a rush, being the center of attention at the baptismal font. It was nice that people came just for me, but I missed Daddy. No, I really didn't feel much different, just pleased I'd done something good for our baby. Still, I had a calm, warm vibe. If it was from baptism, I wanted to feel more of that internal peace. I could be at peace for my baby.

CHAPTER 15

HIPPIES CALL IT "A HAPPENING"

"Would you like to run to the store with me?" Sister Gwen asked via phone. "Maybe we could start stocking you up with baby stuff. My gift," she added with a little giggle.

I looked at the phone with surprise.

Now that I was twelve weeks from my April 1972 due date, the overwhelming checklist of things I needed loomed large. Baby clothes—rompers that snapped in the crotch over cloth diapers and plastic pants. It was a kind invitation and I smiled.

I had been smiling a lot lately. Maybe there *was* something to this church thing and I was now a Jesus Freak, like hippies said. I adored the thought of having a child of my own to love. Having enough of what the baby needed would be a comfort, too, and a shopping trip was a start. It supported my all-consuming desire to give my baby what I'd always wanted. Baby things? Yes, but especially a never-ending love, no matter what.

"Thank you, Sister Foster. I'd love to go, but I can't do much walking these days."

"Oh, call me Gwen. And I promise I won't make you walk *too* much."

I was glad she was coming to take me out. But I was gladder that Dave and I had moved from the little apartment with a Murphy bed and bad memories. Gwen picked me up at our newest digs, a simple one-bedroom duplex.

Since Dave had our one car, I was left on my own all day, which meant Gwen took me to my prenatal appointments weekly as my delivery date drew near.

I'd never been in a Lincoln Continental before and I loved riding in Gwen's. It was a bump-free ride in aqua blue. I slid in on the smooth, leather bench seat and we moved down the street in a warm aquamarine bath. I held my head high; a very pregnant queen being chauffeured.

"This is the biggest car I've ever been in! The front end just goes on forever."

"It's a Mark IV with a V-8 engine," Gwen remarked, stopping at the light. "I wanted the nifty little Jaguar coupe with the mahogany dashboard, but my husband likes this big engine. It'll protect us better if we get in an accident—although you'd have to be blind not to see us coming!" Gwen added with a chuckle. "Let's stop at my house for a minute."

We pulled up in front of a white, colonial two-story with green shutters. It sat up on a small hill away from the street, which made it appear even more impressive. This was a medical doctor's home. Daddy was a doctor, too, a professor, but his house didn't compare. It was an exciting opportunity to see how "the other half" lived.

"Come on in for a few minutes," Gwen offered.

Gwen opened the front door and I walked in on a maroon-carpeted foyer. A polished wood hall tree with hooks for coats and a tufted cushion to sit on stood sentinel to one side. Photos of Gwen's three daughters were on the wall opposite, framed beautiful faces. Gwen and her husband were clearly proud of their children. A sudden wave of sadness washed over me.

There were no photos of me in the Ingalls' home, not even when I was little. I'll have to remember to do this for my child.

I followed Gwen further into her house as I heard a bustle of female voices. We walked into the living room and I stopped cold. A dozen ladies I recognized from church sat on Gwen's matching gray tweed chairs and sofas. My mouth dropped open and I stared.

I must be interrupting something.

"How . . . what—?" I muttered, stupefied.

"Surprise, Janet!" someone called out. I scanned the room as clapping and laughing filled the air.

"We knew you'd need a lot of baby things, so we're all here to help you out!" Gwen announced as she put her arm around my shoulder.

My eyes grew even wider, then a waterfall of tears streamed down my cheeks and onto my shirt.

Gwen led me to an elegant, white, high-back armchair and I plopped my very pregnant self down with a thump. The women were quiet and watched me with affectionate smiles. Near me was a folding table piled high with presents wrapped in paper with baby designs and dangling ribbons with pastel colors.

I was gob smacked. I'd never seen so many gifts. Speechless, I continued to weep, my chest and tummy heaving up and down with each ragged breath. I tried to stop, but the shock of it all wouldn't let me. No one had ever thrown me a party, not even a birthday party.

I hope they won't look down on me for crying. Mother sure wouldn't approve.

Intense gratitude and disbelief gripped me hard. Strangers had planned this party in secret, completely unselfish.

A lady with red hair handed me a box of tissues, a little moistness in her own eyes. "You cry all you want. You and the baby deserve a celebration. It's a lot of fun for us too!" she whispered as she turned to go.

I wiped away the tears and an immense smile filled my face as I looked at each lady.

What do I do now? Is there cake or something? I'm starved.

Another woman approached.

I wish I could remember all their names, but twenty women! They know my name but. . .

The second woman picked up a wrapped present and handed it to me. "You'd better get started or we'll be here all night," she said with a wink.

For the next two hours I opened gifts, all things baby: rompers in many colors with baby animals, eight packages of cloth diapers and plastic pants, baby bottles, pacifiers, diaper pins, and bibs. Someone had crocheted a matching hat and baby-sized sweater of blue, and there were handmade flannel receiving blankets.

Then Linda came up.

Finally, someone I know besides Gwen!

I remembered her because she was chubby with salt and pepper hair. She wore a white dress to church once and I thought, *She's not ashamed of her size. I was always told* fat *women don't wear white or bright colors. This is all so different from how I grew up.*

She offered me a huge, round package wrapped in orange paper with a giraffe motif, all of it held together with brown jute twine.

"Just pull on this end," she said as she offered me a twine end.

I pulled and the paper fell away. *How clever, no tape!*

Lying across Linda's arms was a yellow quilt with orange backing. The appliqued baby giraffe had big blue eyes, long dark eyelashes, and a large silly grin. Green palm tree fronds fell over its head and a small monkey with a banana sat at the animal's feet. All of the appliqued design was sewn in place with small, white stitches.

"Quilting is what I do when I can't sleep," Linda shared quietly, "which is most nights. I thought a baby giraffe would be good for a boy or a girl."

"Wow," I whispered in total wonder. Someone had stayed up nights to make me, make my baby, a one-of-a-kind gift. I looked at the stranger standing before me as tears formed again in my eyes.

Linda's brown eyes held mine with an internal calm. She was a woman you wouldn't notice in the grocery store, never guessing what an artist she was. All I could say was, "thank you" as she walked back to her chair. She gave me a small smile as she sat down, her eyes half-closed. The loss of sleep was part of her gift. I wished I could find the words to say what was in my heart.

Cake (*finally!*), a nut cup, and a 7-Up and sherbet frappe were served with matching paper plates and cups. I continued opening gifts in between bites of sweet mouthfuls. The ladies clapped with each unwrapping and chattered happily among themselves. Their giving personalities was a warm cocoon encircling me. I'd never felt so welcomed.

Afternoon slipped into early evening with wrapping paper, ribbon, and baby items lying in a pile around my feet. I rubbed my hand over my tummy as baby Jenkins kicked and rolled around, making my maternity blouse crumple and pop. Exhausted, I sat back in my chair.

Gwen came over and said, "Okay now, close your eyes. We have one more thing."

I wiped my face with a giraffe napkin, took a breath, and put my hands over my eyes. I heard her walk away, then return in a few minutes. The room went quiet.

"Okay—you can open them now."

I did. There before me was a white wicker bassinet on wheels, with a shelf under and a hood at one end. I glanced up at Gwen, my mouth hanging open and my eyes full of tears *again!* The room of church women cheered and clapped, and I did too.

"We can put your gifts in the bassinet and take them out to the car when you're ready to go," my hostess announced. "The wheels fold under and we can slip it all onto the back seat.

The party finished and the women wished me well on their way out. It would be many months of church attendance before I'd remember which face went with which name, but I'd never forget that incredible day.

Gwen drove me home with the bounty of gifts filling the backseat clear up to the ceiling. I was silent. The intensity of the afternoon was beyond belief, beyond words.

Why would all those women—sisters—do such a thing? Where do women like this come from? Mother never had female friends. Grandy did nice things for others, true, but this was just far out!

Dave returned from work and saw the presents piled all around me . . . and my big grin.

"So they did it," he snickered. "Sister Foster's been planning your party for months. I'm glad for it too; who knew a baby would need so much stuff? It'll save us a lot!"

I nodded. *Well, that was gross. It might have been fun to shop with him for the baby, but come on! It's from compassion and love, Dave.*

That big *X* on the month of April was fast approaching. And on top of that, we'd lost all our hippy friends, though we did have some new friends from Church. Still I was sad my pot-smoking friend Linda and I wouldn't be moms together.

As the days passed, Dave came in and out, mostly going out to play basketball or volleyball at the church; I took long naps while he was gone.

Man, I can't wait to get this baby out of me!

I was grateful we'd completed the birthing course offered at the hospital, I felt less anxious about what was coming. Dave had learned to coach me and I'd learned to focus on my breathing. I had no idea if I was ready or not, but the classes made me less scared.

I'd written to my parents about the baby and shared my April 14 due date, but there were no calls or letters in return. I missed Daddy, but Mother wouldn't even talk about sex, so I doubted she'd have much to say about delivering a baby. Dave's mother, a part-time nurse, didn't reach out either, so it was good to have Gwen drive me to my last few checkups. I could talk to her about giving birth, grateful that she didn't tell me horror stories about her own experiences.

"Tell me about how you came to join the Church," Gwen said as we drove along the first Wednesday in April. "I know you took missionary lessons."

"Oh, it was interesting," I admitted, "mostly because of the change I saw in Dave. In the beginning, he was real nervous." I took a breath.

Should I tell her about how we lived before the Church?

"Umm, you know we were hippies before we joined, right?" I added tentatively. "In fact, acceptance of everybody, promoting love and peace, that's what made me interested in the Church too; the same ideas I already believed in but with a firm foundation now. Our lives, er, the people we hung out with, I'll admit they were more about drugs and sleeping around than being an active part of the peace movement."

I shook my head in dismay and looked out the window.

Gwen was quiet.

"So," I added hesitantly, "and I hope you won't think less of me, but, well, we *did* smoke pot, mostly on the weekends with our friends. Even when the missionary lessons started, Dave still had to light up before they arrived. The missionaries never said a word. That really impressed me." I chuckled, my cheeks turning pink. "The whole place reeked of marijuana the first few times they came."

Gwen pulled up to a stop light and suddenly burst into boisterous laughter . . . and she kept laughing as we pulled away. "I'm sorry," she managed to say, still chuckling and wiping away tears, "but honestly, what you've shared is such a relief."

"It is? Why?"

"Well," she began, "a lot of times the missionaries came over for dinner after they finished teaching you. It was good for the girls to be around them and I figured feeding them once a week at least gave them something to eat besides peanut butter. But a few times I got concerned. I took Gerald in the bedroom one evening and said, 'I'm sure I smell marijuana! You don't think those boys—?' 'Heavens no!' he assured me, 'they must have been somewhere they picked up the smell, you know how potent it is.' Now I know."

Gwen laughed heartily again and I laughed with her.

"I'm glad you told me. I really didn't think . . . but I knew what I smelled. It all makes sense now."

I'd never been thanked for smoking weed. It was so ridiculous I had to giggle.

Monday evening, Dave and I sat playing cards. It was like old times except without beer or smokes. The baby bouncing around made my stomach rumble. A few minutes of pleasure for Dave and nine months of hormones and body changes for me, but at least there'd be a baby. Another sudden kick popped my blouse up. It made me smile . . . until it didn't.

"Bathroom," I said, getting up in a rush. Lately, it seemed like I lived in that tiled room. I untied my maternity pants and sat down on the cold seat.

Somebody should make these things warm up!

Suddenly, a warm gush of water rushed out of me.

Weird!

I stood up and another big gush of water flowed out. It soaked everything right down to my socks! I sat down again, shocked.

Then panic rose up as wetness continued to trickle down my calves. *The baby!* I knew so little, even with birthing classes, but I *knew* this was it!

"Dave! Come quick!"

Dave slammed open the bathroom door, took one look at me, and jumped into high gear. The doctor was called, and the prepacked hospital bag and I were driven to the Seventh-day Adventist Hospital. I was checked in and checked up.

"All's normal. Nothing to worry about," the nurse said matter-of-factly as she gave me a cup of ice chips.

Uterus muscles pushed my stomach up and down in waves, starting and stopping all night long and into the next morning. By 4:00 a.m., the intense roiling had doubled. Eight a.m. Tuesday morning and there still was no baby. I'd been in labor for thirteen hours. The doctor came in at nine as my head lolled to the side and sweat ran down my back and thighs.

"I think you may have a lazy uterus," she stated.

What does that mean? Is it worse than being a horse? I'm so tired . . . can't they let me nod off? Dear Jesus, please let this baby come soon!

CHAPTER 16

IT'S CALLED LABOR
FOR A REASON

ive me a sleeping pill and pull this baby out!
"A slow uterus happens now and again," Dr. Chamberlain stated, pulling off her gloves. "Everything's okay, though. The baby's started into the birth canal, so it shouldn't be long now."

The baby's just starting? That must be why the cramping had picked up. Still no drugs for me; I couldn't stand the thought of chemicals in *my* system that might hurt this baby. I'd heard stories about babies being born with fingers missing, blind, or with heart issues. Would smoking pot or, God forbid, an LSD trip cause those things? Ice water ran in my veins.

What have I done? Think of something else, think, think!

"You're built like a horse" galloped through my thoughts. Maybe that was a good thing. How was a horse built, anyway? *"You have a good, wide pelvis,"* was the other thing I was told. Did horses have wide pelvises?

"It'll be like shelling peas for you. You're lucky," Dr. Chamberlain declared as she left.

By 11:30 a.m., hard labor was a miserable reality. Intense muscles pushed hard with only thirty seconds in between.

Let's sing, let's sing . . . What song? Something . . .

"Come, come ye saints," I breathed out, "no toil or labor fear . . ." I tapped my fingers on the sheets with each word. Dave came over and stood next to the bed, a little snicker on his lips and a big smile across his face. "Ah good, you're singing. Would you like some ice chips?"

"Get away from me!" I yelled. He looked shocked, so I screamed louder. "I mean it! YOU DID THIS TO ME!"

I turned my head away, hot tears splashing onto my damp hospital gown.

"Ah, okay, I know what this is," he replied calmly. "This will pass, hon, it really will. Besides, you had fun creating this baby too. You know it's true!"

Yeah, well, that fun was nine months ago and the memory was long gone. He was all I had to get me through this, so I stopped short of saying he probably couldn't handle this pain. I took a deep, steadying breath, and prayed.

God, if you can hear me, give me strength. Steady me . . .please, please.

"All right," I said as another wave began. "I'm sorry. Yes, ice chips, please! Oh, wow! It's a hard one . . . hurry up, Dave!"

Dave scurried over with the paper cup and tossed an ice chip into my open mouth. The cold ran down my throat, soothing me for just a moment as my husband mopped away sweat with his sleeve. I grabbed his hand as another intense riff drove through me.

Dave ripped his hand away and ran to the door. "Nurse!"

A dark-haired woman rushed in, all masked up in green scrubs. "Let's see what's going on here," she said, pulling away the sheet. "Yep, you've made good progress. Let's welcome this new baby into the world."

Before I could say a thing, I was moved onto a gurney, Dave gowned up, and we all moved into the delivery room. Other nurses scurried about under the blinding lights. My legs went up in the stirrups and my bottom was pulled down to the very end of the table.

"Let's deliver this bundle of joy," Doctor Chamberlain said with a warm smile, sitting at the end of the table, like a baseball catcher. "You've done really well, Mrs. Jenkins. You're almost done. Give a really strong push now . . . that's it . . . again. Ah, there's the head! PUSH, PUSH!"

Dave held my head up and I tightened my muscles and clenched the sheet with my fists.

"That's it. Come over here, Mr. Jenkins. Here's your new baby. Put your hands here to take the head. Here it comes . . . oh, it's a healthy boy!"

I slumped back onto the sheets and the baby rolled into Dave's arms. He cuddled his new son against his gown. Eyes big as saucers, his huge grin was obvious, even behind a mask.

Raising my head up, I threw out, "It's a boy, Dave. Our first baby is a boy." If I'd been royalty, the kingdom would be happy. I was suddenly exhausted, but satisfied too.

The doctor gently took our new son, gave him a slap, and baby wails filled the room. "Good lungs; he's a healthy infant. What's the time? 1:12 p.m. Nurse, here take this baby and clean him up, then wrap him in a warmed blanket."

I was prepped to return to my room as my own warm blankets, straight from the dryer, embraced my weary body. Bliss! Dave walked beside me, holding my hand.

That evening, I held my new child. His tiny face was soft, serene. Sound asleep and tightly wrapped in a soft blue blanket, a matching blue cap cradled his head. I saw the Jenkins' nose, and a light peachy fuzz of hair through his crocheted cap. We named him Alex.

"I made a boy," Dave said, standing over us. "I did a good job."

"You weren't alone in this, you know!" I said, irritated. "Didn't you see what just went on in there?"

"Yeah, you did the work, honey, right . . . but look what *I* did too! My sperm brought in all the important bits."

Really, Dave? I could slap you!

I was too tired to argue. Annoyed, I just closed my eyes.

When I woke up it was 5:15 p.m. Alex was gone. So was Dave, which was a relief. I brushed back my messy hair and ran my hands over my tummy. Part of me was sore, but it wasn't unbearable. That must have meant I really *was* built like a horse. Alex was a healthy child and I didn't need drugs to make it happen. Chemicals would never be a part of my life again.

At seven that evening, the doctor came. I was glad to see her, since I had so many questions.

"How is Alex doing? Is he okay? Does he have all his fingers and toes? I should have unwrapped him to check. What did he weigh? Is he—?"

"Nothing to worry about at all," the doctor replied as she took my blood pressure and checked my vitals. "Your son is a normal, healthy six and a half pounds. That's a good weight for a first baby." She uncovered my tummy and checked it carefully. "And you're doing well, too, although I'd like you to stay here a while just to be sure. We like first-time mothers to stay in the hospital for four days to be sure all is well before you go home."

What a comfort; everything was all right. Maybe God really *did* forgive the sins of mothers who repented.

It was 1972, I was a new mother, and I had four days alone with my child. Tears of gratitude flowed with Alex's tiniest moments. I watched him sleep, and watched him try to focus his blue eyes. *Blue like mine! I feel wonderful! God, thank you for letting me have this miracle.* No one told me I would feel so amazing.

Saturday came and reality set in. The first night home I got up every two hours to nurse my son as Dave slept. During the day I changed diapers and sponge-bathed my crying baby, holding him carefully in the warm water of the kitchen sink. I loved dressing him in new little rompers and matching tiny booties. What pleasure those ladies had given me with their gifts.

Four months gone, I sat in bed one evening nursing Alex with Dave next to us.

"I wish I could do that," he said, frowning. "It's not fair you get to do something with *our* son that I can't share in. Especially when he's doing something I used to do."

I gasped at his bluntness. Abruptly, he got up, dressed, and grabbed the car keys.

"I'm going for a drive," he said as he rushed out and slammed the front door.

Rude . . . nasty, Dave!

A surge of guilt followed and a new revelation: Dave was jealous of the baby. Childbirth classes said nothing about what comes *after* a baby's born. Maybe this was something I was just supposed to know, something a mother would tell a daughter probably. One more secret.

I hadn't seen Dave upset like this since before we started going to church. In the past, he'd get stoned or drunk. I just hoped his leaving would calm him down without chemicals.

I put Alex up to my shoulder and gently patted his back, waiting for the sound of his burps. He nodded off to sleep and I carried him to his crib, a recent new gift. Alex curled his fist up under his chin and wriggled himself asleep.

Maybe I *was* giving too much attention to the baby. How was I to know? Dave and I were intimate again, but now I'd have to figure out this new challenge.

Several hours had passed since Dave left. My worried thoughts were a jumbled mess.

Maybe he went to play pool . . . or maybe he's just driving around. Where could he be? What's he doing? I felt more guilty by the minute. At 11:00 p.m., I closed my eyes and fell into a deep sleep. I dreamed of five-year-old Alex gliding down a slide, blond hair cascading over his forehead, laughing in glee. At the bottom of the slide, a soot-streaked little girl stood watching. My eyes flashed open—that dream! When would that recurring nightmare of a poor, lost child go away?

Blinking, I noticed Dave was back, standing over me. *Was he okay?*

Before I could ask him anything, he climbed into bed. He sidled up close and started kissing my neck, traveling down to kiss my mouth. I was grateful he didn't smell like booze or pot, but his roughness made me shrink away from him.

"Stay still," he muttered.

A shiver ran through me as he pushed up my nightgown, my body still half-asleep. I was afraid. I couldn't move under his weight and it was hard to breathe. He was gruff, insistent. I lay as still as I could until he finished and moved to his side of the bed. "You're a stiff board," he said with disgust.

"I wasn't quite awake, Dave. I'm sorry," I replied. For five minutes, I slowed my breathing and settled my nerves. I curled up against my husband's back and wrapped my arms around him, but he was already asleep. I moved back to my side of the bed and stared at the ceiling.

I needed to do better. Maybe a plan: feed and take care of the baby, then try to take care of my husband. His happiness was my responsibility; wasn't that what the Bible said? A wife was a helpmate in whatever way he might need. My stomach felt sour thinking about it.

I have no idea what I'm doing, God. Please help me. Send me inspiration, direction. How do I make this man happy? No one talks about this . . . Now I have two jobs.

Alex reached seven months in November. His teeth were coming in now, and their tiny edges rubbed against my breast. Monday evening, I nursed him one last time before bed. Because it was natural and my soft flesh was there, Alex nipped me, using my breast as a teething ring. I pulled him away and he looked at me, surprised.

"No," I said sharply. "No, Alex." Then I let him finish nursing until he dropped off to sleep.

Every day from then on, it was the same. I even gave him a pacifier, but it didn't help. After four days of sharp, unpredictable pain from his baby teeth, I couldn't stand it anymore. Alex's next feeding was with bottled formula. I cuddled him close, hoping he wouldn't miss our closeness, but I did. I hadn't wanted to stop nursing. My heart ached.

But Alex adjusted to the bottle quickly and still fell asleep after. Dave even fed him now and I was grateful for the reprieve. I hoped he'd feel more involved now and be less irritated. Maybe he'd help with bathing and changing diapers if I asked carefully.

"That's for the mother to do," he stated at the breakfast table. "Besides, I've finally got back what's mine," he said as he grabbed one of my breasts, a teasing look in his eyes.

I drew back in a hurry, cupping a hand over the pain. "That hurt, Dave!" I cried as hot tears filled my eyes. I pushed my chair away from the table and ran to the sink, my stomach a clenched knot. I gripped the sink as I started to shake.

"Oh, come on, don't be such a wuss. Anyway, I know you like it."

I turned the water on to wash dishes, my back to him, shock running through me.

Dave's arms wrapped around me and he lay his head on my shoulder. "I didn't mean to hurt you, honest. I was just playing," he insisted quietly. "All of this . . . I just don't know where I belong. But I'll get my bearings, I promise."

I turned to face my husband and stared into his eyes. He looked sincere. Maybe the pre-baby Dave was still in there.

But I can't keep up with his unpredictable changes: he's nice one minute, then mean the next.

He kissed me and gave me a hug, then walked over to Alex in his high chair and kissed him on the top of his head. "Off to work," he announced.

The months continued to fly by with regular baby checkups. There were no more incidents with Dave and I thanked God, imagining a white-haired man with a benevolent smile when I prayed and warmth sometimes flowed over me. It was how I'd felt around Grandy. I hoped God was helping Dave and he realized it too. He *was* easier to get along with, perhaps he was also sending up prayers.

I turned my attention to a new worry: monthly periods . . . there weren't any and hadn't been since I stopped nursing. I counted the days since I'd stopped and the reality was sobering. I stood at the window and watched a quiet December snow drift down from Portland's overcast sky. I tried not to think about the possibilities, but the nagging questions wouldn't stay away.

Am I pregnant again? So soon?

Alex was only seven months old and it might be true. Pregnant? Why, God?

I already had a baby. Curse that, Dave! Why does he have to have sex every stinkin' night? I'm trying to be a good wife. I did my wifely duty. So, God, why this?

I paced the duplex living room like a crazy woman. *I could spit nails! How am I going to tell Dave? We're saving up for a house.* I balled up my fists. *It's not fair; I don't* want *this baby!*

"What is God thinking!" I yelled, my face an angry scowl.

I didn't care who heard me. I didn't even care if I woke the baby.

Pressure rapidly built in my head. I had to escape. I tiptoed to Alex's room and looked in. At 2:30 he was still in the middle of his afternoon nap. I left his door an inch open, then walked quietly to my bedroom. Far back in the corner of the closet was my box of freakin' hidden secrets.

Time for first aid before I explode!

I sat on the floor, propped up against the bed, and took the lid off the shoebox. Inside, like glistening pirate booty, were two Hershey bars with almonds. I'd snuck in the contraband when I'd gone to the corner mom and pop store over the last several months. And sneak-eating was always more satisfying.

Contraband! It's so good I could bathe in the stuff. Total bliss out, man! Thank you, God, for chocolate. And especially thank you for Mr. Hershey!

My sugar fix returned me to normalcy; at least, what *I* called normal. I watched the snow drift lazily down from the overcast sky. Winter could be so beautiful. Standing in the quiet, I heard Alex goo-gooing in his bedroom. His babbling made me smile.

I found him sitting up in his crib. When he saw me, he giggled and put his arms up for me. My heart exploded with love for this child. I *did* love being a mom, but another baby? Maybe it would all work out okay.

Dave came home not long after my chocolate fix. I didn't know how to tell him he'd be a father again, but it'd be a while before I was showing, so I had time to figure it out.

"I think I'll go play volleyball at the Church," Dave threw out as he disappeared into the bedroom. "Why don't you come? Some of the other wives sit on the sidelines and you could visit and show off Alex."

I nodded, my energy amping up. I bundled Alex and me in warm coats, hats, and mittens, and followed Dave to the car. What a blessing this baby was right then. He was the center of my attention and, for the time being, it made me stop worrying about what I was sure was coming.

We drove to the church with Alex sitting comfortably on my lap. Dave pulled up to the curb and turned off the engine. "This will be good. I need to work off some stress!"

He jumped out of the car with an anxious intensity and ran into the building. Wrapping the baby snugger in his blanket, I stepped onto the cement curve.

Suddenly, I stopped. Someone was puking nearby, retching hard! I held Alex in a protective hug and looked toward the church building. There was my husband, bent over into the bushes, vomiting like he had the flu. He gave a belch and a dry heave, then looked up at me, wiping his mouth on his sleeve. His face was so pallid, it was almost green. With eyes full of shock, his lips curled in disgust. He walked fast to the car, got back in, and slammed the door so hard it made the windows shake.

"The place is full of gooks!" he snarled, starting the engine.

I got back in the car, too, and held Alex close. "Gooks? What–?"

"I thought I'd left all those bastards in 'Nam!" He gunned the engine and we peeled out. "What are they doing in *my* Church?"

We rocketed down the road, Dave's face red with anger. I kept my face blank, but my body stiffened with worry. I sank deep into my seat, holding the baby closer against me. I'd never seen Vietnamese at church, so what Dave saw must have been from a refugee program. Even though he had bright moments of kindness, there were still deep, dark shadows of the past's pain in my husband's heart and mind.

CHAPTER 17

TURMOIL AND BLISS

At 1:30 a.m. that night I heard Dave quietly weeping. I wanted to comfort him, but nothing I said or did helped. After an hour, his breathing quieted with sleep but my rest didn't come for many hours.

I woke up to the baby crying and sunlight reflecting off icicles outside my window. I threw on a robe and fetched Alex. "Oh sweetie," I cooed. I grabbed up my burbling son and took him in the kitchen. We did our morning ritual of feeding, bathing, and dressing. Grateful for set habits, I knew my brain was too tired to think. Once done, I laid Alex on a blanket on the floor with a bottle and pulled the phone onto my lap. I needed to stop thinking about Dave, and think more about my son. Sons? But if I was honest, I just wanted to hear Daddy's voice.

"Dear God," I murmured with my hand steadied on the receiver, "I feel abandoned, but I really am trying to be a good mother. Please let me feel Your arms of comfort around me. And give me courage, help him to understand, Father."

Courage began to fill me as I dialed Daddy's number. I had questions now. Who was *my* mother? Were there any kind of health issues I should know about for my kids? *And just where the heck* did *I come from?*

"Hello, Daddy . . . uh, hi. It's me, your daughter."

"Janet, yes, hi. You always call when I don't have much time, but how's that rugrat of yours? He must be crawling now." I heard the smile in his voice and it made me want to run to Ashland and feel his arms around me. Would I ever be welcome to visit with my child?

"He's well, Dad. You'd like him," I said, my voice tight. I cleared the emotion from it as I continued, "He has your bright eyes. I'll get you some pictures."

"I'd like that," he said, a little hesitant. Then he added, "Your mother would like it too."

No, she'll just say stop having babies. You're too stupid to take care of an infant.

"Thank you, Daddy. But now that I have a son, I need some extra information about me, if you don't mind. I mean, I'm wondering if there's anything, you know, anything I should worry about for my kids health-wise."

"Listen, I've got to go," he responded in his professor's voice. "But honestly, I don't know anything except your biological father was a sailor off some ship, from the Far East, I think. He met your mother when he jumped ship in San Francisco."

What? I certainly don't look Asian. Maybe I am the recessive gene?

"That's all I can tell you, Janet," he said gruffly.

"Okay, um, I guess this makes you uncomfortable."

"Yes. Please don't ever ask me about this again. There's nothing more to say."

My jaw tightened with frustration. *Does he really not know any-thing else? It isn't like Daddy to jump into something as important as adoption without serious preparation. Secrets!*

I felt nauseous, defeated.

"I've got a class waiting, Tiger. I've got to hang up now. Give that baby a kiss for me."

And he was gone.

The brief chat with Daddy formed a tight lump in my chest, but he *did* call me Tiger.

Still no matter what, I can't make my parents happy. I guess Mother's right about me.

My family with Dave evolved. At Christmas we worshiped and felt joy for the birth of Jesus. My tummy got a bit more round every day with our second child. I was glad Dave didn't pay much attention to my figure; I never stopped being nervous about what might set him off. We had our obligatory roll in the hay at bedtime and he dropped off to sleep. Dave needed it, he said, but for me, it was a wifely chore.

January 1973 rolled 'round and I knew that Tuesday morning I couldn't put off sharing the baby news any longer. Dave ate a fork full of scrambled eggs, then put some on a spoon and gave it to Alex. The baby's face turned quizzical as he took the spoon and gingerly put it in his mouth. He let the egg sit on his tongue for a second, then chewed the tender mass, licking a bit of salt from his lips. His face broke into a huge smile and his eyes twinkled with happiness.

"What a big boy!" Dave declared. "Look, hon, he likes scrambled eggs!"

"He does. He eats more grown-up food all the time." I paused. "And that's a good thing. He's getting more independent. That will help when I have to nurse our next baby."

Dave stared at me and angry heat rose up on his face. "What did you just say?"

I wasn't surprised at his reaction, but I had convinced myself he'd be less upset.

"When?" He scanned my body, then stood up. "We're just getting on our feet. How could you let this happen?" he yelled.

"I wasn't in this alone, you know." I stood up to face him. We stared at each for three seconds. Dave's hands turned into fists and I backed away a few inches.

Without warning, he turned and smashed his fist into the wall. Big pieces of plaster and sheetrock bent inward with a cracking sound and dust filled the air. He drew back his fist, now with little cuts and traces of blood. He cupped the hurt hand with the other, his face grimaced with pain. Then he turned to me with a disgusted look. Grabbing my arms, he shook me as hard as he could.

"Dave, stop! You're hurting me!" My teeth were rattling. "Stop it!"

He backed away and looked at me as if seeing me for the first time. Then he ran in the living room, grabbed his coat, and shot out the front door.

I looked at Alex. His mouth stood open and his eyes opened wide, the spoon stopped in mid-air. "Daddy's a little crazy," I uttered. Willing my head and insides to stop shaking, I looked at the wall I'd have to clean up, then turned to my baby. "Let's get you out of that high chair, bud."

Well, that went well. I never know what I'll get with this man.

It had been two years since the last violent incident in the bathroom. Now, it was clear that his temper had never left.

I laid Alex down for his nap. My head wouldn't stop pounding so I took some aspirin and laid down too.

Dear God, now what? Am I going to raise my children alone? You and Jesus were Grandy's best friends, so please be mine too. I need Your help desperately.

I didn't see Dave the rest of that day . . . or the next. I took Alex outside and let the cold air and snowflakes fall on his face as we walked. My heart was so full of love for this child. He relieved my worries. I knew, despite anything else I faced, that this was God's gift: Alex was my solace.

His face filled with wonder. He brushed the white stuff off his face, gave a short squeal, and buried his face against my shoulder. I picked up some snow and held it in my hand for him to touch as it melted and dripped to the pavement. "Really cold, huh, babe? But it won't hurt you. See? It's just running out of my hand."

As we stood there playing, Dave pulled up. He inched around the car and stopped in front of me. He bit his lower lip and looked like a dog who had peed on the rug. "Sorry," he muttered, then turned and went into the house.

I stared at him and words from my mother popped into my head: *"You've made your bed, Janet. Now you have to lie in it."*

But did I really have to? I considered my options as I took Alex inside to get warm.

Leaving Dave was out of the question. I had no way of taking care of a baby *or* myself. How did mothers take care of two babies under the age of two? Fear of Dave gnawed at me.

It would be a cold day in HE-double-hockey-sticks before I'd trust Dave again. My heart was shattered. I stayed away from him as much as I could and spoke to him even less. We ate together, continued with obligatory sex, and slept in the same bed together, but I was empty inside.

The Bible said we should forgive everyone, turn the other cheek, but I wasn't going to turn mine! Forgiveness right now was too much. I'd have to step carefully with a babe in my arms and another on the way.

Being a Christian should be simple: do things the way Jesus did them. I *wanted* to forgive Dave, but "to love and cherish" were just words now. Dave often said everything was my fault anyway. I tried *not* to believe Dave's insults, but Mother's words haunted me.

At least being pregnant, I could eat what I wanted, especially during anxiety and stress. Chocolate, ice cream, or fried chicken . . . it all went down smoothly with no heartburn.

Mid-April, Dave came home with an announcement. "Listen, you know my friend Jeff from Church? He's got to move to California and wondered if we would look after his house. I'm not sure for how long, but we'd only have to pay utilities while he pays the mortgage. At least a year, he said! Isn't that great? God's blessing us cuz we're bringing babies into the world."

A house! I felt a spark of hope and my spirit lightened. There were two bedrooms and even a dishwasher.

"Yes, amazing, Dave. When would we move?" I asked cautiously.

"The first of May, and the guys from Church will help us." Then he looked solemn. "I'm trying to improve things, babe. I really am."

We moved into the house on Northeast Fifty-Six Street on Saturday May 8th. There were two bedrooms, a large bathroom *and* a large bathtub, a maple tree in the backyard, Kentucky bluegrass, and a run-down wood garage. It wasn't much, but it *was* a house and we were in a real neighborhood away from busy streets.

By late July, Alex was walking. He held on to the edge of the couch, then let go and bobbled over to me, my arms outstretched to catch him. I hugged my son, then let him stumble and sway over to his dad. "Look at him go," Dave said, laughing. "He's really a toddler now, just in time for the next baby's arrival."

At six in the evening on August seventh, Benjamin entered the world weighing an even six pounds. His weight seemed low, but his color was good and I was told he'd gain weight quickly from being nursed.

A scripture from 1 Corinthians popped into my head as I thought about the intense love I had all over again for this new baby. It was resolute love: "[it] suffereth long, and is kind, seeketh not her own . . . beareth all things, believeth all things, hopeth all things, endureth all things." We brought helpless little people into the world, enduring all things, hoping and believing. I'd focus on that. I'd given birth twice and something positive was forming in my spirit: a belief in myself. I felt closer to God, honored that He trusted me with His children.

Not Mother or even Dave can take this hard-earned strength from me.

I just hoped if Father was going to send us more spirits that He would plan their arrival time better.

Our lives changed a lot with Ben's arrival, everyone said it would. I didn't understand what that meant, until the next baby came along . . . and then the next. They kept coming, even though we used contraception. We were way out of step with the 1970s concern about overpopulation. Abortion was a major issue too. I didn't have my head in the sand regarding any of it, but I only had energy to focus on my children.

Time whirled by in a dizzying mix of hormones, sleepless nights, feeding, and caring for my sons, fortunately spaced more apart. I thought of how they'd just left God's presence and felt a joy as I envisioned them walking with Jesus. By 1978, there were *five* of them: three boys, finally a girl, and then one more son.

Still, with the joy of birth came disturbing regrets. It seemed every time a child was born, Dave lost his job. After Ben, he was laid off from Western Electric. He got a job selling insurance, then lost it, followed by another job somewhere else. Babies arrived every two years, and every two years, Dave started employment over again. He was too opinionated or insulted a customer or he was too pushy. "I'm not going to be somebody's patsy just to keep some abusive customer happy," he spewed at me over dinner. "You've got your world of kids and I have to put up with a bunch of ass—er, stupid men who try to put one over on me." When a job ended, he'd just say, "Besides, I can always find another one."

There was never enough money now. At least I nursed the babies. I did the best I could making meals from scratch for the older ones. I was exhausted by 8:00 p.m. and dropped into bed the same time as the kids, fear of an unknown future an ever-present ache in my heart.

One night in June after Dave fell asleep, I slipped out of bed to my knees.

Dear Father, these are Your children and You trust us to take care of them. So I pray You will bless Dave to find dependable income. I'm running this household by myself. I'm not ungrateful, truly. There are many selfless, good women from Church as examples to me, thank you. I'm learning so much from them, but every day, it's just me taking care of these little ones. I am open to Your impressions, Father. I promise to work harder to hear You.

Alex age six, Ben age five, and Chris age three slept through the night now. Daisy shared a room with baby Eric and even slept on when he woke for his 2:00 a.m. feeding. I nursed him in the living room and rocked him to sleep in our Goodwill used lounge chair. It was quiet and I felt angels were near, perhaps even Grandy. I treasured those nights of peace.

When Eric was four months old, we moved to Woodburn, Oregon near farms owned by Bird's Eye. Friends at our new church managed their fields of green beans, corn, and strawberries. I scrimped and saved, baked my own bread, bought raw milk for $1.25 a gallon, and learned to make my own butter. I was a real pioneer. But pinching pennies as a young, hippy couple was one thing. Doing it with five kids mostly by myself was a different matter.

Dave ran in and out of our lives on his new-to-him motorcycle, played racquetball with a club membership we couldn't afford, and went to work at his latest job an hour away in Portland. Dave's money was Dave's money. He portioned out a small amount to me for living expenses. The day I ran out of toilet paper and laundry soap was the day I had had enough. I stopped him in the driveway as he prepared his next "run away from home" recreation trip.

"I just don't have enough, Dave. I can't take care of these kids without more money. These are your kids, too, you know!"

"Sure, hon, I know. But it'll be okay," he offered as we walked out to the carport together. "When I get paid next Friday, we'll pick up the things you need. Hang in there," he said as he mounted his motorcycle smiling. "You can make do, I've seen it . . . and I love you for it. Gotta go, my racquetball partner's waiting for me."

He jetted out of the driveway as I fumed! He went where he wanted, when he wanted, and I cleaned bottoms with washcloths because there was no toilet paper and washed diapers in the bathtub with dish soap because there was no laundry detergent. We were down to oatmeal, a package of hot dogs, and homemade bread. Our old car sat in the driveway dripping oil. There was no way out, and I realized Mother's curse had come true: I *was* lying in the bed I'd made.

CHAPTER 18

IT'S ONLY FOR A LITTLE WHILE

I n Woodburn, Oregon with five children, I saw members of my Church more than my own husband. I was the *real* parent who stayed home and managed it all. The one advantage was, so far, no more babies came. *Thank you, God!*

One afternoon, Harold Duncan knocked on our back door. A loving, Grandpa-type with gray fringe that hung down around his ears under his well-used cowboy hat, he visited once a month with a spiritual message or helped when I called him.. He always shook hands with the boys and shared stories with Daisy on his lap. I opened the door with Eric on my hip.

"Come on in. Sorry the house is so messy. You know, three boys, a baby in diapers . . ."

"Oh, Sister Jenkins, you're raising children, not a house. There'll be plenty of time to have everything nice and neat later on." I could have kissed him for that.

Two-year-old Daisy came and stood in front of him. Her light brown hair curled naturally under her chin and freckles popped out all over her nose. "Freckles are angel kisses, did you know that?" Brother Duncan said as he propped her up on his knee. "Now, I have an idea to share with you all. Bird's Eye machines come through the fields and harvest the best of my crops, but when they're through we have lots of fruit left the machines didn't get. We need gleaners to clear the fields for the next season, so I wonder if you and your kids would like to come by and do that for us. You could bring home what you pick. My wife could entertain Eric while you and your mob fill up boxes. What'd ya think?"

Free food and a chance to get out of the house? God used people to do His work, and this was definitely Him working through this kind man . . . an answer to prayer.

"Of course!" I said, tears in my eyes. "The boys would love helping, although I suspect they'll eat more berries than we bring home."

"Oh, that's part of picking," he chuckled. "Let's plan on Friday. I imagine Dave will be out of town working so my wife Jenny will pick you up."

On Friday we bundled into Jenny's car in sweatshirts and jeans. Even though it was summer, there was a little chill in the air at eight in the morning, so I wrapped everyone up good. The Duncan red station wagon was an improvement over our faded blue VW square back with a bent hanger for a radio antenna. The boys sat in the backseat with their uncontainable energy, teasing each other. Daisy squeezed in next to them and quietly watched scenery pass by, totally ignoring her brothers.

She's such a quiet little thing, but maybe she's just used to all the noise.

"Make him stop, Mom," Ben yelled. "Alex is breathing my air . . . quit pinching me!" He punched Alex in the arm.

"Boys!" I leaned over the backseat and moved Alex and Ben apart. I looked at Jenny with embarrassment then, but she just smiled. It was a relief when we finally reached her house next to a large expanse of fields.

Brother Duncan brought out buckets, then showed us how and where to pick. The boys scampered off to the rows of strawberry plants while Daisy and I found our own row. The strawberries were big, sweet, and juicy. Daisy and I put one berry in our shared bucket and one in our mouth, the red juice dripping down our chins, big grins on our faces.

By noon the breeze had picked up and clouds threatened rain. We scurried to the car with three boxes of fruit and boys with full tummies. If Dave came home with a paycheck, maybe we could have strawberry shortcake and ice cream.

We pulled into the driveway at 1:00 p.m. and Dave's motorcycle was there, which meant only one thing: another lost job.

The boys ran into the house while I brought in Eric and Daisy. Jenny sat the boxes of food on the counter and quietly left as a familiar awkwardness like choking weeds grew between me and Dave. Daisy sat on the kitchen tile floor and tried to keep her eyes open, her head nodding to one side. I took her hand and pulled her up, then settled her and Eric in their room for a nap.

Dave sat on our bed, averting his eyes. I stood over him, trying to burn a hole in his head with my fury.

"I have a job interview tomorrow," he said sheepishly. "Ah, I'll need you to iron my good shirt." With that, he quickly walked into the living room and turned on the TV. "Let's watch *The Electric Company*, boys. You know what that lady says, 'Hey you guys!' Right?"

Another go 'round with jobs. Did he even bring home his last pay-check or has he already spent it? I was too irritated to ask.

I checked on Daisy and tucked a blanket up under her chin; there were little beads of sweat across her forehead. I wiped them away gently and felt her fevered brow. But she was sleeping quietly and her breathing was normal. Someone at church said the flu was going around. Maybe that was it; it had been a chilly morning, then the rain-filled breeze . . .

I checked on my daughter before dinner and she still slept.

It's probably just a cold coming on, sleep is good, and fluids when she wakes up.

At 2:00 a.m. June 16, something woke me.

My head had barely hit the pillow after nursing Eric. I wanted to roll over and pretend I didn't hear anything. It was a Friday, and I just wanted to sleep before I had to iron Dave's shirt.

It's way too early for a child to need me. But there it was again, a mournful whimper . . . Daisy. I tiptoed into her room.

Eric slept on in the dark as I tiptoed into the living room with Daisy in my arms. I sat us down in the rocking recliner and she cuddled in close, resting her head on my arm. Her body felt warmer than normal through her nightie. She hadn't eaten dinner, so maybe her tummy was upset. Or the flu? I grabbed a cold washcloth from the bathroom and put it against her forehead, then we cuddled once more.

I wish we had money for some baby aspirin at least.

"Oh, darling girl, you'll feel better soon. Having a body means some-times you just won't feel good. But it'll be okay soon. Just go to sleep, sweetie. Mommy's got you."

As I held her close, she fell into a peaceful sleep. With the quiet, I nodded off too.

I woke up abruptly to find Daisy still sleeping, snuggled tight against me. How much time had passed I didn't know, but I gently put her back to bed. I pulled the covers up around her face and tucked her in.

The clock by my bed said 3:17 a.m. *If I get up at six, I can get Dave's shirt ironed before the boys bounce in for breakfast. Maybe I can catch a nap later when Daisy and Eric go down.* I fell into a deep sleep.

"It's six, Janet. Get up!" Dave groaned as he clicked off the alarm button. He pushed me to the edge of the bed with his bottom and rolled back to sleep. I dropped my feet over the side of the bed, put on my bathrobe, and headed to the living room.

Glancing at the recliner, I remembered the night and rocking my feverish little girl. I tiptoed into her room and blinked hard at what I saw; my face went pale. Daisy had inched her way out of her covers and rolled at an angle toward the wall. Her pink-flowered nightgown was all twisted up and her light brown hair was scattered and damp behind her head. She was very, very still.

Startled awake, I stared hard at the form of my child, trying to make sense of what I saw. A horrible reality sank in and my breath caught in my throat. I couldn't move. I wanted to touch her, to pick her up, but my body was rooted to the carpet. I fell back against the doorframe.

Finally, my mouth opened and I screamed. "Dave! Dave! I think Daisy's dead . . . Hurry, I think something's—"

Dave rushed in, still dressed in his gym shorts and T-shirt.

"You're lying! What are you saying? Get out of the way!" he yelled as he pushed me aside. He looked at Daisy and his face went white. He grabbed her up, ran in the living room, and laid her on the floor. I watched as he shook her a little, then began mouth-to-mouth CPR.

"Do something!" he roared at me between breaths. "Call 911!"

I must have called because suddenly four paramedics in blue were there with their equipment. They shoved Dave aside and surrounded my child. I watched their backs as they pressed against her little chest and lowered their heads to give CPR.

IT'S ONLY FOR A LITTLE WHILE

They'll bring her around, though, they always do. Daisy will start crying . . . any minute now. Come on, baby girl, COME ON!

Word spread quickly through the ward. Brother Duncan hurried in the front door with the bishop, followed by a sister from church. She came over and gently put her arm around me. We stood in the kitchen doorway together and watched.

Just as suddenly as they showed up and worked over my child, the EMTs stopped. I blinked hard, my whole body numb.

What are they doing? Try something else, hurry!

Now they pulled back from Daisy's body and knelt there, completely still. They shook their heads and began to gather up their equipment.

A paramedic approached Dave. "I'm so sorry. If we'd been called twenty minutes sooner, perhaps . . . but she's been gone too long. There was nothing we could do."

The weight of his message smashed into me.

Dave's face was blank, his lips slack.

They can't be done! What about those paddle things they use on TV?

The paramedics picked up their medical things and left. Our only daughter lay silent on the living room carpet, her face a pale gray, her eyes closed. I knew what it meant . . . but my brain wouldn't accept it.

"I don't think I should bless her to come back," Brother Duncan said as he stood next to Dave, trying to make eye contact with my husband.

Why not? Lazarus came back . . . why not Daisy? What's the matter with you?

Dave didn't react, didn't speak, didn't move. He'd seen dead bodies before during the war, but this was different. It didn't make sense. Children weren't supposed to die before their parents. He seemed to stop breathing as a gush of tears flowed from his too-wide eyes.

Tiredness hit the back of my neck like a brick, but adrenaline raced through me like morphine and kept me shocked awake. Were there other people in the house doing something? I slumped into a kitchen chair, placed my arms on the table, and lay my head down on them.

I rocked back and forth, faster and faster, willing the horrible pain that ran to ends of my fingers to stop—stop! I heard a hum of quiet talk. People were out there somewhere. I threw my head back and tried to scream, but no sound came out. Jumbled thoughts rolled round and round in my mind.

Where are the boys? What time is it? They have to have breakfast and get off to school. I need to iron Dave's shirt for that interview.

I looked up to see Lois, the sister from church who had put her arm around me. She laid a hand gently on my shoulder. "Janet, Nancy took your boys to feed them and get them away from all this. She was able to scoot them out without having to see Daisy."

I looked at her, stunned.

Of course. Good, the boys need breakfast. I hope Nancy won't mind feeding my kids.

"But I think Eric needs you. I can hear him. Shall I get him for you?"

What did she say? Eric?

She placed a crying Eric in my arms, wrapped in a handmade blue receiving quilt. It was small enough to cover him head to toe but not drag on the floor.

Isn't this nice? Who gave us this blanket? Did I thank them? I should send a card.

Eric started rooting, trying to find my breast, so I took him to my bedroom and nursed him privately. It was good to be away, but my brain wouldn't work. I held my baby close as he nursed and let hot tears splash down my cheeks and onto the receiving blanket. When Eric stopped suckling, his head dropped back in sleep. I lay down with him tucked against my side.

Father in Heaven, help me now. What should I do? I don't under-stand what to do. Should I call my parents? I thought about that for a long moment. *Yes, maybe I'll call Dad.*

When I awoke, it was 1:00 p.m. The house was deathly silent. Slipping away from my sleeping child, I walked to the living room and found Lois on the couch reading scriptures. She stood up when she saw me and wrapped her arms around me.

"They took Daisy's body to the funeral home, Janet. Everything will be okay," she stated as she looked at me compassionately. "When you're ready, we can talk about all this. Just know there are others who understand what you're going through."

"What? What I'm going through?"

The words hung in the air between us. Slowly my brain took hold and the morning events came clear. It was a horror movie going across my mind.

"Having a child pass on is an experience many of us know, myself included." Lois's face was empathetic and she embraced me again. I stared at the ceiling as the truth slapped me alert.

That moment was like a memory I cherished. It was like Grandy's arms around me when the house next door to ours burned down. Tears cascaded down my cheeks as reality set in.

"Daisy's dead, isn't she? My only daughter is gone." My heart exploded and I sobbed against Lois' shoulder.

"Stop that blubbering or I'll really give you something to cry about." Mother's words attacked my brain.

But I couldn't stop. I cried harder. Nothing would ever be the same. I pulled away from my friend and sat on the couch, my eyes burning with dryness.

Lois quietly left leaving me to my grief.

The boys came home for dinner. Dinner . . . someone had brought it and left it in a warm oven. Dave pushed his food around with his fork and time slowed to a crawl.

I was too alert; everything was in Technicolor. I had cried a waterfall, but what about Dave? He didn't look at me, he didn't speak, he didn't cry.

Our sons left the table with their normal energy, pushing each other, laughing. I cleared the dishes into the kitchen sink and watched Dave through the window as he started his motorcycle and roared off down the street. He didn't return until after dark and the boys were in bed. His face was flushed, hair windblown, and eyes bleary. He walked past me into the bedroom and fell on the bed fully dressed and was out cold.

I wanted to fall apart, too, but I couldn't. I had a four-month-old baby to feed. And nursing my baby stopped chaotic thinking, a great blessing.

Does he know I need him? He just left where Daisy has gone . . . so maybe he remembers something beautiful—maybe Daisy's in Grandy's arms. Wonderful thought, that!

I nursed Eric at 12:30 a.m. Late and the house was quiet. We rocked in the recliner where I had comforted my daughter just a few hours before. It felt like weeks had gone by. Wolfman Jack's raspy voice pulled me into the TV world of *The Midnight Special*. Lionel Richie, glittery in his white sequined suit, wrapped me in a euphoria for a few precious moments with his sultry, smooth singing. The world really *did* go on without Daisy. How dare it, the nerve!

I put a sleeping Eric in his crib and I laid back down in the place where that morning's nightmare had started less than twenty-four hours ago. I was exhausted even though my heart kept up its visceral, tearing pace. I closed my eyes and willed my system to shut down. Drifting into a troubled sleep, I hoped I'd never wake up.

Stop . . . quit it! You need to rest so you can be there for your sons. Stop it!

My eyes popped open at 2:30 a.m. and I sat straight up in bed as if I'd never been asleep. I was confused, groggy. I turned my head towards the doorway where a soft illumination greeted me. And, in the brightening light, I saw a young woman. Floating just above the floor, an ivory-colored robe flowed around her. Her feet bare, light brown hair curled under her chin. Her eyes, still bright and blue, her whole being radiated a luminous glow.

Peace swaddled me with warmth as I gazed at Daisy in awe. Words came then, impressed upon my mind as she lovingly smiled at me.

"Mama, it's all right now. Please don't worry. I'm Home where I'm meant to be, right on time. And it's wonderful. I love you, Mama. This is only for a little while . . . I'll be near you 'til we meet again."

I *felt* the truth of her words, as if they were spoken aloud. I nodded my head as I took in her beauty and watched her fade into the light. My pain softened as I pondered—*all is well, it's only for a little while.* I lay back on my pillow, closed my eyes, and floated into a dreamless slumber.

We had a short funeral and tried to return to some kind of normal the next two weeks. Dave went to Portland every day for his newest job and was gone 'til late at night. The boys got off to school every morning, seemingly still unaffected by our family change. Alex, almost eight, Ben age seven, and Chris age five, resumed life with their boundless energy. I nursed Eric, made meals, and cleaned the house.

One day, Chris asked, "Mom, when are they bringing Daisy back?"

Stunned, I knelt down and hugged him. He pulled away, gave me a puzzled look, then ran off. *I want Daisy back, too, Chris. I want my dreams of a happy future back.*

The first week of April a woman I'd seen at church meetings knocked at my door. "Hi, I'm June," she said with a warm smile. "Can I visit with you for a while?" We sat down together on the living room couch and she bowed her head for a minute. Then she looked at me with a kind intensity. "I didn't know if I should come, but the Spirit nudged me, so I'm here. I want you to know there are at least six other women at church besides us who have lost a child."

My eyes grew big as I took in her words.

"Amy's baby never came home from the hospital after six months in the NICU. Carol's baby *did* come home but died of SIDs. My son had complications with his lungs and was on oxygen for eleven months . . . until I found he had returned to Heavenly Father in his sleep. I think it's no accident that you moved into our ward."

Tears fell freely down June's cheeks, I joined her. "The thing that helps me, Janet, is knowing our little ones go straight home to God and receive all His glory. They don't have to stay and go through the challenges of life like the rest of us."

No words came, yet what she shared aligned with seeing Daisy.

"I think of my son as being in another country I don't have the passport to yet," June shared with a slight smile and I nodded in agreement. After a tender hug she left as quietly as she came.

Other women had found the strength to move past their losses, so perhaps I could too. After June's unselfish sharing, I felt determined, as God used people to bring comfort.

July arrived. It had been four months since Daisy had left. Each day I felt a little more accepting of where she had gone and what my life had become without her.

On a warm Tuesday morning the phone rang.

"Mrs. Jenkins, the autopsy on Daisy is completed now. We have the results, if you'd like to have them."

CHAPTER 19

DOWN THE RABBIT HOLE

Startled, I gripped the phone so hard my fingers turned white. "Yes, what are the findings?" I asked, trying to steady my voice and stop my shaking.

Did I cause my daughter's death because I didn't turn on the bedroom light to see how sick she was? Will the police come and arrest me? I'm glad the boys are at school.

I dropped to the floor and waited for the news, kitchen cold tiles against my fanny. It seemed like an hour passed before he spoke again.

"Daisy had pneumonia," the coroner answered matter-a-factly. "It was fast moving, Mrs. Jenkins. There was really nothing you could have done. There's no culpability with you or your husband. Have a nice day, now."

Click.

There it was, the authoritative truth. I had seen Daisy's spirit and accepted that she was gone; even my mother's guilt had left me, and now it was back. I held my breath. The phone's disconnected tone penetrated my ear, snaking into my brain. The peace I'd clung to the last few weeks disappeared, replaced by shame and sorrow. I stood on jelly legs and hung up the phone.

Out the kitchen window, the trees were summer green wrapped in dappled sunlight. But my heart was cold to the sight. Daisy had died all over again.

I paced the shag carpet as confused thoughts raced through my mind. I sat on the couch, wrapped my arms tight around my middle, and rocked.

After a half an hour, I stilled myself then I went to dial the phone.

"I was just thinking about you," Lois' voice sounded far away. "I was wondering if you'd heard from the medical examiner yet. Hope you don't mind my nosiness."

"Daisy died of pneumonia," I blurted out. "I . . . I could have done something if I'd turned on her bedroom light, but I didn't want to wake up the baby. If only I'd—"

"Stop this now!" Lois said a little sharply. "Don't you do that to yourself, Janet."

I gulped and clammed up. "All parents who have lost a child say, 'if only.' I did. But that thinking will make you hate yourself, hate life, hate Dave and that's not God's way."

I was stunned by Lois' tone of voice but more so from her words. After two minutes of silence, her insights take hold—I wasn't alone in my grief and guilt. God loved Daisy, loved me, and had sent compassion.

"Think about it," Lois continued. "You'd just gotten the baby to sleep a short time before you heard Daisy, so of *course* you wanted him to stay asleep. And didn't you say you had to get up early and iron Dave's shirt? Daisy wasn't feeling well, so you did what any mother would do. You comforted her 'til she went back to sleep so you could get some sleep yourself."

But if I'd known more, maybe . . . No. You . . . did . . . nothing . . . wrong.

I held the phone against my ear as tears streamed off my chin.

"Why don't you talk to Heavenly Father about this?" Lois suggested quietly. "That's what I did when my son died. He sent me comfort, filled my heart with a gentle peace."

"Thank you. Okay, I'll think about that," I replied sheepishly. I was glad to share this disturbing news with my friend, but I didn't want to talk to God. He took my daughter.

Early in the afternoon, I found myself in Daisy's room. I'd only ever gone in there to put Eric in his crib. I couldn't look at where I'd found my dead child, but it felt like the right place to pray, so I closed my eyes and knelt next to her bed, glad that Eric was asleep in the living room. I wanted to scream and yell at God, but my throat was dry and my mouth wouldn't work. I laid my arms on the bed and dropped my head down on them. I stayed there for ten minutes, collecting my thoughts, my outrage. Then. . .

God. I am so angry, more than words can tell. I could do this life with a crazy husband as long as I had Daisy. So why did You take her? I hate you. . . I took a breath. *Okay, maybe I don't.*

I opened my eyes, stared at the ceiling and yelled, "I know You don't do anything without a reason, so . . . did I, did we, do something wrong? Are we being punished!?"

I stopped and hung my head. And a voice spoke, as if someone was standing right next to me. He said, "It feels unfair when a child dies, I understand. Trust in Me. I too lost a Child. I know your pain, my Son knows your pain. You are a loving mother and your heart is broken. You hurt because you love intensely. You have every right to grieve. But, my child, which one of your sons would you rather have had come Home to me?"

Silently I offered with eyes closed again— *None, of course. Just none! But not Daisy either. Any of them dying would be just as horrible, terrible. But now, how do I manage this pain, Father? I can hardly breathe. My chest hurts all the time.*

"Blessed are they that mourn for they shall be comforted. Remember June's words, remember Lois. I've sent them to mourn with you. Cry as you must, then go to your sons. Daisy is with me, surrounded by unending love. I sent her to bring you comfort. All is well. I love you, dear daughter . . . I'm only a prayer away."

I opened my eyes and put my hand to my chin. I had heard Heavenly Father, I was sure of it. His voice was tender, compassionate, and deeply kind. He gave me permission to cry, no matter what Mother said.

Didn't the scriptures say Jesus wept?

I had to be a mother now and comfort my sons.

Then the mother dictator in my head spoke: *See, you are too stupid to take care of a child. That's why she's gone. You can't do anything right. It's your fault she died.*

I grabbed the side of my head and squeezed as hard as I could, pushing away Mother's screaming voice. "Shut up!" I yelled at the ceiling.

God was near me, and my direction had to be for my children, to serve them. I wouldn't let her harping stop me.

Determined, I watched for signs of sadness in my sons, but they returned to their happy ways: teasing, racing each other to school, hiding their peas under their dinner plates. None of them asked questions about their sister, at least not to me. And I had a baby to care for, so I pushed along with the boys as best I could.

Money was still tight even though Dave had work in Portland. He had an hour commute one-way on his motorcycle and was gone until seven most nights. He ate dinner with us, talked to the boys at the table, and went off to play volleyball at church. I wanted to talk about Daisy, but he stayed away from me as much as he could.

It had been four days and nights since the coroner had called. I laid down in bed, exhausted at 10:30 p.m. after rustling Alex, Ben, and Chris to bed, picking up the house, and taking care of Eric. I was "normal" mother tired now, not grieving mother exhausted. Keeping busy pushed away the anguish.

Dave came in at eleven and I made sure I was rolled away from him as if asleep. He still expected his nightly intimacy, but maybe tonight he'd leave me alone. When he just fell into bed and didn't bother to grab for me, I breathed a quiet sigh. I'd never shared the autopsy report with him and he'd never asked. I hoped he'd grieved, somehow, but he certainly didn't cry with me.

Now near the end of July, Ben's birthday was coming and I wanted to ask Dave about how we could celebrate. Maybe we could talk about that, at least. This family could use a party. Ben wanted a bike and I wanted to give it to him.

Late Saturday afternoon, I followed Dave out to the carport through the kitchen doorway. I got ready to speak, but before I could get a word out, he said, "I think we should have another baby. We should go back to having five kids, ya know?" He grinned. My blood turned to ice and I clenched my fists.

He's crazy!

"What? We can hardly take care of the kids we have now!"

"Oh, I'm doing great at my job and we *do* have insurance now, so why not?"

Angry heat started at the base of my neck and pushed up into my skull. "You just want to replace Daisy," I spat out. "That's what this is! We *have* a baby, Dave. He's five months old in case you forgot. I'm *not* getting pregnant!"

Dave scowled at me, then grabbed me by the shoulders, his fingers digging into my flesh. "Listen, Janet, you *will* have another baby!" he hissed. "If you don't, the Church says I can divorce you."

I yanked away and stepped back into the kitchen doorway. He climbed onto his bike, fumbled with the keys, then gave me another hard look.

"I'm *not* having another baby so I guess I'm going to hell!" I yelled as I backed into the house and slammed the door. He flipped me off, lowered his goggles, started his bike, and roared off down the street. I pushed my back against the cold refrigerator door and shut my eyes tight.

"This isn't the way things are supposed to be. It's not right!" I shouted.

"What, Mommy?" Alex asked as he walked toward me. My oldest son stood close, holding out his truck with a wheel spoke sticking out and the wheel in his other hand. "Can you fix this?"

His questioning blue eyes were beautiful.

"Alex, give it to me and go find something else to play with. Mommy doesn't feel well, but I'll fix it for you soon, okay?"

He dumped his toy on the counter, then walked away with a frown. It wasn't fair that *I* was the one who had to deal with everything while Dave rode off somewhere and pretended he wasn't married. I hated him for that. He had his orgasms and I had the results.

Something had to change and change now. I had been a member of my Church for seven years, trying hard to be a Christian, to follow the Savior's example. Marriage was a sacred thing, but this? This wasn't *even* a marriage. I was alone and felt it in every cell of my being.

Okay, I have all the kids, and that's not going to change. How do I take care of them? I've had one decent job in my life because Daddy got it for me. I don't have anything to offer an employer. I don't have a bank account; I've never written a check . . . but there's got to be a way. What would Grandy do? Did she have to tough it out in her life?

I could hear Eric crying and Chris and Ben fighting over Fisher Price people in the living room. I took the toys away from my stunned boys and let my temper erupt.

"You guys share or go to bed!" I ordered. "Chris, you take the fireman, Ben you take the black and white dog. And you *both* can go take a bath with the boat that these toys go with. Now go before I give you a swat . . . Now!"

My sons stared, then gathered their toys and ran off to the bathroom. Alex sat on the couch staring down at his book, inched up to cover his face. I'd deal with him later. I grabbed Eric from his playpen, changed his diaper, got him into his footed PJs, and put him in his crib with a pacifier.

If I get a job, I might have to stop nursing, my mind whirled. *I'll think about it later.*

I got the house quieted down and the kids in bed by eight, although I could hear them whispering. I made a decision. I'd sleep on the couch from now on. No more babies.

I hated thinking about *any* of it. I grabbed a pillow and wrapped a blanket around me as I lay down on the couch. The shadows from the streetlights paint odd shapes on the wall. I watched them move ever so slightly. Now was a good time to pray.

God, I need you. What should I do? I can't tell women at Church about this pregnancy thing. Do I really have to get pregnant again? I waited, hoping to hear His answer, but nothing came. *All these kids, they deserve better. If I go to work, how . . . who . . . I don't want to leave them with someone else. There's no one to talk to about this except You, so please, help me find the answer, Father. In Jesus' name, amen.*

I laid there in the quiet. There wasn't anything more to say or anyone to say it to. I closed my eyes and stopped thinking about Dave and his selfishness. As I fell asleep, that now familiar a warm feeling came. Maybe everything would be all right.

Another week passed, full of the usual flurry of household duties and dirty diapers. Hungry boys were like birds with their beaks open, waiting for food. I fed them, cleaned up after them, and moved through the days in a trance. Wednesday came with no sign of Dave. I was glad at first, but wondered if I needed to call the police or a hospital. I had plans to go to a Tupperware party on Friday, but without Dave, I couldn't leave the kids. Finally, Thursday night, he called.

"Listen, babe, I've taken an apartment in Portland so I don't have to run back and forth every day. Riding the bike has really played havoc with my kidneys. I gave up my health club fees so I could get a place."

What?

Stunned, I stood at the stove stirring macaroni in boiling water, Eric on my hip.

"Are you there, Janet?" Dave asked.

"Yes, I'm here . . . I'm always here . . . with *your* four children. How am I to get money to feed them and keep a roof over our heads? I hope you've considered that," I said, clenching my teeth.

"Of course. You'll get house money when I'm home on the weekends. It's not a big deal. It's just like what we do already anyway. Let's talk about it Saturday . . . love you." He barely finished that meaningless phrase before the dial tone hit my ear.

"NO, YOU DON'T!" I yelled into the dead phone.

I hung up and turned to see a wide-eyed, worried Chris standing there. I knelt down, put my arms around him, and hugged him and Eric together tightly.

The Tupperware party was Friday evening at Sherry Bowman's house and my neighbor Elise watched the boys. There were three card tables with matching plastic blue tablecloths set up in front of her fireplace, with all the Tupperware displayed. Pastel pink, blue, green, and yellow bowls were there to lock in freshness with burpable lids. I had no money to buy, but I was away from the house, the kids, and thoughts of Dave. I sat and listened to Sherry's pitch with five other ladies.

After the demonstration, there were refreshments. Our hostess excused herself to prepare them, leaving us to talk and, hopefully, buy.

I looked at the happy faces nearby and watched them chatting. Clearly, they were happy women, at peace with their normal, married lives.

Children's noises floated toward us from the hall as three little girls came skipping out of their bedroom, their dad right behind them.

He'd been in the back bedroom entertaining the children while his wife did her Tupperware thing. Remarkable! Now this is a marriage! People who support each other, who actually like each other. This is what I want . . . certainly not what I have.

I wasn't even sure if I loved Dave anymore, but I was pretty sure I didn't like him. I wanted to excuse his behavior, chalk it up to the death of our daughter or his troubled mind from what he faced in Vietnam, but lately his behavior was more extreme than ever. If he'd only talk to me and share his grief. Instead, he had pulled even farther away and was now absent five days a week. What were my sons learning from all this? Did they miss their father? Did they notice he wasn't there?

On Saturday Dave was supposed to show up with some much-needed money. With Dave gone during the week, I slept in our empty bed, but I kept the pillow and blankets behind the couch just in case.

The days were summer warm and the boys played outside in the backyard. It was a good time to go over information Sherry had given me about starting a Tupperware business. I began to read the material when the back door opened and Dave ambled in. He looked like he hadn't bathed for a week.

He stopped at the fridge, took the milk out, and chugged down what was left. Irritation bubbled through my bloodstream.

"Did you bring the house money?" I asked, working to keep my tone even.

"Of course. I'll leave it here on the table in an envelope. But I need the car keys so I can take stuff down to Portland," he said, standing over me.

I stood up. Fear wasn't going to get the better of me even though I could feel Dave's craziness pouring off him. I'd given birth to five babies and I was determined and strong.

"Can't you get someone to help you move your stuff? I can't be all week without a car. What if one of the boys gets sick? I need transportation to get groceries too. Maybe someone from Church—"

"Nope, not gonna happen," he snapped. "I can't ask anyone else to help me move out."

I didn't reply. He glared at me, then went to the kitchen to grab my purse, but I got there first and yanked it from his grip. He pushed me and a tug-a-war began, pulling the purse back and forth 'til the contents fell out on the floor. I grabbed the car keys and ran for the bedroom, but he grabbed me and pushed me down on the living room carpet, the shag rough against my neck. Sitting with his full weight on top of me, he pinned my arms down.

"Give me those keys or I'll knock your teeth out," he hissed, his eyes on fire.

I closed my mouth tight and shook my head. Then his fist hit my face and jarred my head to the side. I wanted to get away, but I could hardly breathe with his weight on me. His eyes rolled back in his head, and I knew he was on automatic, a soldier fighting a war.

Dave grabbed my neck and started banging my head against the floor. Bright stars of pain flashed around me. I tried to squirm free as the keys dropped from my hand. Dave snatched them up, jumped off me, and ran out the back door, leaving it wide open. I heard the car start up and he drove away.

Slowly, I stood up. I put my hand on the back of my head and closed my eyes as the pain rose up. I tenderly touched the sore places on my face and knew bruises were forming. Opening my eyes, I looked through the open back door. The carport was empty except for a motorcycle and three little boys standing in the doorway staring at me with shocked faces.

CHAPTER 20

I MADE IT STOP

"**M**ommy, did you fall down?" Chris shouted, running toward me.

"Did Daddy *knock* you down?" Alex asked seriously as he reached out to touch my face. I put my hand over his and the pain throbbed a little. Another warm touch came next, and I realized Ben had taken my hand.

"Guys, come here," I said as I quickly wiped my wet face. We went to the living room and sat close, their faces filled with concern. I took a deep breath. What could I say? I didn't know what to even tell myself.

"Um," I began, "your daddy and I had an accident. He's not feeling very well these days. So, I think he's going to stay near his work for a while and maybe . . . we can go visit Brother Duncan at his strawberry fields. You guys could play in the dirt and swing on his big ol' tire swing, maybe have a sleepover. Let me see if we can do that. Wouldn't that be good?"

I hoped something fun would lighten their mood.

"Could we eat more strawberries?" Ben asked, grinning.

"Yeah," Chris jumped in. "I like berries a lot, Mom!"

I looked at Alex then and saw the question in his eyes. Almost eight, he wasn't easily put off. I gave my oldest boy's shoulders a squeeze and whispered in his ear, "It'll be okay, sweetie, don't worry."

His blue eyes serious, he gave me an intense once over, then a nod. I quietly sighed in relief. My insides were still shaking, but one thing was for sure: change was coming. I didn't know how I'd make it happen, but I'd figure it out. I wasn't going to let anything like this happen again and I *certainly* didn't want my sons to think that what they might have seen was okay.

"Why don't you boys get some pajamas to take with us? Grab your toothbrushes and anything else you want. I'll call the Duncans. Since your dad has the car, let's see if Jenny can come get us. We can ride in her great big station wagon again! Won't that be fun?" I asked, trying to muster a smile, even though my head was really pounding now.

The boys took off down the hall and I walked to the kitchen. It was almost six and the sun was setting, hopefully not too late to bother my church friends. After all, we were stranded.

Is he gone for good? Wait . . . did he leave any money on the table like he said he would?

A rumpled envelope was on the table where he'd thrown it. I opened it and four fifties and a hundred-dollar bill fell out. It was more than the usual, but I had no idea how much Dave's salary was these days.

Or maybe he gave me this much because he doesn't plan to come back.

Tenderly, I touched the area on the back of my head and felt a large bump. That was gonna be a reminder for some time. I moved my head from side to side, at least I could do that.

Father, please, don't let me find any more damage, there's no health insurance, and I have to take care of these boys.

I dialed the Duncan's number and Brother Duncan answered. We said our pleasantries and then I added hesitantly, "Ah, we've had some trouble over here. Dave and I had a bad argument and he took the car. The boys and I . . . well, I'm pretty shaken up."

After a long silence, Brother Duncan replied, "We'll be right there!"

The phone went dead and I slid to the floor, a place I seemed to be at a lot those days. The boys were laughing and wrestling around in their room, *thank you God*. In spite of their ruckus, I heard Eric starting to cry in his crib. My mind was spinning. I wanted it all to just go away and my head to stop pounding.

Some normalcy came with motherhood responsibility. I nursed Eric and held him close, taking in his baby smell.

When he finished I laid him in his playpen and packed a few things for him.

"Brother Duncan will be here in a few minutes, guys, so quit fooling around and get your stuff ready!" I yelled.

Instead the three jostled into the living room, wrestling and falling on the floor.

"Okay, guys, sit your bottoms on the couch!" I tried to yell, but now nothing more than a loud whisper came out. The adrenaline rush gone, The physical agony came full force.

The back door opened and Jenny and her husband hurried in. Jenny took one horrified look at my face, now with my red blotch turning to blue. I'd seen in the bathroom mirror Dave's finger marks that showed near my ears where he'd grabbed my head.

"Did your boys see him do this to you?" Jenny whispered angrily.

"I think so," I whispered.

"Harold, that man's going straight to hell!" Jenny shouted.

"Who's going straight to hell?" Alex asked as he came over, his eyes huge.

"Jenny, little pitchers have big ears," Brother Duncan said quietly. "Uh, that's not a good word, Alex. We just meant some people do bad things."

Alex looked at me questioningly again. I caught him in an embrace. "Yes, honey, sometimes grown-ups say things they don't really mean," I shared, trying to sound convincing. I took his face in my hands and added, "Hey, help your brothers get their things together."

"Yes, let's get you boys in the car," Brother Duncan said cheerily. "Janet, we need something to put all these items in."

Jenny and I gathered up the boys' things and stuffed them into pillowcases as her husband got the boys into the station wagon. With them out of hearing range, Jenny repeated, "I mean it, Janet! Don't you make excuses to anyone at church! Tell the truth, you hear me?"

I did hear her . . . and I loved her for it. *Don't make excuses for Dave!* Yes, time to get the real truth out in the open. He was disturbed, no question. I didn't know if it was his war experience or Daisy dying or both, but I knew I couldn't live with what had happened and I wouldn't have the boys watch and learn.

At 8:30 p.m., we got everyone tucked into sleeping bags on the large living room floor of the Duncan ranch house. Leather tufted chairs, a matching sofa, and Indian pottery with dried flowers decorated the room. All my Arizona memories flowed in and panged my heart.

With Eric in his playpen and the boys snuggled down, I crawled into some blankets on the couch.

The next day, Sunday, I went without the boys to see the bishop in the evening. Jenny drove me to the church and parked. "Listen," she began intently, "the bishop is a good man. He'll understand, so just be truthful."

I was a bundle of nerves because of how I now looked, with dark bruising on my cheek and finger marks on my neck. It had even frightened the boys for a moment, but there was nothing I could do. I fussed with my hair and adjusted my blouse as I sat down across from Bishop Lewis.

I shared everything: how Dave was never home, how he now had an apartment in Portland, and left me to take care of the children. Finally, I spoke about Dave's attack. Sobbing, I remembered Jenny's words. "He was out of his mind, Bishop. He kept after me 'til he got the car keys. He took the car and left us stranded." I hung my head to hide my bruises and wrapped my arms around my very upset stomach.

Bishop Lewis was about forty, younger than most bishops. He watched me through his thick glasses, his face full of compassion, but I couldn't fully meet his gaze.

He shook his head and reached out to pat my hand. "I don't understand how a man can do what your husband has done," he said gently. "No, I can't. Why would—does he drink?"

I looked up at him. He was genuine. My face got hot as my anger burned. "No, he doesn't drink—at least, I don't think he does. He used to . . ."

It had been seven years since Dave chose to quit drugs, booze, and cigarettes. Thoughts of his kind behavior when he was stoned flashed across my mind. But now that he was straight, he was mean and unpredictable.

"You know, I've had your husband in here a few times since your child died, just to give him a chance to talk," Bishop Lewis shared. "I tried to impress on him how much his family needs him, especially now, but it didn't do much good, it seems," he said regretfully.

I sat up straight and my eyes wide. "You did . . . what? I never knew." Dave never talked about visiting with the bishop. "Did he talk about losing Daisy, or maybe, the pressure of taking care of us? Anything?"

Maybe he was having a breakdown and I got caught in the worst of it.

"I wish he *had* talked openly, but mostly he just listened, agreed with me, and left the office as fast as he could. This is quite a sorry mess, isn't it?" the Bishop added.

I pumped up my courage and took a breath. "Yes, it is. I know marriage is sacred, Bishop, I do. But this isn't a marriage. I hope you can see that."

Bishop Lewis nodded sadly.

"I'm afraid for my safety. More than that, for the boys' safety, for what they may see and think is an acceptable way to treat a woman. If you've been talking to him and it hasn't had an impact, well, I think divorce is my only option."

Tears threatened to fall, so I ducked my head again and pressed my hands against my eyes.

I am such a crybaby.

Deep inside, I felt responsible. Shame was a hard ball in the pit of my upset stomach. I could hear my parents reminding me about my bad choices. I was a failure at my marriage and one of my children had died under my care.

"In light of what you just said . . ." the Bishop took a breath, "it's my personal opinion that you're making the right decision. I'm not supposed to say this, but I've watched for some time, tried to reason with him. No one can tell him anything."

I looked at the bishop, astonished. I hadn't expected him to agree with me. In fact, I was sure he'd say, "forgive him, try to make the marriage work," all of it my responsibility . . . a pious slap down. Once again it seemed God was using someone to show His deep understanding. I was relieved and gave my minister a weak smile.

We drove back to Jenny's house without speaking. She didn't pry and I couldn't make myself share. Emotions cycled around in my mind at a frantic pace even though I had made an internal shift in the bishop's office. My stomach still fluttered—fear, yes, but also anticipation.

At the house, Brother Duncan was feeding the boys; he was totally at ease taking care of kids. It made me smile. Even Eric had a bottle of milk and was completely happy.

"We had pancakes with chocolate chips for dinner," Chris shared, his eyes twinkling.

"Yeah, and bacon and oranges," Ben added. I looked at Alex, but he just shrugged.

That boy's heart is hurting. I know he sees what's happening. I need to be careful.

Jenny took the boys for haircuts on Monday, with the promise of ice cream if they behaved while Brother Duncan and I sat and talked.

"I have a lawyer friend in Salem, not expensive," he offered. "And I have some funds put aside that can help. No, don't object, it'll be a privilege. And hey, call me Harold, okay?" he said with a grin. How wonderful to have friends and not just rescuers.

"My neighbor Elise is going to let me know when Dave's back at the house, so I'll go talk with him about all this" I responded, trying not to shudder. "Not sure what will happen . . . I hope Dave won't contest, but he really acts like he doesn't want a family."

"Well, one step at a time. Take the old '60s truck to go down there," Harold offered. He took my hand and looked at me intently. "Listen, sister, there are a lot of folks around here who will help you. This is a hard bargain, but you've come through a lot, and I know you can handle this. God's here. Never forget that He's waiting to hear from you when you need Him."

The following Saturday, Elise let me know Dave had returned. It had been a long five days with the boys out of their element. They were restless and most of the time I was breaking up their squabbles, trying to keep them quiet with toys or TV. I was completely out of diapers and clean clothes for them too. Jenny helped so much with meals that I hated to ask for anything else, like using the washer. We just *had* to get back in our own space.

I drove the old truck down to the house that afternoon. The VW square back sat in the carport, as if it had never been taken. My nerves beat a rapid staccato as I turned off the engine.

Okay, God, please let me feel Your presence. Strengthen me and keep me safe. You told me that the boys need me and I'm here. But we all need You. I hope what I'm doing is right, that You'll bless me and the boys now. Amen.

I sat dead still on the truck's bench seat, my eyes closed, waiting for my courage to rise and my accelerated heartbeat to slow down. I took a deep breath . . . then another. And ever so peacefully, a quiet calm encased and strengthened me.

"Are you coming in or what?" Dave yelled. "Where are the kids?"

Startled, I glanced at the open kitchen doorway. There was the man I had lived with for nine and a half years. His big grin was the same as it was when he stood up to Mother. *Maybe we can work this out.* I had to hope; there were four kids to consider.

I followed Dave into the living room and watched him plop down in the recliner. He rocked back and forth, eyeing me with suspicion.

"Where are my kids, Janet? What kind of games are you playing now?" he snarled.

Ah, there it is. His *kids!*

"Your kids? Since when? What do you know about *your* kids?" I shouted. "You're never here, Dave! You've got some nerve . . . you don't give twenty-five cents for anyone but yourself!"

"Well, whaddya expect me to do, hang around here all the time? You're no wife! I said let's have another baby. But 'oh no Dave, you want too much,'" he mimicked. "You've gotten fat and ugly. I don't *want* to be here and we both know whose fault it is."

Everything wrong was "my fault," that same broken record playing the same old tune.

"Okay, Dave. You can have what you want," I said decidedly, hands on hips. "You're free to get the hell out. Go back to living single. I'm filing for divorce."

A terrible heartache ripped right through me down to my toes, but I stayed aloof.

Dave's stare was full of hate. His face went white as he gripped the arms of the chair. "You'd better get out of here now or I'll kill you!" he spat out through clenched teeth.

I knew that look . . . I backed away toward the kitchen.

"And I want Chris," he seethed.

I shook my head vehemently. "I'm not splitting up these kids so you can get through this mess, which, by the way, you've made for yourself!"

I gulped. *Whoa, be careful.*

Dave eyeballed me and started to get up from the chair. His face red, his lips tightened, and his eyes black. He clenched his fists tight, then yanked them behind his back.

"You'd better get out of here right now, bitch!"

He took a step toward me. Shocked into action, I ran out the kitchen door, got in the truck, and peeled out. Shaking overcame me as I neared Duncan's. I pulled over and turned off the engine.

"Stop this!" I told myself. "The boys can't see you like this. You're their only parent now so get a grip."

I couldn't stop my hands from shaking, so I plastered them tight against my face. I let out the loudest scream my breath could carry . . . then another. I pulled my hands away, shook, and screamed harder, shrieking 'til my energy failed and made me stop.

I opened my eyes and gazed out the truck windows. There were the strawberry fields that bordered the road to the Duncan's home. The sun shone through nearby filbert trees and daffodils by the ranch house waved their happy yellow heads in the slight breeze. Life was all around me; real life, peaceful life.

I had been fighting an internal battle for a long time. I dropped my head and let one last deep moan travel up my spine and into the air. It was done.

CHAPTER 21

GRENADINE AND ROCKY ROAD

June 1980 I sat alone in a courtroom in Salem, Oregon; there was no sign of Dave. The divorce was granted and filed. The bishop and Brother Duncan finally convinced my now ex-husband to leave the house and car, even as he insisted it was his place because he paid the lease. He took his sorry self back to Portland and the boys and I returned to our lonely house.

I'm never going to marry again, not unless you're a part of it somehow, God.

Trying to get things back to normal, I read to my children at bedtime, washed their clothes, fed their bodies, and gave Eric bottles of formula. Then I cried myself to sleep.

One Saturday afternoon I stood in the driveway talking with my neighbor Elise. "Listen, let's go to the bar and go dancing," she proposed. "I don't drink, you don't drink, but we could just get away for a while and have some fun. We can get that teenage girl from down the street to stay with your boys after you get them to bed."

I hesitated, but then her encouraging smile egged me on. "All right, I'll go with you if you'll drive."

I hadn't gone somewhere with a friend since high school. Even a trip to the grocery store meant the company of four children. And truth be told, guilt and shame over the divorce and responsibility for four small human beings was almost drowning me. Mother's voice was in my head playing liked an unending tape, telling me what a loser I was. Maybe rock 'n' roll and dancing would drown it out, at least for a little while.

I put on my best pair of jeans, a white button-down shirt, and some strappy wedge peep-toe shoes, red. I'd found them at the Goodwill a few years ago but had never worn them to church because I couldn't be taller than Dave. But wearing them now, being taller, I felt almost majestic. Anticipation, excitement, and a sense of freedom rippled through me. My strawberry blonde hair was in the current shaggy style, with one side pulled back behind my ear. Farah Fawcett hair was what I wanted, but all I could manage were flippy bangs like hers. Still, it was better than my "I don't care" hair.

At 9:00 p.m. Saturday, the boys were asleep, a babysitter sat in the living room, and I drove off with Elise. The last time I'd been in a bar was with Dave in Portland and it still made me uneasy. It felt a little dangerous and something my religion warned against. But my neighbor and I would have our 7-Up and listen to music. What was the harm in that?

I'm not sure about dancing, but having someone be nice to me would be a great change.

We pulled up to the Raven Bar and Grill and heard music before we even got out of the car. I loved rock and roll. Maybe a local band was playing; that would be even more interesting.

The room had five round tables, the bar, with every barstool filled, a jukebox that blared music, and blue lighting for ambience. It was hard to see people, but that was for the best. My naivety showed in my flushed face and wide-open eyes.

Elise and I sat at an empty table close to the bar, then she went and ordered us a couple of 7-Ups. We sat together, crossed our legs, sipped our drinks, and tried to look like we'd done this plenty of times, although two females sitting alone was obviously unusual. Male heads turned and stared. Elise's soft brown eyes and auburn hair was her real attraction, although her sparkling red blouse and tight Levi skirt accented her figure.

Three men at the table behind us were talking softly in a lilting Spanish cadence. The tone and rhythm of their speech was appealing. When blaring music changed to a slow tempo, a Latino man from the group came over to me.

"Senorita, would you favor me with a dance?" he asked, holding out his hand. His manners guaranteed that I was instantly smitten. Tall with black hair, his brown eyes were like liquid chocolate. I looked at Elise, who smiled her approval, then let the man lead me to the dance floor.

He held me in a firm embrace as we moved together, not tight against his body, but close enough that I could smell his aftershave. The scent of patchouli from my hippy days mixed with a woodsy pine fragrance, Arizona intoxication. His face was a smooth sepia brown and his smile warm and inviting. It seemed we'd been friends before. He romanced me with his charm and accented words. A tingle ran through me, something I'd never felt, not even from Dave.

I was a little scared and a little excited, just like when I heard Jimmy Morrison sing. I stepped right into his foreign enchanted world. Without the fear of a husband hanging over me, I felt alive and special.

"Has anyone ever told you, you are beautiful, mi amor? Mi corazón es enchanted," he whispered. His Spanish words charmed and put me at ease. We had two dances, then he escorted me back to my empty table.

"Here, sit and let me get you some refreshment," he offered.

As he walked away, I looked for Elise. She was on the dance floor with a slim, tall cowboy with a bushy mustache. I caught her eye and we waved at each other.

My Hispanic friend brought me a scarlet-colored drink in a tall glass. Alcohol and drugs were something I promised never to consume again. I was about to share that fact when my new friend announced, "You looked like a Shirley Temple lady, so I got you one to drink while I have my rum and Coke."

He took a sip from his drink as I stared warily at mine. "It's just some grenadine with 7-Up. I saw your friend order that earlier."

The cranberry color of my drink was new and different, so I took a sip and tasted its sweet/tartness. It was delicious and a bit strange, but I'd never had grenadine syrup before, so that must be what I tasted.

We watched Elise and her cowboy dance and savored our drinks. She looked so happy, and I imagined that maybe I could be too.

"Can I drive you home?" asked my new friend. "I love to show off my brother's big car."

It was going on 10:30 p.m., and I had promised the sitter I'd be back by eleven.

"Yes, that would be nice, thank you."

I walked over to Elise and told her I had a ride home.

"I'm glad! I want to stay a little longer. Be careful though, k?" She waved me on and turned back to her dance partner.

I felt a little woozy as I walked, holding the arm of my new acquaintance. Dancing with a good-looking dark man who found *me* attractive made me feel giddy.

I'll ask his name when we get in the car. It might be nice to have someone in my life, if this does turn into something.

He opened the car door for me, another first, and I slid into the passenger seat. My head was spinning a little, so I rested it against the seat's headrest. I gave the man my address and he started the engine. "This is my brother's Cutlass," he bragged with a big grin. "I love the powerful engine."

"I'm not surprised," I said, speaking slowly and carefully. "It has such a big front end."

He nodded and reached across the console to take my hand. I closed my eyes as a warm happiness slid over me.

It wasn't long before we pulled into the driveway and under the carport. He turned off the engine, came around to my side, and opened my door. I thought he might walk me to the door, but he gently pushed me against the car instead and placed his warm lips on mine.

Surprised, I responded with intensity. We kissed and embraced for several minutes, wrapping our arms around each other. I didn't realize how hungry I was for affection.

"Hey, you guys, I'm going home now," a young woman's voice announced. I turned to see the babysitter coming out the kitchen door. She gave me a wink. "You enjoy yourselves," she added with a snicker as she walked away.

Heat climbed up my neck and my head was even more fuzzy.

What is this guy's name? I'll ask him when we get in the house.

He smiled, took my hand, and led me toward the kitchen door. "Come on, let's go in."

Yes, I need to go check on the boys.

We walked through the kitchen where a single light shone down from above the sink. It threw beams on the nearby living room floor as he sat on the couch.

"I should check on my kids," I said shyly. "I'll . . . I'll be right back."

"Of course, take your time," he replied, crossing his legs and giving me a tender look.

I walked toward the boys' rooms, then leaned against the wall for a minute. Eric was sound asleep in his crib. Down the hall to the back bedroom, Alex and Ben slumbered in their bunkbed and Chris slept soundly in his single bed across from them.

I feel weird. I better tell this guy to leave. I'm too tired for romance. I just want to sleep.

I woke up to the morning sun streaming in and shivered in spite of it. I tugged the blanket closer up under my chin. I opened my eyes then quickly closed them again as a terrible headache hammered my temples.

I must have fallen asleep on the couch. Wait . . . where are my clothes?

My memory began to wake up. Warm, inviting lips, a handsome man dancing with me in a fragrant cloud of patchouli and pine.

Suddenly, I bolted upright and clasped the blanket tight. Reality wrapped its tentacles around my brain, but I pushed the thoughts away fast.

The clock on the kitchen wall said 6:12 a.m. I listened intently, but there was no sound of the boys, a tender mercy. I ran to the bathroom and gently closed the door. I turned on the water as hot as I could stand, sat down in the tub, and let the water fall over me.

I just wanted to dance and get away for a little while. Why did I let Elise take me to a bar? A bar! Alcohol . . . just what did that guy give me?

I cried until my eyes were sore and dry.

That's enough, I chided myself. *The boys need breakfast . . . get moving.* I toweled off and went to my room for fresh clothes.

7:30 a.m. and the boys were chattering at the table as I moved automatically, making scrambled eggs, pushing bread in the toaster.

Fifteen minutes later, three boys left for school and I put Eric in the playpen with his morning bottle.

You're so naive and gullible! Mother's voice screamed in my head. *Stupid! You let that guy slip something into your drink! You have no way to earn money and four children to take care of. What a mess you're in. I told you so. If you go to work, who'll take care of them? You never thought of that, did you? That's because you don't think!*

I sat in the recliner and rocked, my hands clasped on top of my head, thoughts rolling around at a frantic speed. "SHUT UP!" I yelled at the ceiling.

I have to keep busy with housework and children's needs. If I stop moving, I'll feel the disgust I deserve.

Mother was right. I *didn't* know what I was doing. Divorced and alone, what was I going to do? My insides started to shake. Where *would* we go? I needed to tell my parents– no, not them. Maybe Dave's parents. Dave's mother didn't like me, but his father was always nice.

That evening, with the boys in bed, I made the call. "Yes, Dave told us," his mother answered stiffly. "I'm not surprised, really. You didn't do anything to help my son. He was under a lot of pressure with all those kids you popped out. You should have gone to work, been supportive."

"I *had* a job: the children were my full-time job."

Then Dave's dad came on the phone. "I'm sorry about this, Janet. I wished you'd called us before you got a divorce. Don't you know this all happened because Daisy died? Marriages often fall apart when a child dies. You should have tried to work it out."

I had hoped for some understanding. Where was their compassion, even concern, for their grandchildren? And why hadn't they come to Daisy's funeral?

I should have realized. They're Dave's parents. What could I have expected?

The days came and went. I took care of my kids and I went back to bed when they left for school, keeping Eric close by. I had freedom from violence, but I was in a dark cave of regret and dejection. When we were all in the living room with the TV on, Eric was in his playpen and I laid on the couch with a blanket over my head. I couldn't climb out of the rabbit hole.

One day as I lay in my bed quietly weeping, I looked up and saw Alex standing in the door watching me, his eyes full of alarm.

"Honey . . ." I began.

He turned and ran off. With a deep sigh, I turned away and wrapped blankets around me more tightly. I couldn't help him, I couldn't even help myself.

On Thursday, Lois walked into my mess. She stood over my prone body on the couch and shook her head. "Sit up, sweetie. Come on, give me room," she said as she pulled me into a sitting position. Lois wrapped her arm around my shoulder and smiled at the boys who watched her intently. "You know what? Maybe you guys could go over to Brother Duncan's and play on his big tire swing. Would you like that?"

The boys whooped and jumped up and down. They were probably as tired of me as I was.

"Jenny's on her way over," Lois told me. "I haven't seen you at church for a while so I thought maybe you needed a break from your parenting duties."

"Thank you," I said sheepishly, looking at the nightgown I'd worn for a week. "Maybe I should go change."

Lois gave me a smile and nodded.

My two friends took over that afternoon. Jenny took the boys to her house and, after I'd changed, Lois herded me into the kitchen. "Let's talk about what you can do with your life now. But first, let me scramble you some eggs."

Miserably, I swallowed down some of the food even though I didn't want to. What I wanted was to scream until the pain in my heart and the depression in my head left me.

"You've got a lot on your plate," Lois observed with a small grin, trying to lighten the mood, "and I'm not talking about those eggs."

I looked up at her with heavy, drooping eyes.

"Take another bite," she encouraged. She took a long breath, then added, "I've been thinking about what I'd do if I were in your shoes."

I swallowed another small bite, glad to skirt around sharing my latest experiences. A half-gallon of Rocky Road ice cream couldn't stop my searing shame. I'd lost a lot of faith in mankind married to Dave, but now I hated myself too. When I thought about what *could* have happened if the man who'd taken me home had been violent, my children . . .I was so disgusted with myself I could've puked.

I drank some water out of a glass Lois washed and handed to me. A little food and fresh water began to wake up my senses.

"I know you have a lot to come to terms with. I'm so sorry," my friend said kindly, patting my knee. "One way to see your life is that you're a victim, but you can also say you've received a strange sort of gift that's given you freedom."

What? Are you nuts?

I raised my eyebrows with skepticism. "What did you just say? Look around you, Lois! I have four kids, no money, no job, and let's not even talk about what needs my constant attention in this house," I whined, my voice dripping with self-pity.

"Yes," Lois nodded as she took in the sink full of dirty dishes. She looked to the living room and the jumble of scattered toys, PJs on the floor, and the grocery bag by the couch full of dirty disposable diapers that should have been thrown out days ago, the stench hit my now awakened faculties. I winced.

"Aren't disposable diapers the invention of the century?" she said with a smile, getting up from her chair. "Still, you have to actually *dispose* of them, don't you?"

A flush of embarrassment colored my face as she walked into the living room mess. Carefully grabbing the edge of the bag, she gingerly picked up the stinky stuff, marched out the kitchen back door, and tossed it in the garbage. When she sat down next to me, I pushed away the plate of mostly uneaten eggs and stared at the floor. Lois covered my cool hand with her warm one.

"Here's something else," she stated quietly. "How do you think God feels as He has watched you during these last heart-wrenching months?"

A tenseness rose up in me like a threatening storm. I looked out the window, my eyes full of bitterness. I'd never shared with Lois about Dave's behavior or my feelings about it.

Yes, where are You, *God?*

CHAPTER 22

GOD IS IN THE DETAILS

I took a deep breath and willed myself to calm down, grateful that Lois wasn't judging me. She took both of my hands in hers. "All good people want to know why they suffer, and you *are* a good person, Janet. You are loved right now, just as you are. Father has blessed you with the freedom to choose for yourself, to choose with the end in mind."

As comforting as her words could have been, I still kept my eyes on the kitchen floor. *She doesn't know what I've done, where I've been. I don't deserve to be around all those good women at church. God must be so disappointed in me.*

"Wait a minute," I said heatedly, "I just—"

"I recognize your choices were few when you were married to Dave. But you chose to stick it out and take care of your boys above all else. That was unselfish. God saw that."

I paused my self-deprecating and thought about my responsibility, where I was at that moment. *I did choose to marry Dave because he helped me run away from home—I've cared for my boys with every life's breath, too. Someone had to.*

"Yes, Lois, but I'm the one in charge of it all now, and I don't feel anything. I just want to sleep. It's all I can do to get up every day for my sons."

"You will always be a mother, that's never going to change. And if you want to be there for your boys, you'll have to start taking care of yourself right now—eat right, sleep enough, get some fresh air. And pray."

I knew Lois was right, though I didn't want to admit it. With Dave gone I really did have freedom. *Oh man, I'm no one's wife or daughter now. Yeah! Maybe . . .*

Lois' "come to Jesus" talk had kicked me in the pants. It was hard to hear even though she spoke with kindness, *that* was a revelation. The following Monday, I made a start and tried to talk to Father, imagining He was listening with sincere interest.

"Dear God, it's a new day, so please send angels from above or angel friends down here. I don't know how to mother these boys by myself. I have no husband to support me, but you know that. . .I'll keep trying to feel Your impressions, God, even when I'm too tired. Amen."

Saturday, July 12th, Dave called. He had left Oregon for California, even before the divorce was final. I was relieved he was gone but angry that he could just walk away. And now he was calling to tell me he'd fallen in love with a sweet LDS woman.

"She's divorced like me with three kids. We got married last Saturday."

Wait, what? How many months have we been apart? He left the house last November. And now it's almost August . . . well, he's *really broke up about the divorce.*

I straightened my spine as I gripped the phone.

"We're coming into town next Saturday and I want you to meet her. She's a real angel."

My eyes narrowed as I focused on the length of the hallway where the boys were playing. My chest tightened with indignation and I ground my teeth.

Heavenly Father, this isn't what I meant by sending me angels!

"Great," I snapped into the phone. "I guess I'd like to meet your next victim—oops! I mean your next companion."

"Very funny. See you at Denny's Saturday."

The phone went dead. Whatever Christ-like feelings I tried to muster toward the father of my children died too. I closed my eyes tightly as my temples throbbed, anger racing through my bloodstream. I went for the only cooling agent I knew. I took down the box of Hershey's with almonds from above the refrigerator, then looked around . . . no boys. *Safe!* I took a bar out of the box, peeled off the wrapper, and stuffed it in. Relief . . . chocolate was still magic.

Saturday arrived and Elise stayed with the boys. I drove to Denny's in the beat-up VW square back. It was ugly, but it was all mine. I parked next to a white Ford station wagon with California plates. It had to be the new victim's. It wasn't brand new, but it wasn't filled with empty fast-food garbage, so I knew it wasn't Dave's.

I walked into the restaurant wearing a straight black skirt, a light pink blouse, and fake pearl earrings and necklace. I looked like someone who went to church.

There they sat, snuggled together in a booth, my ex and his new girlfriend. He was "happy" Dave again. I looked *her* over: short brown hair, glossy clean, not too thin, an inch shorter than Dave, about thirty, and glasses. I had to admit there was something attractive about her. I wanted to hate her, but the feelings wouldn't come. Adrenaline pushed through me instead, mixed with pity for this new woman.

She gave me a warm smile and offered her hand. I never thought I'd face a situation like this so soon. I politely shook it, then quickly let go.

"Thank you for meeting us. I'm Carole. I'm sure this all feels a little strange. It is for me, but Dave said you were a good mother who took his kids to church, so I knew you'd be someone I'd like and want to meet. We all go to the same church, by the way."

Dave said something nice about me? Shocker! Carole and I are sisters in Christ though, so that's good.

"Thank you," I uttered, trying to think. "Uh, I hope you had a nice trip from California."

Light conversation ensued, passing in one of my ears and out the other.

"Where are your kids, Carole? Dave said you have three."

"They're visiting with their dad. We have free time till the end of the month. We want to get all settled in Portland. Dave has his job there and he'll be able to come see the boys."

My face tightened.

They're planning to flat out take my kids, I know it!

I looked down at the table, then took a big gulp of my soda. The carbonation made me cough and hurt going down. The thought of Dave with the kids pained my throat too. I hacked and convulsed, trying to clear the passage, then ran to the lady's room. I closed the stall door just in time to lose my breakfast into the toilet.

Sweat popped out across my forehead as I leaned against the wall. Dave and a new wife, my kids spending time with him, and them living close by. Carole seemed halfway intelligent, but them together? It was all moving so fast.

Someone entered the bathroom. "Are you okay, Janet?" Carole asked.

I straightened my clothes, flushed, wiped the damp off my face with the edge of my skirt, and opened the stall door. Carole's eyes were huge with concern, magnified through her glasses.

"I hope I can help make it okay somehow, for the boys too."

As I looked at her my heart softened a little; she actually was sincere. "Yes, well, it *is* a lot," I managed to reply. "Thank you, but I'd better go home now. My stomach's really upset."

I said good-bye to the new couple and almost ran out the restaurant door. It wasn't fair that crazy Dave got a new wife. Maybe Carole could be a mediator between us, but it was too soon to tell.

That night, I went to bed the same time as the boys when the sun was gone at 8:30 p.m. I lay on top of the covers in my bathrobe, staring at the ceiling, waiting for the kids to drop off to sleep. Half an hour later, I crossed my arms over my chest and let the tears fall down the side of my face as thoughts buzzed in my head like mosquitoes.

I've been alive twenty-eight years! I should have it together by now. My sons should see their dad. I have full custody, but Dave has reasonable visiting rights. I hate this, I reflected. Carole will be there, so maybe they'll be okay. It's an awful adjustment, I don't like it.

The last weekend of summer, Dave and his new wife took the boys to the lake for a picnic. Even Eric toddled along, holding Carole's hands as she walked him in front of her to the car, his diapered behind wiggling with each step.

The quiet house was a dark cloud hanging over me. It was weird to be alone. *When was I ever alone before?* I sat on the couch for a minute or two pondering, then fell into a troubled nap. When I woke up, the sun was almost gone. Shadows moved across the living room walls and the clock said 6:30 p.m.

Where are they? Did they just take my kids and aren't bringing them back?

Nervous energy pumped through me as I stood up. Then I saw the station wagon come to a stop in the carport. I pushed out a rugged breath of relief.

Before I could open the back door, the boys jostled in with happy jabbering. Carole came in behind and Dave followed with Eric in his arms. "Your boys are a lot of fun," Carole said. "I'd love to have them come spend some time with my three."

Dave bounced Eric and made him giggle. "Yeah, Janet," he said, "In fact, we'd like to have them come stay before I start back to work. Carole can take care of this little guy too. The boys like Carole and it would help them get used to our house." He sidled up to me, his face closer than I liked. "What d'ya think?"

I looked at my now "happy-to-be-married-again" ex-husband.

My thoughts? You have ulterior motives and it makes me twitchy.

But the boys were happy with their dad *and* Carole. It might also be true that with the boys gone for a short while, I *could* start to make plans. Insecurity pushed in then, followed by irritation.

"I'll think about it," I replied, gritting my teeth. "Don't push me."

Carole nodded at my terse response, then carefully stepped an inch closer. "This is awkward, I know, but I can't figure any other way to plan upcoming visits. I have an ex-husband, too, and he gets my kids for visits because I trust his new wife. And, well, I realize you don't know me, Janet, but I *am* a Christian. I'll take care of your boys like they were mine."

"All right, Carole," I responded, my annoyance settling. "Call me tomorrow."

I'll try to pray . . . and talk to Lois.

Dave's face went all cheerful as he looked at Carole, took her hand, and walked her toward the back door. With them gone, I sat down in the recliner and gazed at the back of my sons' heads as they sat in front of the TV.

The kids going to Portland . . . when? How? Time to myself sounds nice, but I want what's good for the boys. And what is that?

As bedtime approached, I put a very tired Eric to sleep in his crib. He was almost asleep before he snuggled under his blanket. With Alex, Ben, and Chris in their own beds, I sat on the floor in their room and prepared to read to them. I looked at their expectant faces, then took a long breath.

"So, guys," I said casually, "would you like to stay at your dad's for a week, maybe meet Carole's kids?"

"Really?" Chris asked, his eyes sparkling. "Yeah, let's do that! I wanna go!"

"Me too," Ben said, smiling.

I glanced at Alex in the top bunk. He gave me a confused look, then rolled over on his back and stared at the ceiling.

"Your dad wants to spend time with you in his own house, so you can feel like it's your home too. And you guys like Carole, right?"

Alex turned over and looked at me, thoughts crossing his face. "Well, she does make good egg sandwiches, Mom. But if we go, it would just be for a week, right?"

"Sure, just for a while, Alex. Your brothers would be glad you were there."

"Okay, Mom." He rolled back over and stared at the ceiling again.

"Are you going to read or what?" Chris demanded.

"Oh, yeah . . . okay, Chapter Three: 'Huck and Jim Travel South . . . for some days everything went along quietly, but we were getting bored . . .'" I read for fifteen minutes, then looked up. Every boy had conked out.

I went to my room and dropped to my knees by the bed. "Father in Heaven, I don't want to let my sons go to Portland," I pleaded. "They *are* Dave's sons and I like Carole, but it feels terrible. What's best for my sons? I feel sick. Please help me know what's right. Help me do what's right."

Reality arrived on Saturday August 22nd. It was God's answer, and I knew it, Carole was now the *new* mom and I did grudgingly like her, but my stomach still hurt.

The day before each boy had rushed around and packed their favorite toys and some clothes in the backpacks Dave had bought them. Now, with extra toys and games piled by the front door, they knelt on the couch, excited, and watched out the front window for the white station wagon. It pulled up in front of the house at eleven, and the boys whooped and ran to the screen door.

"They're here, they're here!" Ben shouted. I stood against the wall, out of their way, stunned to see my sons so lit up with delight. My heart was in my shoes.

Carole walked in with a warm smile, then stopped abruptly as she saw the piles. Dave came in right behind her and stared too. "We can't take all this stuff," he growled.

"Oh, there's plenty of room for these things," Carole remarked quickly, before I could put in my two cents. Ben went to Carole and hugged her. "We'll make it work, won't we, guys?"

"Yep!" Chris yelled. "Let's go!"

He ran out the door to the car dragging his backpack. Ben followed next, an eager grin on his face. Alex looked at me annoyed, then walked out onto the grass with his pile of things. Eric watched his brothers go, giving me a bewildered look. Before I could comfort him, Carole picked him up and gave me a hopeful smile as Dave began hauling out the collection.

"I wish I could say something to make you feel better, Janet. But here's our phone number. Please call anytime you want. In fact, why don't you call after church tomorrow?"

"Right," I muttered. She gave me a tender look and hugged up against my side.

I watched her go to the car holding my baby. She settled Eric on her lap, pulled him close up against her, and kissed him on top of his head.

Without a glance back at me or even a wave good-bye from the boys, the car took off. I watched it go until I couldn't see them anymore.

Lois arrived at noon. She dropped her purse on the couch, then wrapped her arms around me. I cried for a minute against her shoulder, then pulled away, determined not to sob.

"I guess I'd better get used to all this, but I let Carole take the baby. What was I thinking? I'm trying to be positive, trying to see the good, but it hurts so much."

"It is a hard, no question. But it's also the start of a new future for all of you." She looked straight into my face. "And I've been thinking, what about going back to college? If you're going to support your kids, education could be the right direction."

"Going back to school. That would please my dad. And I need to get out of Oregon somehow, too, maybe to a different state for that education."

"Yes," Lois said hesitantly. "I've prayed about that as well and I agree. What about Las Vegas and UNLV? Or maybe Henderson to live in. It's less expensive than Vegas, not far from the college, and I have friends there who could help you and the boys get settled."

"Henderson! Thank you, Lois, it would be good to have someone to help me get oriented. And there's got to be work there. The further away from here, the better. When I look around at this house, my stomach—"

Lois squeezed my shoulder and we fell silent for ten minutes.

"You'll want to keep close to Church there and stay away from the Strip," Lois added. "I haven't been there in a while, but I'm sure the neon lights still blaze day and night. There are herds of people, crazy traffic. It's a lot coming at you."

I nodded, a sense of dread forming in my stomach. Still, anything was better than staying here.

"You've got a lot to think about while the boys are gone," Lois stated. "Let's have Brother Duncan give your car a once over while you decide. Nothing worse than a broken-down car and kids screaming in the back seat, whether you stay here or not."

I gave her a strong hug. She had been my confidante, had seen me at my worst, and never judged. An approving smile was on her face. She *was* the angel I'd prayed for.

With seven days to myself, I examined all the stuff in the house—worn furniture, clothes, dishes, even an old washer and dryer. I drove to the grocery store, got boxes from the produce section, and started packing, realizing I'd decided.

I'd get the deposit money back if the house was cleaned before I left. Telling Lois my decision, she brought church ladies over to help. When they left, the place was spotless, even the baseboards.

I called Carole that evening to share my new plan. When she answered the phone, I heard the boys and other kids playing in the background.

They're having fun. That's good. It was an assurance things would be okay.

"How are you doing, Janet? Did you go out to a movie? Or maybe you just stayed in bed and read a book and ate chocolate," Carole giggled.

"What a great idea, but no. I did a lot of thinking and planning for me and the kids. I'm going to go back to college and finish my degree."

"Oh," Carole said, suddenly quiet. I could almost hear her thinking. "Um, that will be a challenge with all the boys, don't you think?"

"Yes, but I know sisters in the church who'll help. I've seen it around here, even in this small town. So, when I go to Henderson, Nevada, I'm sure I'll find support there too."

"Henderson?" The shock in Carole's voice was unmistakable. "Don't you think you should talk to Dave about taking the kids out of state? I mean, well, I have to stay in the vicinity of my ex and I suspect you have the same requirements too. You should talk to Dave."

I felt good about my decision, and I was sure God was in the details. In the last week as I'd cleaned and packed up the house, and my love of life returned along with fresh new goals. I heard Carole talking to Dave in a hurried, irritated tone, then he took the phone.

"What are you thinking? What about what's good for these kids?

You can't just take them out of state. You'd better check out the divorce papers before you go off half-cocked like you usually do."

After all the unstable, crazy behavior I'd had with *him* in the last year? I wanted to throw that back in his face, but I resisted instead and hung up.

If you let him push you around, you let him control you.

The divorce decree said nothing about where the kids had to live, so I kept the new plan. Staying busy made the rest of the week fly by. My adrenaline soared as I made progress. I liked the rush. I was finally in charge of my life.

It was Saturday before I knew it, and the boys were due back at three. When the clock read 2:45 p.m., I stopped packing to catch my breath and tried to ignore the tenseness in my chest. At 3:20 p.m., I went to the front doorway and watched out the screen door. *Where* are *they?*

Then the phone rang . . . I didn't want to think about why, but I knew.

"Listen . . . Dave and I have been thinking, praying, about your last call," Carole shared. "The boys, well, we're all having such a good time here, all the kids getting along and everything. So how would it be if we kept the boys while you go to Nevada? You could get everything set up first. I made Dave realize you have a right to pursue your own life."

My mouth went dry as I held my breath.

"School will be a challenge here, but I can homeschool them like I do my kids."

I jolt of surprise ran through me. My heart beat so fast it made me dizzy and I slid to the floor. Sweat beaded on my forehead and my hand went white as I clutched the phone.

"Okay," I croaked. "You have the boys anyway, so what can I do about it?"

"Oh, please don't think like that," Carole said hurriedly. "We want your move to be easy on you, truly, and easier for the boys."

Her voice sounded genuine, but I felt sick. I *had* asked God to help me figure all this out, so maybe this was it, but it felt terrible. I'd have to count on Carole now.

"I need to talk to Alex, then," I said as evenly as I could.

I waited and finally heard my oldest son's breathing come through the phone lines.

"Hello, son. How are you doing? What is your dad's house like?"

Alex stayed quiet for several seconds, then finally said, "Oh, it's okay. He has a new TV and I only have to share a room with Ben. When do we get to come home?"

"Well, I'm going to go to Nevada right now and you boys will stay there while I do that. Once I get settled, then you guys will join me. Uh, you getting along with her kids?"

"They're okay . . . why Nevada? Can I go with you?" The longing in his voice was clear and his tone filled me with a terrible sadness.

"Hon, I need you to stay with your brothers. I know they'll feel better with all of you together. It's only a few more weeks. I'm sure we'll be together by Thanksgiving, okay?"

"Sure, Mom," Alex replied, his irritability pouring through the line.

"Time will go by fast. Then you guys can come join me in some warm weather, away from rainy Oregon. It'll be a lot better!"

I waited for a reply. "Alex?"

He was gone.

Brother Duncan gave the car a tune-up, then went to Portland and took the boy's things to them for me. He said they looked happy. That made me smile because I hadn't had the strength to go with him. It already nearly broke me once, when I thought I wouldn't see them for a week. I couldn't bear the idea of saying good-bye now.

CHAPTER 23

A NEW BEGINNING

There was only a folding chair left to sit on in my house when Brother Duncan and the bishop came to my door. "We thought a blessing would help you on your way," the bishop offered. "A blessing of protection."

I let them both in and sat in that chair with an uncertain smile, *Will this help my currently freaked-out state? I guess it can't hurt!*

The two Christian men placed their hands on my head as I folded my arms.

Brother Duncan spoke, "Heavenly Father, we are grateful to know Sister Janet. We know she is Your daughter and You love her dearly. She's passed through many hard times and has been uplifted and strengthened by Your son. As she goes forward now, please bring her peace. Help her to believe in herself and Your inspiration. Provide her with insights, God, as she makes decisions. And let her feel Your all-encompassing love."

When Brother Duncan finished, I stood up, wiped away escaping tears, and shook both their hands. I had a sense that everything would be okay.

Out in the driveway, the two of them with arms crossed, looked over the VW.

"I wouldn't even drive this car to the market," the bishop said, chuckling. "But I'll bet you can drive it to Nevada with no issues because Someone's definitely watching over you."

I gave him a weak smile.

Brother Duncan put an arm around me then and said, "Yes, Janet, you've had the crap beaten out of you, we all know that, but you've also passed right through it all. Angels will go before you and protect you on this trip."

Early Wednesday morning, September 10, 1980, I jumped onto the freeway with a fierce urge to cross the border into California. I left my daughter buried in Woodburn cemetery and my boys with their father and stepmother. I discovered an envelope with money in it on the passenger's seat. Gratitude made me smile and softened the grief I was determined to ignore.

It was one long sixteen-hour drive with a break at a rest stop after eight hours where I slept with the windows up and doors locked. Waking up, I hit the hot road singing in harmony with The Eagles, Gordon Lightfoot, and Blood, Sweat, and Tears, all their music blaring out my rolled-down windows. Too bad they didn't know what a fabulous addition I was to their bands.

I passed through Eugene, Oregon and on to Susanville, California. Eight more hours motored me up to the Lake Mead Highway. I arrived in Henderson Thursday afternoon and pulled into Elaine Session's driveway. Across the dry desert Las Vegas sparkled in the blinding late afternoon sun and I wondered aloud, "What have I done? I must be crazy!"

I wasn't sure if God had inspired me to move to Nevada, but Elaine's dinner made me forget any confusion I had. Spaghetti with homemade sauce and meatballs followed by a from-scratch angel food cake, a welcomed reprieve from road trip food.

"I'm glad Lois reached out to let us know you were coming," Elaine said as she made up a bed for me on the living room couch. "The bathroom's over there and I'll make sure it's just for your use while you're here . . . you know, kids," she added, smiling.

We had a quick hug, then she disappeared upstairs to bed down her six children. I snuggled under a thick blanket as the air conditioner cold blasted over me. An exhausted melancholy fell on me as I drifted away, imagining Carole putting my boys to bed.

Friday morning, barely awake and bleary-eyed, I watched Elaine's kids run out for the school bus. I stood and stretched cramped driving muscles, then had to sit down fast. A sour gurgling started in my stomach and a sick mass bubbled up into my throat. I ran for the bathroom, slammed the door behind me, and threw up Elaine's dinner, sadly, even the angel food cake. I retched 'til there was nothing left.

Wow, I hope nobody heard that. Driving for sixteen hours did a number on my digestion.

Feeling shaky, cold sweat under my arms, I stood up and drank some water. A little bit of energy returned and my body calmed down. My stomach ached a little, but it was much better than the flu-like nausea from a few minutes before. Gazing in the mirror, my face was more pale than usual. I patted a towel on my face, pinched my cheeks for some color, then opened the door.

Elaine stood there, eyebrows raised, her eyes wide with concern.

"I think the trip took a lot out of me," I said with a faint smile. "I've never been car sick before, but then I've never driven by myself for such a long stretch."

Elaine nodded and gave me a searching look. "Well, it's none of my business, but how long since you've, um, had intimacy with your husband? I know you're divorced, but still . . . cuz really, that sounds like the kind of throwing up I know all too well."

"Oh no, that's not possible," I assured her. "It's been at least a year," as I remembered sleeping on the couch to stay away from Dave.

When was my last period? It's been a while, but I have been under a lot of stress.

"Well, you could be right about the driving, but you might want to get a checkup. I know of a free clinic where you can get a pregnancy test," Elaine offered. "In the meantime, why don't we drive around and look for apartments? Maybe you'll start to feel better."

I nodded, then went with Elaine to the kitchen, grabbed a banana, then followed her to the car. I gave her a smile, grateful for this woman who was helping me, a stranger who had wandered into her life.

"Lois said you're planning to go back to school and need to find work. The new Levi factory just opened here in Henderson and I think they're hiring."

She chattered on and I wrote down phone numbers for apartments as we drove past Henderson properties. My tummy had been calm all morning, but by afternoon the nausea was back, and I barfed up my lunch when we returned to the house.

I hope Elaine isn't right, I thought worriedly, *but I'd better check.*

The next day I went to the free clinic and peed in a cup. I knew a woman couldn't get pregnant if sex was forced on her, so I was dead sure I wasn't with child. Sitting behind curtains on the examining table, I swung my feet back and forth as I waited. The posters on the walls around me said free contraception or, alcohol and birth defects, and then an ad for Planned Parenthood, all things about birth—or not.

After an eternity, just twenty minutes, a nurse pushed back the curtains and stepped up to me. Clipboard in hand, glasses on the bridge of her nose, she was energetically proficient. "You're three months pregnant," she announced. Looking down at her clipboard, she continued, "I can see you're not married, so, we can schedule your abortion—"

"What? STOP!" I nearly fell off the table. "I don't *want* an abortion!"

The nurse gave me a startled look. Her eyes were large behind her glasses, then irritation passed across her face. "That's what we do here," she said curtly. "Isn't that why you came?"

I shook my head no. She gave me a disgusted look, then turned and marched away down the hall.

Stunned, I drove back to Elaine's, focusing hard on the traffic, confused about this new direction my life had taken.

Dave would say, "You don't plow under the corn cuz you don't like the farmer." I had to agree, conception wasn't the baby's fault. *Honestly, that night at the bar's a blur. . .will I ever quit having babies?!*

"I'm pregnant—again!" I yelled at the car ceiling. "What am I going to tell my kids?"

The familiar lump of tears was in my throat. Once more, I needed someone's help to survive. *Humiliating!*

"No. I am going to handle this by myself, I've been through worse. I'm strong. I'm capable," I muttered out loud, not believing any of it.

At Elaine's house, I told her everything, every thing.

"This baby must really want to be here. It's a lot to manage by yourself," she murmured quietly. After a moment's thought, she continued.

"We'll find a way, Janet. God will provide direction if we ask Him," she said kindly.

I hadn't thought to ask God to help; I was too ashamed. *I'd* made the poor decision to go dancing at a bar, I was the one that went somewhere I shouldn't have. Anyway, I'd learned growing up when I did something wrong, I had to change before I was worthy of help or forgiveness. *But how do I change this?*

Sunday, I met with Bishop Garner. In his sixties with a receding gray hairline that exposed his shiny front scalp, he gave me a kindly smile and offered me a seat.

I took a deep breath, stared at my shoes, and silently thanked God that Pepto-Bismol was keeping my nausea down. Then I confessed all: divorced, pregnant, alone in a new state.

I looked up hopefully. The bishop stared at me intently, then an accusatory frown crossed his forehead, his brows knit together, his eyes dark.

"You have quite a story," he stated abruptly, "but I can only take you at your word that what you've said is true, Sister. I've met others pregnant out of wedlock and, to be honest, I don't know you. I don't know *what* to think . . . I'll have to call your Oregon bishop."

I left his office feeling like Hester from *The Scarlet Letter*, with a sign hung around my neck with a big red letter *A*. I had hoped for understanding but left feeling stupid and judged.

Better keep this freakin' secret to myself, at least from everyone but Elaine.

I still had no place to live for the next six months, no health insurance, and very little money left. I was embarrassed and ashamed. The lump of tears had returned along with morning sickness. That evening, Elaine and I sat together on her porch watching a purple and orange Nevada sky.

"I'll have to talk with Denny," she said gently. Perspiration dotted my forehead as we sat in silence. After ten minutes, my new friend continued. "I'll bet it will be okay for you to stay with us 'til the baby comes, we do have a spare room. We store things there right now and there's not much cool air circulating, but all of that will be easy to fix."

I looked at Elaine with surprise, my mouth ajar. The woman hardly knew me.

"Now, you might want to talk to Family Services. They're a church organization that offers counseling and resources for any expectant mother on her own. They'll help you decide about the baby's future too. Just a suggestion, but that's what I would do."

A tear ran down my cheek, the rest of them balanced on the bottom of my eyelids.

"Wow, are you sure? The bishop wasn't very nice, but here you are, being so—gosh!"

"The bishop's a good man," Elaine replied, "but we do live near Vegas, and immorality is something he hears about all the time. Don't worry about him. He probably doesn't know what to do or honestly, what to say. He's just an imperfect man, but that's all God has to work with, right?" She finished with a knowing grin and we broke into laughter.

Here was God putting another wonderful woman, another angel, in my life.

I need to remember how this feels so I can be a giver if I ever get a chance.

It was a promise I determined to keep.

On Tuesday, I took her advice and went to Family Services in Vegas. I parked in front of a light yellow building with frosted glass panels in the front door. The receptionist ushered me into an office with an older woman and I took a seat on a padded folding chair near her desk. The woman's mass of white hair looked like she tried to comb it into a Jackie Kennedy bouffant, but most of it just went any which way it wanted. Her round, broad face held a smile and her brown eyes said "hello" from behind big glasses with clear frames.

"My name is Wanda," she said in a confident voice, shaking my hand. "I'll take your basic information then explain about our services." She took out a yellow pad and pencil and sat behind her desk. "Before we start, let me assure you there's no judgment here. We help women however we can in whatever circumstances they may have.

I nodded okay. I hoped she was telling the truth. I could use a break. "Tell me about your situation."

Wanda's appearance reminded me of Grandy. She had the same rounded body, creased hands that had known a lot of work, and tiny wrinkles around her eyes, but it was the acceptance I felt that put them together in my thoughts.

Just like Elaine, I told Wanda everything, I couldn't help it; everything just gushed out of me. Lastly, I told her about how the pregnancy happened. Wanda wrote briskly, continuing even after I'd finished talking. A relief from spilling my story made me feel ten pounds lighter.

She finally stopped and looked at me thoughtfully. "So, what we do is cover medical expenses for the mother if she chooses to put the baby up for adoption." Wanda looked at me intently. "God chose you to bring this baby here; I know He has a plan. Choosing to give this baby up for adoption could be an answer to a prayer for a couple who so much want a child."

God certainly hadn't entered my thoughts about this conception, but it eased my heart to think I could be an answer to someone's prayer.

Wanda stood up, came around the desk, and sat in the chair next to me. "If you have someone in your life you trust, you might talk and pray about this together. It's a big decision. Several lives will be impacted by it."

I nodded in agreement and stood up to leave. It *was* a hard decision, but without health insurance, adoption seemed the only answer.

By the time I was four months along, I was sure. This infant would have a better chance at happiness with parents who longed for a child of their own.

As the months went by Wanda continued to counsel me, teaching me concepts I wished I'd learned at home. "It's simple," she began, "there's real power in saying to yourself, 'this is what I did, and this is what I learned.' With honesty, take charge of your life and do things in a healthier way, for youself. As for other people? What they think of you is none of your business."

Surprisingly refreshing.

In November, my sixth month of pregnancy, I called Dave and Carole with the news.

"Is it mine?" was Dave's only question.

"Are you okay? Do you need money, anything?" Carole asked next.

"Yes," I replied with heavy emotion. "I need you to keep the boys a bit longer, if that's okay."

"Of course, Janet . . . and I'll keep you in my prayers."

I hung up the call and cried. The boys would be taken care of by someone who was in my corner. Father had provided for all of us, especially my boys, in spite of me.

On March first, labor came and didn't last more than an hour. In fact, the baby came on the gurney while I was being wheeled into the delivery room. I had to look away. I knew if I saw this new baby boy, held him, I might not let him go. When I was told he was healthy, relief washed over me.

Thank you, God, that all is well, and now he'll have a life where he is cherished.

Wanda came to visit with the closed adoption paperwork to sign. Her kind words and praise helped solidify the truth I'd come to recognize: it was the right thing to birth this child and let him go.

"I was just thinking, I was put up for adoption myself," I began as I deliberately wrote my signature. "Now I'm the one giving a baby up for adoption. It's kind of a full circle, isn't it?"

Wanda gave me a knowing smile. "Yes, I hope you have compassion for your birth mother now." She gave me a hug and reminded me as she left that we'd meet in two weeks.

I hadn't thought much about my birth mother since I'd become a mother myself years ago. Who was she, why was I born? The desire to unbury family secrets grew.

But right now, what I did know was that God was still in the details of my life. He'd blessed me in ways I couldn't have imagined. In the last twenty-four hours, I'd given birth with a pain-free labor that lasted less than an hour. The baby was healthy and now had a home where he would be treasured. God had brought amazing people into my life again with unconditional love. Since my days with Grandy, I wondered how many others had helped me that I'd missed.

"What are your plans now?" Wanda asked, during that next meeting.

"I need to see my boys," I replied with a visceral ache, "then I thought I might take some college courses since we're so close to UNLV. I'm glad the boys have two parents to care for them, but I feel guilty. It's awful not to have them here."

"You're not the first who has had to let their children go live with others," she offered. "Give yourself some credit for doing the best you could at the time. As we learn to do better, we usually do better. You have done well and you will continue to do so in the future, I'm sure. I have faith in you."

Wanda's point of view was encouraging. I'd come to trust her insights.

"Something else," she continued. "I've worked with young women for many years. Most of them I never see again and I understand why. I'm connected to a situation they don't want to remember. So, if you feel the same, it's okay."

" No," I said with intensity, "I'd like you to stay in my life."

"I'm glad, I feel the same," she replied taking my hand.

"I hope you know it's no accident that you are on the planet right here, right now, Janet. Figure out that 'why.' Your future depends on getting the answer to that question."

It was a good wrap-up visit and I was grateful to return to making plans. But what *was* my why? Wanda's counsel supported my determination to get answers about my past.

When I got back to Elaine's, I called Dave to arrange a visit with the boys. "It's not a good time. Call us again in a month." The phone went dead, I stared at the receiver.

My heart sank with this new reality—I had no say now about my sons' lives. Heat filled my chest. I was well and truly pissified, and slammed Elaine's dishes around in the sink. I'd have to let it go for a while, but *only* 'til I got on my feet. I prayed for my sons every day and tried to focus on serious plans for our future. First, I needed money.

I got a job cleaning and fixing meals with a single father and his daughter. It gave me a private room with bathroom, and a small salary. That gave me some free time and a little money, but what would I do with my life without kids? Could I enter the world of Peter O'Toole and Audrey Hepburn, be a part of the film industry in some small way? Movie scenes still flashed through my mind all day long as I vacuumed and cooked. Along with God and good women who seemed to show up in my life, movies were still my secret healing balm.

Every Friday afternoon, I went to the movie theater to let the same story carry me away from the real world for two hours. I needed its over-the-top intense adventure. It didn't hurt that the lead actor was everything Dave wasn't. Masculine like Bogart, he wore dark brown everything—a fedora, leather bomber jacket, leather boots, and a whip that hung from his belt always handy to use in the nick of time. I traveled in his 1936 world munching popcorn, with extra butter, and a Diet Coke to balance out the calories. After twenty-five viewings, I knew most of the lines: "It's not the years, honey, it's the mileage."

In August, Wanda went with me to see *Raiders of the Lost Ark*, too.

"I think my favorite scene is Indy and the beefy bare-chested guy near the plane propellers," she shared afterwards as we drove to her house. "Well done, very realistic. I've seen fights like that. My four brothers were always scrapping. One of them would run out of breath and try to back out of the fight, but his brother had to win and wouldn't quit."

"And I like that Marion wasn't a screamer and could hold her own!" I added.

"Absolutely," Wanda agreed. We laughed.

"So, have you figured out what you want to do with your life?" she asked as we walked into the kitchen.

"I don't know; I sure love movies, but I doubt I'll ever be in front of a camera. Maybe I could pull cable for the camera person or work with props."

We sat down to a lunch of grilled cheese sandwiches and tomato soup.

"Did you know Brigham Young University has a film program? It'd be a good place to get your feet wet and decide if this is a career you really want to pursue," Wanda offered as she spooned in some soup.

A thrill of excitement ran through me. All I knew about movies was what I liked to watch. The use of camera, lights, sets, I really knew nothing. Could school prepare me for a career making movies? I felt like a giddy kid at the carnival thinking about it. I grinned at my friend, my eyes bright as the possibilities ran through my mind.

"Courage, dear heart," Wanda smiled, "eat your lunch."

CHAPTER 24

GEOGRAPHICAL CURE?

"I'd love to be a part of stories on the screen. Stories have changed my life—books, movies, even the Bible is made up of stories. Stories change the world."

Wanda and I walked to the living room and sat down together. "Well, all journeys start with a first step." She patted my hand. "Why not give it a try? If it doesn't work out, you won't be any worse off than you are now."

We hugged tightly for several minutes. I didn't want to let go. "You might as well call me Mom," Wanda whispered. "I'm here for you no matter what."

I held Wanda at arm's length and studied her face as she nodded with a warm smile. My heart swelled with joy. Her acceptance renewed my energy. Someone actually, finally, believed in me and loved me in spite of my mistakes. It changed everything and I hugged her intensely.

I applied and was accepted into the BYU film program and began in fall 1982. For the next two and a half years, I eagerly soaked up everything I could.

I loved learning about the history of film; it actually started in the 1890s in France. I devoured the knowledge that there were seven elements needed to make a good film: acting, cinematography, set design, lighting, sound, costume, editing, and makeup. Just as important, good directors cared about the story's influence on the hearts and minds of their audience, even more than making money. Story and character was what mattered most from the 1920s through the '50s in movies. I watched a lot of films from those decades: film noir classics, suspense from Hitchcock, Frank Capra's "love of America" films, and Billy Wilder's romances, drama, and comedies.

Then *Citizen Kane* was on the screen. Released in 1941, written, produced, and starring Orson Welles, it was startling. One of the most iconic directors in the Golden Age of Hollywood, Welles was still living. He was known for his innovations and experiments with the camera. He'd even had a hole jack-hammered in the bottom of the sound stage to get the camera as low as possible to make his *Kane* character huge on the screen.

Fascinated, I learned as much as I could about that incredible man. A law only to himself, no one outside the production was allowed on his set. Nobody did that in 1940 except Welles. He had been a success in New York, so RKO studio heads grudgingly accepted his terms. Thinking back to *Raiders,* I realized a lot of the camera techniques used were invented by Orson Welles.

In class, we watched him act in *The Third Man, The Stranger*, and *Othello,* films often written and directed by him as well. I wanted to be a part of putting stories on the screen that would have a positive influence just like what Welles had done. Film was powerful.

Carole and Dave were now living in Utah, too, and I got to see my sons often. They were happy and secure in their home with two parents. I helped whenever I could with my school loans money. I was living on it, so why not help when I could? It was a small way to stay involved and do my share to support the boys. I helped purchase their school clothes, they had visits at my place, and I even took them to see *Return of the Jedi* when it hit the screen May '83.

Carole and I coparented very well during that time; we had made a pact that we would never talk about Dave, we were there for the kids. My four and Carole's three made a big family: five boys and one girl. Together, we coordinated family outings, church, and school. I was happy for them, as long as I didn't think about it all too much.

I loved film school for over two years but then got frustrated. A new department head for the film program changed getting a film education a competition. "It's already hard to be taken seriously as a female in this film program," I complained, frowning to Jim D'Arc, head of the BYU Film Archives Department. I worked there part-time helping to catalog Jimmy Stewart's film and memorabilia donation. "I've been told my screenplays have to be as good as male students. I mean, males, *really?* I thought I was just competing with myself, to improve my abilities, not to be as good as–whoever."

"Then why not just go to LA and see if it's what you really want to do?" Jim remarked. "There are a lot of talented women in the film industry. Did you know a woman, Anne Coates, edited *Lawrence of Arabia?* She won the Oscar for it."

A woman edited *Lawrence?* Far out! My mouth dropped open. Jim chuckled. Editors had as much influence on a final film as the director. Imagine watching Peter O'Toole for hours.

If she could do that, maybe, I could become a woman director. Why not?

I finished the school term, packed up my car, then went to see the boys.

"Have you prayed about going to LA?" Carole asked when I came to say good-bye. "I know you're strong and you've been through a lot, but this is a big leap into the unknown. LA, wow."

"I feel sort of directed to do it, no pun intended. Still, it could just my being impulsive," I admitted. "I'll pray and see what God impresses on me. I hope you know I wouldn't even attempt this if I didn't know my boys were happy with you."

We had a hug good-bye and I thought, *You'll never know how grateful I am for just you, Carole.* I wiped away a few tears as I drove away.

Forty miles out of town, I parked under the shade of a Ponderosa pine at a rest stop. "Dear Father, I know You know I'm moving to LA," I began. "I'm a little scared, so please be with me or send angels. Help me see myself as You see me, maybe as someone who could do some good somewhere. But if it's not the right direction, please put a road-block in my way. I'm impulsive, I know, but it feels right. I pray Your Spirit will guide me. In Jesus' name, amen."

I sat quietly for a few moments and felt that now familiar warm surround me.

"Okay," I told myself. "Let's freakin' do this."

Pumped with caffeine from Diet Cokes and some BBQ chips, I drove five hours to Las Vegas to tell my volunteer mom my plans and have an overnight stay. Wanda gave me her approval, a small loan, and a road map. "If you want to pay me back, that's up to you. I never expect loans to be paid back because I don't want money to ruin relationships," she said as we stood at the front door. "Just be frugal. Los Angeles is more expensive than Provo. And one more thing, don't let anyone tell you what to do. You've got plenty of insight, trust yourself."

With an encouraging hug and kiss, I was on the road again. As I drove through the dry, barren desert, I daydreamed of me on movie sets. Maybe I could be a script supervisor and sit next to Steven Spielberg. Anything was possible in LA and I was determined. Better yet, once I got established, I could even have the boys come live with me again.

It was the middle of August, and after five hours of driving, I rounded the last hill on the freeway and saw Los Angeles laid out in front of me. A light smoggy haze hung over the city and the traffic looked hectic. *Glad it's not rush hour.*

My bishop in Utah had connected me with his brother in LA, who had found me a room to rent in an older Hollywood neighborhood. Trees along the street shaded elegant stately homes built in the 1940s. My room was the library on the second floor of a two-story colonial. I had a queen-size bed, my own bathroom, and books of every kind surrounding me.

That first week, I put in applications with employment agencies to get contract work at the studios since they were the biggest businesses in town, which suited me just fine! By my second week, I was a receptionist at Paramount Studios for ten dollars an hour. As the months went by, I worked other contracting jobs at other studios: Walt Disney Studios in Burbank, Universal Studios in North Hollywood, and Sony Pictures at the old MGM studio lot in Culver City.

I built a solid reputation for being dependable and respectable. It meant I kept my distance from TV or film talent, production crew members, directors, or on-the-set writers. Maintaining my distance was more important than my typing speed.

Almost a year later, however, the work felt tedious and boring. Negative feelings about myself returned to bite me in the fanny. What Buckaroo Banzai said in his movie was true: "No matter where you go, there you are." I'd moved to LA to pursue my dream, but I'd brought my past miseries with me.

Mother's voice still attacked my brain: *You can't make movies, Janet. You have no talent and you never did. Who do you think you are?*

"Oh, shut up!" I yelled to my bedroom walls. It was becoming a litany.

I ate away my disappointments. I was just a receptionist traveling from one studio to the next. I couldn't figure out how to get on a sound-stage. There were already plenty of goffers everywhere; I couldn't even get work with film caterers. Instead, nachos on my way home from work and half a gallon of ice cream on the weekend soothed my unhappiness . . . at least until the next Monday.

With the mild California fall hitting the southern coast, I found myself as yet another receptionist for one of the many producers at Merv Griffin Enterprises on Vine Street, in the heart of Hollywood. My boss often had a four-hour liquid lunch around 12:30 p.m. and I wouldn't see him the rest of the day. He had his booze and I had my large-size Hershey's chocolate with almonds as soon as he left, always with a Big Gulp—to balance out the calories. As I chewed and swallowed, I looked at the show's production sheet.

Orson Welles would be interviewed on Merv's 3:00 p.m. show . . . today. *What?* I was so excited I stopped eating. At 2:45 p.m., I wandered down to the production set and stood behind the audience seats. Every chair was filled and the audience quieted as the lights went down and the taped introduction started. We all clapped as Merv came out and introduced his first guest.

"He captures our attention with every word he speaks. Would you welcome, the one and only, Orson Welles," Merv announced. We all clapped again and I nearly stopped breathing.

In a dark blue suit, blue button-down shirt, and blue polka-dotted scarf about his neck, Orson entered from stage left, walking with a cane, a warm smile on his face. He gave a small hug and kiss to Merv, then turned to the audience who were still clapping. He bowed with a huge smile and said, "Thank you," seemingly surprised by the intense reaction.

Can he see me and my star-struck face? I'm friggin' fifty feet away from Orson Welles!

I began breathing normal again as he sat with Merv and began chatting. He was seventy and happy about it because he thought he was seventy last year and this year's birthday was a huge surprise. We all laughed along with him and applauded.

"Thank you! Believe me, it's nothing to applaud about," he retorted. The two men fell into the host/guest patter and Orson talked about his life, his love for Rita Hayworth, and his career.

"There's certain parts of every day that are joyous. I'm not essentially a happy person, but I have had all kinds of joy," Welles shared. "And there is a difference, you know . . . because joy is a great big electrical experience. And just happy is, oh I don't know, a warthog can be happy."

I leaned back against the studio wall in the shadows, unable to take my eyes from him. *That's exactly how I feel right now, Mr. Welles, warthog happy.*

"What about painful times?" Merv inquired.

"Enough of those exist too," he responded. "There's all kinds of pain; bad, conscience pain, too, ya know? That's the worst, the things you think you did."

It sounded like a eulogy. I hung on to his every word, listening to stories of his loves, his work, and his insights.

I have to meet this man. He has to know how much I admire his work, how greatly he has influenced me to dream . . . that even I could work in this business.

As Orson walked off stage, I hurried out the side door and went around to the back of the studio. As I entered the parking lot, a security guard stopped me. "What are you doing here?" he demanded gruffly.

"I want to say hello to Mr. Welles and thank him for his extraordinary work."

The guard looked me up and down.

He thinks I fell off the turnip truck.

"Okay . . . if anyone asks, I didn't know you were here." He turned and walked away.

I let out a huge sigh. *After all, I'm just another fan that nobody knows or will remember. Probably a good thing.*

A black Chrysler pulled up and parked near the building as Mr. Welles came out the studio side door. In a black caftan, he looked a bit thinner than he seemed on TV. As he walked toward me with his cane, his eyes crinkled up and he gave me a smile.

He could have played Santa Claus with that smile and his full gray-white beard and hair. He stopped in front of me and I extended my hand. He grasped it warmly, gave it a little shake, and waited for me to speak.

"Mr. Welles," I stammered, the adrenaline making sweat trickle down my sides, "I just want to thank you for all the work you've done in the film industry. I've learned so much watching your films."

He looked at me seriously. "You're not from around here, are you?"

Oh man, he thinks I'm a rube too.

"No, I'm not," I confessed. "Uh, I just left film school."

"Which one?"

"BYU."

"I've heard that's a good school."

"It is. We do a whole section on your work," I told him emphatically. "So, when I say I'm a fan, I know other films besides *Citizen Kane.*"

Orson looked at the ground and didn't say anything for a couple of awkward moments. Then: "I didn't think anyone cared anymore."

Stunned, I gathered some more of my courage. "Oh, not true," I insisted. "Not at all. We care a great deal!" I laughed unevenly. "It's such a thrill to meet you."

He looked up at me then. "So, what are you doing here young lady?"

"I want to do what you did, write and direct movies," I said boldly.

Why did I say that? I'm an idiot.

He looked steadily at me and I gave him a weak smile. I hoped he wouldn't say, "What, are you crazy? Don't you know what they've done to me? And *I'm* a genius."

But instead he quietly replied, "I wish you good luck. Some of the best people I've worked with in this business have been women."

Amazed by his encouragement, I asked for his autograph, which he gave, then he walked toward the driver who was standing by the Chrysler with a black Pomeranian dog. He handed the dog to Welles and they both got in the car. As the car backed out of the parking lot, Orson gave me a nod and a smile. I watched until the car was out of sight, unable to move.

I have to tell somebody about this! But who?

The next morning, I came in the main doors of Merv's studios, having decided to share my Orson experience with my friend Phil, the guard at the main desk. He'd understand. I was eager to share every tidbit of the wisdom and encouragement the great man had given me.

But before I could speak, Phil said, "Did you hear about Orson Welles? He died last night."

What did he just say? A cold shiver ran through me.

"What? N-no!" I stuttered. "I talked with him in the parking lot yesterday. He was just fine . . . I must have been one of the last people to talk to him. I—"

Phil nodded, his eyes full of tears. "He was a genius. We have jobs because he invented new, better ways to tell stories with a camera. The makeup man told me his color wasn't good before he got him ready to go on stage. What a loss."

Orson's smile and twinkling eyes filled my thoughts as I took the elevator to the office and my desk. The rest of that day, I typed, answered phones, and filed papers in a stupor. The weekend newspapers and TV specials told everything they could dig up about Welles' life. *The New York Times* said, "Orson Welles, the Hollywood 'boy wonder' who created the film classic, *Citizen Kane*, and who scared tens of thousands of Americans with a realistic radio report of a Martian invasion of New Jersey, changed the face of film. Welles's death appears to be natural in origin. He had been under treatment for diabetes as well as a heart ailment."

I worked the rest of the month for Merv, remembering Orson's words; the man who thought no one cared any more about his work. I hoped he had found real electrical joy now and for always. It was hard to stop thinking about him. He came in and out of my mind for weeks.

One weekend, I went to dinner with Sally, a coworker. The Merv Griffin contract work was ending and I didn't want to lose contact. We planned to gorge ourselves with Mexican food, then go to a free presentation about eating disorders; we loved the irony. We had become instant friends over the mini-Snickers candy bowl in the employee lunch room. Sally had unusual green eyes, and a cynical wit she used to poke fun at the celebrities who came on Merv's show—the bodybuilder who hawked his movies or the 1950s actor with a scarf tied high over his neck to cover his wrinkles and age. Sally called them high-paid pitchmen for the movies they were in while the studios raked in most of the money.

At the family-owned Mexican restaurant, we slid into a booth, ordered our entrees, and talked while we polished off the chips and salsa. "We might as well hear what the eating disorder people have to say," Sally said in between bites. "I mean, we can sneak out if it's boring, right? Besides, with all this food in us, we're insulated from getting too emotional."

"I doubt they'll say anything I don't already know, but hey, it's free, right?" I offered as I rolled my eyes.

At ten minutes to seven, we entered the Evolution and Recovery Therapy Center in Santa Monica. A man and two women sat at the front of the room, watching potential clients wander in. We sat behind about forty people, mostly overweight women.

I hope they don't ask questions. Back here we should be pretty invisible. I'm not like these people anyway. They all look kinda sick and unhappy.

I studied each speaker, hoping they really *would* have something to offer, but I kept my face unemotional, with just a touch of interest.

One of the women speakers gave me a friendly smile. A slender woman with wild short red hair and twinkling brown eyes, she came over and extended her hand. "Hi, I'm Raina. I hope we can talk after. I have a real sense we could work well together. You look like you're interested."

I gave her a silent nod. *You're mistaking weird for interested. You just want me to sign up for therapy.*

"See what you think and let's talk after," she said, returning to her associates.

She has a "sense?" What does that *mean?* I squirmed uncomfortably. I was just here to check things out, not have someone make me feel that I needed "fixing."

Damnshithell (DSH). Why'd she focus on me? *She probably just needs clients.*

The presentation discussed bulimia, anorexia, and Karen Carpenter. Refusing to eat definitely was *not* my issue, and neither was throwing up everything after I ate it . . . if only. I admired Karen Carpenter and wondered why someone so gifted would have an eating disorder. She was famous, loved, and had lots of money. She sure didn't have the life *I* was living.

I listened attentively to the presenters, then walked with Sally to her car. The information actually sounded interesting, but I kept my thoughts to myself.

"I thought they'd explain how we should eat, like 'here's the diet for your eating disorder,'" my friend chuckled.

"If they'd done that, I'd have left long ago," I countered. "I already know how to do that *and* go to the gym. My problem is what to do when I eat twelve donuts *instead* of working out."

CHAPTER 25

WHO KNEW?

I didn't tell Sally, but I'd agreed to meet Raina the following Friday at 4:00 p.m. I'd tried OA (Overeaters Anonymous) when I first got to LA, but that lasted all of a month. Raina was pretty, slender, and confident. What could someone who looked like *that* have to offer *me*? I looked down at my large thighs and stomach. How could she relate to someone who binged to stuff down poor self-esteem and past heartache?

Raina greeted me in a midi-dress with a blue flowered print and a welcoming smile. I sat in a chair next to her desk while she wrote down basic intake information, her licensed mental health (LMHC) license above her desk and one large framed photo of the San Gabriel Mountains covered with pine trees. The walls were light blue, probably to calm down clients.

"Pine trees are my favorite," I offered, trying to find a connection with Raina besides food.

"I agree," Raina shared. "They remind me how much God loves us."

I nodded and squinted my eyes, trying to think of a clever response.

"I felt a connection to you the other night," Raina added with an intense gaze. "I'm glad you're here, though I wasn't sure you'd show up. Why did you decide to come?"

Swallowing dryly, I tried to get comfortable in my seat. *Here goes; she'll probably say, "sorry, can't help you."*

"Well, I *have* had some counseling before now but not about an eating disorder. Maybe you guys can help. Besides, I think I'm turning into my mother."

Raina nodded. "Oh, we all deal with 'the mother syndrome,'" she said knowingly. "An eating disorder is a preoccupation with food and weight that has deeper roots, sometimes like mothers. Overeating hides the things we don't want to deal with. If you choose to work with me, we'll talk about your background, what triggers your binging, and how food helps you cope."

Dread formed a hard knot in the bottom of my stomach.

I'll probably have to discuss things I don't want to. I don't know if I can, but . . . I took a moment to inhale slowly and tried to remember why I'd come. I wanted to be independent, to have my own career doing something I loved so I could support my children. But I also wanted a better life for myself, free of the bullies in my head, free of overeating, free from heartache.

"Um, that sounds like months of work," I muttered worriedly. "I don't have much money to pay for these kinds of services."

"We offer a special ten-week program if you're low income," Raina offered. "You could give it ten weeks and then we could decide what to do after that."

She gave me another compassionate smile and a curious look.

"Well, honestly . . ." I started slowly, "you're really too slender . . . pretty. I'm not sure you're the right person to help someone like me in my size 18 jeans."

Raina rifled through a few papers in a desk drawer, then handed me a photo. A pudgy young woman with mousy brown hair and a sullen face stared back at me. She stood next to a long buffet table, plate in her hand, and some sad-looking adults behind her.

"I am sixteen in that picture and totally focused on what food I could use to swallow down my terrible feelings," Raina shared quietly. "I was raised Jewish and food is important in our culture."

I stared at the photo, then up at Raina, my mouth an *O*, my eyes wide.

"Therapists face their own issues first. It can be a long road to travel, but yes, I can help because I've been there. Can you come back this time next week?" she asked, turning to her desktop calendar, pen in hand.

Okay, I'll try one more time.

Four p.m. on a November Thursday, I sat in Raina's office again, this time in an overstuffed blue chair. Raina walked to an easel with a large tablet of white paper. "We're going to create a family tree. Let's start with your parents, then grandparents, and add in anyone you grew up with who was important in your life. Share anything about each one that comes to mind."

I started at the beginning, being adopted in 1953, age thirteen months. I gave her names, places, and vivid events: a house fire, a bad dream, and fear of snakes. Hot tears threatened to spill as I talked, but I held them back.

Raina turned to me. "I want you to know, you're safe here, Janet." "Really, you can cry if you want to—scream, even, or jump up and down. Emotions buried alive never die, so let's dig them up."

I nodded, then began again. Mother was first. It took the rest of that therapy session to get Mother's characteristics on the paper. Our relationship was horrific. Watching all the truth written out by a therapist certainly gave me perspective. I coughed up details as fast as I could. Raina scribbled "Mother" in red pen across the white tablet. The color choice was perfect. Then she wrote, "crazymaker" in capital letters, which made me like this therapist even more.

"Mother's parents were Lithuanian and her father always smelled like liquor," I shared. "He'd escaped Lithuania in 1913 hiding in a hay wagon, or so says one of the familie's freakin' secrets. Monday nights he sat and watched boxing with his beer and highball. No one went near him when he was in that state. Angry man, he scared me."

Raina was quiet for a few seconds, then turned to me. "Holy-! your grandfather was an alcoholic!"

A chill ran through me as we stared at each other. I knew alcoholism was bad, a disease. But was Grandfather *that* guy? I only knew he was mean, nasty, and unapproachable.

"This explains some things," Raina said as she wrote. "Alcoholism in the '50s was considered a sin, a lack of willpower, even a lack of character. All of that shame no doubt added to your grandfather's misery. We now know the disease can be hereditary, often provoked by life events. He probably had an angry, maybe even violent, alcoholic father himself. What about your grandmother?"

"Grandmother worked hard all the time, no doubt picking up the slack from Grandfather," I shared. "She and Grandfather rented out bungalows behind their house. Grandmother was the one who painted, repaired, and cleaned them, then went to Latin mass on Sundays. When I was bad, she slapped my hands."

"An enabler. Alcoholic families live by the unspoken motto, 'Don't ask, don't tell.' Protect the alcoholic from the consequences of their behavior no matter what and make sure the family looks normal to everybody on the outside."

I let out a big sigh. "Look normal," was a concept I knew very well. Keep those family secrets secret. "I kind of liked Grandmother," I said. "Well, most of the time. But what do I do with all this stuff we're dragging up?"

"Just ponder on it for a while. Your mother grew up as an adult child of an alcoholic with a mother who was codependent and enabling. Adult children of alcoholics, ACOA, develop ways to survive. They keep their emotions to themselves and hide them, especially from the drinker who is unpredictable in their reactions. As adults, ACOAs *have* to have control because they had none as children. They can be critical and judgmental, with a black and white perception of the world—things are either good or bad. Your mother was controlled verbally, maybe was physically abused too. Controlled by fear, living in unpredictable circumstances. She had to learn how to stay safe."

"Yep," I replied with a nod. "And now controlling with fear is her special talent."

Raina walked to her desk and sat down, her face meditative. "Listen, you deserved to be treated with respect and kindness, just for being you. You were yanked from one, probably unstable environment, and thrown into an unknown situation. You should have been loved by your parents, not forced and manipulated with fear."

Raina watched me. I went poker-faced as I thought about her revelation.

She continued, "You have a right to feel your real feelings about how you grew up—anger, disgust, sadness, even rage. Seeing situations clearly and honestly is truth. Anytime you feel something that makes you angry or hurt, it's because you're believing a lie. Now that you can be real with yourself, you're free to feel your feelings as they really are."

Nausea bubbled up in my gut. Remembering the past, talking about it, made me want to knock Mother down and punch her in the face. Confusion, conflict, and anger, those were real.

"I'm a Christian, Raina. I'm supposed to forgive," I responded, shaking my head.

"That's a good goal, and I applaud you, but feel your real feelings first," she replied. "Forgiveness will come later."

When I got home, I pushed back the emotions and nausea with Häagen-Dazs chocolate chip. I sat in my bed and swallowed bite after bite until my stomach felt as smooth as the ice cream I'd swallowed.

Untighten knot, stop hurting! Man, if that was the first real session, what am I in for?

At the next session, Raina picked up where we'd left off. I was shaking, but I wrapped my arms around my middle, stared at the family tree on the pad resting on the pedestal, and maintained a false front of calm.

"I can see how you survived your childhood using food," Raina began, "and that was really very smart. You survived. You didn't get strung out on drugs or alcohol or even get pregnant in high school. Give yourself credit for being smart. If you'd gone down those other paths, you might not even be here today."

I took a deep breath and wrinkled my forehead.

"Being adopted, your role was scapegoat in the ACOA family," Raina continued. "If you did something right, it was a given. Nothing was said. But if you didn't meet expectations, you were wrong and bad. W*ham*, consequence! Hitting, yelling, emotional abuse, black and white thinking. Your mother's own childhood experiences were projected on you."

My eyes flooded with tears. Right away, I remembered how Mother had treated me and Connor very differently. I thought it was because he was a boy and their own birthed child.

Raina turned away from her notes and met my eyes.

"I don't want to go back to that time, thinking about Mother . . . or even Daddy and Connor. I'd rather eat—"

"Ice cream or chocolate, I know," Raina cut in kindly. "It's what you've always done. It's what you knew and it worked. Your mother was an empty well, and you can't go to an empty well to get your bucket filled. You deserved to have your needs met, unconditionally."

I looked at the floor.

"Let's leave the mother stuff for a while. Tell me about your father," Raina offered.

I thought about Daddy for a few minutes, then looked up at my therapist. "He was fun when I was little," I began. "We had to drive our garbage to the dump since we lived out of town and he always sang along to the radio." I took a long pause. "When Connor was born, *he* became Daddy's favorite and he took him on errands instead. I missed Daddy . . . still do."

Raina was writing as I talked. "What else?" she questioned.

"Daddy was a physical fitness professor, so we were all expected to be physically fit. No matter how I tried, I couldn't get my size down to the acceptable size 10, Mother's size. I was a size 14 and felt ashamed, especially when Daddy looked at me. One time we were in a restaurant and a chubby lady was at the next table enjoying a milkshake. Daddy said in a low voice to Mother, 'Where do you think she got her clothes? From Achmed's Tent and Awning?' Then they snickered. I felt bad for the woman and glad she couldn't hear them. His words made my stomach wrench. And I *felt* the insult, especially when Mother glanced sideways at me."

"You have good instincts," Raina offered, "and you were probably right. But you couldn't talk about it, could you? Not safe. You weren't the right size because you weren't the right person. You came from someone else's body so of *course* your body wouldn't be like your mother's. There was no way to meet those expectations," she finished, her face an angry scowl.

I closed my eyes and dropped my head. If Raina was angry, maybe I could be too. I covered my face with my hands, rocked back and forth, and let tears fall like a dam bursting. After several minutes, I looked up at Raina, my lips a hard line, my eyes red and swollen.

"You haven't told me about your father's parents," Raina said quietly.

I looked out the window and let the sunlight warm me, then wiped my sleeve across my eyes. "Grandy and Gramps. They lived near us in Prescott. I spent every weekend with them until I was ten and we moved away to Oregon."

Raina gave me a kindly gaze, then turned and wrote in green ink on the family tree as I continued.

"Grandy smelled like lilacs. She had warm hands, fluffy arms, and gray hair braided around the top of her head like a crown. I went to church with her and read all kinds of books at her house. She often said, 'Oh, Janet you can do anything.' I adored her."

I took a breath and Raina stopped writing. "Go on."

"Gramps looked a lot like Norman Rockwell and he also painted. He loved Arizona deserts and Indians. They wrote a book together called *Indian Folklore Tales*. Grandy collected the fables and Gramps sketched the characters."

Raina scribbled as fast as I shared.

"Grandy died the year we moved to Oregon, '62. After that, we weren't allowed to talk about her dying or even anything else about her. Mother said it upset Daddy so the subject was closed, period. Everything she did was about Daddy," I spit out. "I hated him for that."

"And her," Raina added.

"Yes, both of them. They took us away from Prescott and Grandy died. We broke her heart when we left and it killed her."

My heart hammered with vicious pain and guilt. I'd never admitted that aloud before.

I killed her. I was her favorite, Connor was just a baby, so when I left, she died.

Tears trickled down my cheeks again and I quickly brushed them away. Raina took both my hands in hers. "I can see how much Grandy means to you. She was really your support, a loving mother. How wonderful that God put her in your life." She stopped for a moment, then said, "I don't think you've grieved her loss."

"No, but I'm not supposed to cry about it," I replied. "I'm thirty years old! It's too late to cry over something that happened when I was ten."

"Well, that's just stupid," Raina said angrily. "I don't have to ask where you learned *that*. Crying is a gift from God, Janet! Our eyes are made to show how our hearts feel. You weren't allowed to cry because your mother couldn't handle it. So, what did you do instead?"

"What? Two months after she died, I made a 3:00 a.m. raid with a family friend and gulped down six regular-sized Hershey bars with almonds. . .and the pain stopped."

When I looked at the clock and noticed our session was almost over, I was relieved. I'd just admitted my first binge and I was embarrassed. Heat crept up my neck and tinged my face.

"Chocolate affects the brain like marijuana," Raina assured me with a small laugh. "I enjoy it myself. It produces chemicals that create a happy sensation. Of *course* you'd consume as much as you could. You covered Grandy's dying in chocolate."

Raina paused, giving me time to process, then looked at her desk calendar. "Let's meet next Thursday. Here's some homework for you in the meantime."

I cringed. "Homework? Do I have to give up chocolate now? No way, José."

"No, I won't torture you."

"Phew," I uttered. "Nachos maybe, but not chocolate. We all have our limits!"

Raina looked seriously at me for a second, then we laughed together.

"What I want you to do is concentrate on your thoughts and feelings for Grandy over the weekend. Don't try to control your tears or your body's reaction. Just let it happen. Then we'll talk about what you experience next time we meet."

I nodded and left Raina's office, glad I didn't have to give up what I needed to survive.

How do I grieve for someone who died twenty years ago?

I hardly thought about Grandy these days. Divorced, with my

children living elsewhere, all I could focus on was my weekly work as a studio temp.

Friday evening, alone in my rented room, I comforted my heart with as much junk food as I could. Just the idea of letting buried sadness surface made my stomach churn and my brain whirl.

This is gonna hurt. Better stock up while you're still able to think straight.

Saturday, I took twenty dollars and bought a half-gallon of rocky road ice cream, nachos, a hot dog, a day-old apple fritter, and four almond Hershey bars. I sat on the floor near my bed, eyes half-closed in a daze, and inhaled every bite as fast as I could. Hand-to-mouth nonstop, I stuffed it all in 'til my stomach was aching and bloated.

Empty wrappers and containers covered the carpet. With nothing left to swallow, I sat statue-still, eyes closed. Five minutes ticked by slowly as tears filled the bottoms of my eyes. I put my hand over a throbbing temple and arched my aching back.

I took three heavy breaths as my heart thumped rapidly. I couldn't hold it in any more. Tears gushed out, a Niagara of rage and grief. Weeping as hard as I could, I fell over on my side and let them soak my shirt. The ingested food, now a burning hard ball in my gut, threatened to burst up and out. I scooted back up to sitting and laid against the wall.

My mouth was dry sand as stomach contents began to climb up into my throat. On hands and knees, I crawled through the nearby doorway into the bathroom. Just in time, I bent over the toilet and vomited up nachos, chocolate, and a half-digested hot dog.

I sat back on the floor for a minute, then bent hurriedly over the toilet again. A retch of nasty-tasting yellow-green bile followed one more round of food puke. Exhausted and sweating, I flushed the nasty stuff and lay back on the cool bathroom tile.

"Well, that was attractive, Janet, "now you know what it means to be bulimic . . . and how much misery a person can hork up.""

Dizzy and lightheaded, I rocked onto my knees and pulled myself up holding on to the sink. Moving slowly, keeping my hand over my mouth, I tumbled into bed fully dressed.

I opened my eyes Sunday morning, my face sticky with dried tears. But my stomach was empty. My heart was empty too.

I lay still until I could let Grandy's image float into my mind. Smiling, she seemed to say, "All is well, granddaughter . . . just let go."

Thank you, Grandy. Thank you for still being in my life, helping me to keep going.

CHAPTER 26

AFTER ALL

C rying all weekend over Grandy opened emotional flood-gates and immobilized me. Two weeks went by, and it was mid-November before I could hype myself into enough frenzy to see Raina again. To get there, I ate chunks of apple fritter, swallowed down with Diet Coke, as I steered down the road to her office, my fingers sticky with sugar. I forced the drive, my insides shaking and my forehead moist with sweat droplets. I arrived at Raina's office ten minutes late. I sat and hung my head like a bad dog waiting to be scolded.

"Uh, hey. I'm sorry I didn't show up on time. It's just, Grandy . . ."

"I thought so." Raina took my hand. "I understand, but we still have fifty minutes, so tell me about your experience. It must have hit you pretty hard."

I shamefully admitted I cried until I threw up. "I didn't know I had that much pain. I couldn't breathe. I couldn't eat either, that was new."

I closed my eyes and the impression of Daisy as a young woman came into my mind. She was holding Grandy's hand. "I have some peace now," I added quietly. "It seems her spirit has moved on to be with my daughter."

That made me smile and I opened my eyes. "But I've just dragged myself around the last two weeks. I'm all over the place; I don't know *what* to feel. I hate myself, but well, no, I actually hate my parents. I never want to see them again, but maybe I should give them a chance. And I hate Dave. I really *do*!" I took a breath and thought a little harder. "But I guess he *did* help me escape Mother and brought me to a church where I found Jesus."

Raina nodded. "When we've carried around heartbreak like losing someone we deeply love, it's like spewing poison when we grieve. It brings up all kinds of other buried gunk. You looked grief square in the face and that took guts. You have more strength than you know. Embrace that. You'll never have that kind of pain about Grandy again."

I sat up a little straighter in my chair. *No more pain.* I hadn't thought of that. *But it makes sense. She's not in pain now; she's enveloped in love. So why should I stay in pain?*

"Thank you," I told Raina. "But, umm . . . I'm back to overeating."

"It's okay to eat what you want. It's helped you for a long time. We'll get to that later."

Raina paused and looked at me thoughtfully. I sat patiently waiting for whatever wisdom she'd give. "Other than your past, I think you're also dealing with a chemical imbalance that's causing depression," she theorized. "It's biological, a brain misfire. Please hear this: it has nothing to do with your character or willpower. If you deal with it, what I teach you will be easier to implement in your life and you won't have to use so much energy to just keep functioning every day. I'd like you to try an antidepressant."

I frowned, feeling let down. *Drugs,* I worried. *I am so done with those! I promised myself that a long time ago.*

"You look stunned," Raina observed.

"I'm the one who brings on my gloomy days," I threw out. "It's not my brain. Drugs were a part of my early marriage with Dave. I don't want to go back there."

"If we're going to work through your other challenges, antidepressants will keep you from sinking so low that you're paralyzed," Raina encouraged. "You have a lot of courage, Janet, but I sincerely think you have a brain that's cross-wired. It's *not* your doing."

Thinking about drugs with Dave made me twitchy. I clenched my fists and frowned.

"Tell me about your drug use with your ex-husband."

I sighed, shut my eyes, and let my mind wander back to the years that now were a bad dream. "I guess we'd have to get to this part sometime."

I told Raina about how Dave and I met, getting kicked out by my parents, and getting married. Next came the story about my bad trip, Dave's sobriety for church, and the assault that followed when he lost control.

After sharing all of that, I rocked back and forth and cried so hard it made my head hurt. There was no sound in the room except my sobbing as I buried my face in my hands. I cried like I'd cried over Grandy and I couldn't stop.

The torrent finally turned to a few heaving breaths and petered out. The clock had ticked away twenty minutes. Raina handed me a wad of tissues to wipe my eyes and nose. "In the middle of all that, you just blew the biggest snot bubble I've ever seen," she chuckled.

I broke into a smile, then laughed with my whole body, shaking my head, the remaining tears spraying off my face.

"I'm glad you trust me enough to share these hard experiences," Raina added gently. "Truly, I know it's hard. I feel privileged."

I didn't know *what* to say to that. I nodded and wiped my face with more tissues.

"It sounds like your husband had post-traumatic stress disorder," Raina said slowly. "It used to be called shell shock or combat fatigue. PTSD was entered into the manual of mental disorders just two years ago. It occurs after prolonged stress from a traumatic event. Without his drugs or alcohol, his self-medication, he couldn't keep his illness under control. I'd say the day his anger was triggered had very little to do with you. It's important you recognize that. Just like your mother, your husband had a mental health disorder."

I felt my face heat up with anger and my stomach tighten. "He has an excuse now?" I snapped.

"No, not an excuse," Raina replied quickly, "you have every right to be furious. This information about what drove him is just to help you. It's *not* more proof that everything is your fault."

I stood up so fast it pushed the chair back against the wall. "Well, I just don't want to talk about this anymore!" I yelled. "I wish my kids weren't with him. What have I done letting them go live with that man again? Why did you make me think about—?"

I ran out of the office and got home as fast as I could. Then I called Carole. When she answered, I heard kid commotion in the background.

"I'm just calling to see how things are," I began, trying to stop the shivers running through me. "Are you and Dave getting along? I mean, is his job okay? Are you guys, uh, do you have enough of what you need? How are the boys doing?"

Carole gave a slight laugh. "Yes, all is well. Can't you hear the guys wrestling around? Why are you asking?"

"I was just thinking about some things that happened when Dave and I were together," I said, masking the truth. "I thought I'd check in, see if everything . . . if the boys are okay."

"It's always noisy, but my kids and yours get along great. We're always a little tight for money since I'm a stay-at-home mom, but we're getting by okay," Carole said somberly.

What do I hear in her voice? What is she not *saying?*

"You should come back and visit sometime," she offered next. "Ben misses you a lot and I know the other three would love to see you."

Carole shared a little more about their home life, I promised to visit soon, and we said our good-byes. I hoped Carole was being truthful. I silently prayed for God to bless her and the boys.

I mulled over Raina's words about my ex as I went to a free clinic to get some samples of Prozac, just 20 milligrams. It was a month's worth. I'd have to figure out how to get them on my own with her prescription, if they *did* help. The medicine was $150 without health insurance, which I certainly didn't have. I had no savings and lived paycheck to paycheck.

When I got home, I cranked up The Police, slipped off my shoes, and thought about what I could eat. I felt a little better after telling Raina about my hippy drug use, but intense feelings of remorse still made my heart pound. I stood in front of the refrigerator, glad no one else was around, and stuffed down my feelings with food. When I felt full and groggy, I went to my room, fell into my bed, and passed out like a drunk.

The following Thursday's appointment started as if I hadn't left all pissified the week before. Raina greeted me warmly, per usual, and waited for me to speak. I thought for a few minutes, then looked at Raina who looked back at me expectedly.

Is she waiting for me to apologize? Maybe therapists expect anger from patients, I hope.

"So," I started, "here's what I've been thinking about. Everyone in this town knows who they are, what they want, and where they're going. But I don't even know my favorite color. What am I doing in LA? I know nothing about directing a movie. The film people I've met are creepy. I temped for a commercials director once and watched him put his hand under his assistant's dress when she was standing on a chair. She just giggled. What kind of business *is* this?"

"Ah, a good place to start today," Raina replied with a nod. "You're right. It's a tough business with some who do ugly things. But there are also *good* people in the industry."

Raina paused, then gave me a thoughtful look.

"Maybe God has something else planned for you, Janet, something that matters. Working with me is part of His plan; how we met was no accident. Figuring out who you are and learning about the wonderful future He wants for you is the other part. Your first step is learning to love yourself so you can love others. That's what the scripture says, right? Love others as you love yourself."

I nodded. *But God has plans for me? Maybe, but working with you is so DSH hard!*

"You've already decided to *not* be your mother," Raina continued. "That's a powerful break in the family's dysfunctional cycle. Let's see if we can wipe out more of your mother's influence and help you figure out how to be *you*," Raina added. "I want to take you shopping. Can you meet me at the Beverly Center Mall Saturday? You can buy something just because you like it," she offered, smiling from ear to ear. "It'll be fun to take you on an adventure."

"The mall?" I repeated. A tiny fear started to crawl up my back. "I've never been in a mall. There's always a lot of people. I dunno . . ."

"We'll just go into a couple of stores, like The Broadway or Bullocks. Staying at one end of the mall will make it easier," she assured me. "I'll be with you and we can go sit in the walkway if you need a break. Think of something you'd like to buy, something you don't need."

Raina was full of enthusiasm which made me smile, although my nerves were jumping and my stomach was full of butterflies. I'd always wanted a shopping trip with a mother who actually wanted to spend time with me. Mildred's philosophy was: sew your own clothes and shop only when needed, like for underwear. Shopping was a waste of time and money. Raina might help me bust through my shopping barrier, if I could stand the cure.

On Saturday I managed to find parking underground at the mall, although I felt edgy parking under tons of concrete buildings. I took the escalator up to the second floor and met Raina, who was sitting outside The Broadway. My throat was dry and my palms moist, but I pushed myself forward, holding my head steady like I did this sort of thing every day.

"I'm glad you came," Raina said as she walked up to me. "Have you thought about what you'd like to buy?"

"Yeah, I saw some flowered tennis shoes on a girl at work. I've never worn anything but solid, dependable shoes. I'd like to buy something pretty for my feet that's not clunky."

"Perfect! Let's go," Raina said with a little laugh. We walked into the store through a large, open doorway and passed display cases with glittering jewelry. Mannequins in the women's department were dressed in the latest '80s style, black dresses with white colors and tiny belts or white blouses and square-necked, navy-blue jackets with matching slacks. It was all too sophisticated for me even though I'd stopped wearing hippy clothes. At the shoe department, we sat down in comfortable cushioned chairs with rounded backs.

As I looked at the display of expensive shoes, dread formed a hard knot in the bottom of my stomach. A shoe salesman came over, gave a short introduction, then took out a metal instrument and measured my foot.

Slightly bald, he left to find me some shoes. Panic became rising nausea. I gasped for breath with big heaves and began shaking nervously. "Get me out of here!" I shouted. "Now!"

Without Raina, I walked as fast as I could toward the big open doorway, trying not to run. I fell down onto one of the small backless sofas in the mall. Breathing fast and hard, I rocked back and forth, wringing my hands.

Somehow, Raina was next to me. "Put your head down between your knees . . . that's it. Close your eyes and let your breathing just come slowly. Count, Janet—one, two . . . inhale, exhale . . . that's it." The pressure of Raina's arm around my shoulders helped me forget where I was as I followed her instructions.

"One, two, three . . ." My breaths began to slow to normal. I clasped my cold hands together and opened my eyes to see speckled tile beneath my feet. I heard people coming and going, talking and, thankfully, ignoring me. I raised my head and looked at Raina. "I didn't get my shoes," I managed to stutter. "I feel stupid."

"No, you didn't get your shoes, but you did walk into the store, you sat down, and had your feet measured. That's a good beginning. Maybe you can walk into a little shop on Melrose where there are less people and find those pretty tennis shoes. You certainly don't have to do your shopping in a mall," Raina offered soothingly.

We stood up together and she gently guided me toward the escalator. "This was a big challenge, but I'm really proud of you. You showed up and walked into a store in the mall. That's progress! That's breaking a link in the toxic mother chain."

I let her words soak in as I shuffled to my car alone, opened the door, and got in. I started the engine, then felt something weird that made me grin.

What is this . . .? Am I pleased with myself? Raina sees success where I see failure and panic. Cool! Maybe I won't *be put in a nut house.*

At home, I ate a tuna sandwich and washed it down with a glass of milk. Raina's words circled around in my thoughts and I smiled between bites. Maybe this therapy thing *was* working. I hated spilling my guts. Talking through the horror show of my past hurt like an open wound. But the last two weeks I'd gone to bed without memories swimming up behind my eyes. I dreamt about my sons instead.

I climbed the stairs to my room and saw the red light on the answering machine flashing. The phone number was my parent's. I hadn't seen them since Daisy's funeral.

Daddy seems to always know where I am. I guess I should be happy about that.

I played the message, relieved to hear Connor's voice. "Janet, hi. Hey, Dad's retiring and having a congratulatory dinner next month. He wants you to come. I'd like to see you too. They have a spare room at their new house where you could stay. Please call me back and say you'll come. Love you, sis."

I backed away from the machine, shocked. I wanted to see Connor, yes, and maybe even Daddy. But to stay there? I put my hand on my heart to steady my breathing.

"I don't know what to do," I told Raina at our next appointment. "I'm less angry at Mother now, but I dunno. Yet . . ." I slowed down, thinking it through in the safe space of her office. "With Dave out of my life, maybe she's mellowed a little. And Daddy *was* nice to me last time we talked, so maybe. . ."

Raina was quiet, her hand on her chin. She thought intently as three minutes ticked by on the clock. "You *are* stronger emotionally now," she finally replied. "But I'll admit, I feel protective of you. I wonder if going back is a good idea . . . but, really, you'll have to decide."

CHAPTER 27

THOMAS WOLFE WAS RIGHT

Return to Ashland and be around Mother? Two words came into my mind: *No way.*

But then, I also heard, "Pray." So, I did when I returned home that evening.

"Dear God, you know my heart," I whispered aloud, "you know my real feelings. I'll try to do what You want, even though I don't feel like it. In Jesus' name, amen."

That warm feeling came over me as I finished. Then He spoke to me, spirit to spirit, "I *do* know your heart, my child. Trust in Me and know I only want is best for you. I love you."

I let out a slow breath. "Ah, Father, I knew You knew. I guess I'll go to Ashland. Thank you, Father. Thank you for loving me as imperfect as I am . . . and please stay with me on this trip."

I had to admit, I *was* curious about how things were with my parents and I really did want to see Daddy. With Connor there, I'd have more confidence, maybe stand up for myself.

"I always clam up around Mildred, er, Mother, and I always think of a comeback way after the incident has passed," I told Raina at our next session. "She's ambushed me more than once and knows exactly how to get to me, especially if she can tell I'm vulnerable."

"Seeing her is a scary thought," Raina agreed, validating my concerns. "Bad memories. She's a 'this is for your own good' parent. It's a European child-rearing belief and we know where she got that. The parent is always right, it gives her a sense of control. But she *doesn't* control you or *your* life now. You've given birth, buried a child, and divorced an abusive husband. You have more strength than she'll ever have because she is chained down to her past. You're breaking free, but let's prepare, just in case. What do you imagine you'll say when she sees you?"

I felt my stomach cramp up as I remembered Mother yelling and name calling.

If ye are prepared, ye shall not fear, I reminded myself. *God says so.*

"She'll probably say something about how fat I am or, at the least, give me a disapproving look. I just hope Daddy doesn't gang up on me too." I sucked in my breath and crossed my arms, rocking in my chair, fat shame washing over me.

Raina looked at the ceiling and squinted her eyes, clearly deep in thought.

"You have two choices," Raina finally said, looking at me intently. "You could throw it back at her with a big smile, and say something like, 'you're sure right. Wow, I didn't notice! Thanks for pointing out how fat I am,' then walk away."

I smiled big and repeated her words to myself, stashing them for potential future use.

"Or, you might just give your mother a disgusted look, shake your head in disbelief at her stupidity and small-mindedness, and walk away."

I perked up a little more. "That's really good too!" I replied. "I never know *what* to say, so planning is a good idea. Still, I sometimes wish I'd been anorexic instead of a compulsive overeater. They'd accept that."

Raina's expression turned dark. "Don't you *ever* wish for that," she said grimly. "I have a client in the hospital right now on a feeding tube. She's skeletal. Anorexia will kill you . . . like it did Karen Carpenter."

I nodded silently.

"Anything else?" Raina said, regaining her demeanor.

I thought for several minutes. There was no telling what Mother might throw at me. "Maybe something about my divorce or even about going to my ex-husband's church. Mother was raised Catholic. A whispered family secret was that she was excommunicated when she married Daddy, a Protestant. But who knows?"

She might even blame me for Daisy's death. I swallowed dryly.

"Do you think you could tell her it's water under the bridge and none of her business?"

I laughed without much emotion. "Wow, she might slap me for that."

Raina stared in disbelief.

"Yep, she'd really do it too," I added.

"An assault puts her in control, I can see that. Then for you, your biggest defense will be your prayers. God will be with you in this challenge, so I'd check in with Him. Let Him tell you what to say before you have to say it," Raina advised. "That's the best ammunition you have."

Nodding, I tucked away those nuggets of wisdom to draw on when I needed them. It was all good support. I felt buoyed up and less panicked. I just hoped how I felt now with Raina would stay with me during the visit.

"One more tool for you," Raina offered before our time was up. "Pretend you're a reporter. Ask questions and get others to talk. Most people like to talk about themselves, and I'll bet that's true even for your parents. There will be less questions coming at you that way."

I felt so much gratitude that I hugged Raina before I left the office. She smiled at me with genuine compassion.

"This trip is for you, Janet," she reminded me. "A trip of discovery."

On Friday, May 11, 1984, I rode the Greyhound bus for sixteen hours straight from LA to Medford, Oregon. I slept some of the time, lulled by the quiet rolling along, the steady sound of tires on pavement. We passed the "Welcome to Oregon" sign as we crossed the state line and it occurred to me that I felt less anxious about the trip now than I had for all of the last week.

It must be the antidepressant I've been taking, I mused as I looked out the window. *Perfect, one more gift to strengthen me as I face people from my past. Thanks, God. You rock!*

A boost of positive energy ran through me.

Connor picked me up from the bus station and we drove ten miles into Ashland and to the Ingalls' house. It was good to be with him. I loved seeing his auburn hair tousled over his forehead, his confident smile, and his intense blue eyes with their mischievous sparkle.

Handsome guy. I'm glad to call him brother, even if we're not bio-logically connected.

Thoughts turned to interacting with the parents. It made a muscle in my face twitch.

"You gonna be all right?" Connor asked, giving me a quick sideways glance. "I know Dad will be glad you're here, and honestly, it's just good to see you, sis."

Connor's warm, genuine affection radiated from him. I hadn't felt any kind of family affection since I'd been with my kids. I took hold of Connor's hand and he let out a chuckle.

"I think I'm okay. What happens this weekend could change that," I replied, "but yeah, for now I'm fine. Glad you're here, though; I wouldn't have come otherwise."

The Ingalls' new home was on the other side of Ashland now, not up past Lithia Park. I was sorry we wouldn't be driving through it, but we did go through downtown and that hadn't changed since I'd left in '71. The Mark Anthony Hotel was still there and the Lithia fountain with iron-flavored water still bubbled in the roundabout by the police station.

As we passed Ashland High School, a cascade of memories flashed across my mind. Back then, I never fit in, was miserable at home, and I held a python. *That* made me smile.

I still hate snakes.

Further up Siskiyou Boulevard was Southern Oregon College, now Southern Oregon *State* College, Daddy's employer, and where I'd met Dave in biology class. Buff and confident, just back from 'Nam, there was an instant attraction. Those places had changed my life. I closed my eyes and let sadness run through me.

I'm different now, I thought with determination. *It's called the past because it's passed. I can do this.*

We drove up the driveway to the house sitting back off the main road. Between the main road and the house was a small fish pond surrounded by grass and well-tended bushes. Daddy, Connor, and Mother had built this home together. Bay windows jutted out from the living room to the left of the front door with the dining room and a large picture window on the right.

We walked in the front door, the ascending stairs right in front of us. An expensive mahogany hall tree stood against the opposite wall and Mother stood next to it. A thin smile was on her lips and her arms were crossed tightly against her chest. She gave me a cynical once over.

Here it comes, I thought, trying not to wince. *Let's get the fat comments out of the way. I'm ready!*

Still a size 10, her auburn hair now dyed blonde (to cover the gray, Connor said) was still in a 1940s pageboy. Her face was without makeup but her glasses, an oversized, modern brown version, magnified the mocking sneer she threw at me.

"Now that Connor's left home, Joe and I decided to invest in some vintage furniture," she stated, admiring the hall tree, running a hand over the polished wood. "We can finally spend money like we want rather than on family."

I stayed silent, translating her words: *"So glad you're out of our lives, Janet."* Well, at least there was no fat insult . . . yet.

"Your room's at the top of the stairs and to the right. Dad will be glad you're here, Connor. He's out back," Mother declared as she walked past us to the living room.

"I'll carry your bag up," Connor offered. I followed him to a small room behind the stairwell. A single window looked out to the driveway and a small bookcase was under it.

So that's where my copy of Tom Sawyer ended up. Beautiful Joe, too . . . into my suitcase.

"I'd better go say hi to Dad. You all right?" Connor asked again as he put my bag on the bed. "I know you and Mom . . . well, I know Dad will be happy to see you," he offered as he gave me a brotherly hug. It had been too long since we'd done that. I hugged him back earnestly.

After he left, I sat on the bed and covered my face with my hands. The intensity of being back in the Ingalls' environment hit me like a brick. I was a condemned teenager again. I couldn't stop the tears and I wept silently for several minutes before regaining my composure.

At dinner with the family, I was grateful they talked among themselves and not to me. I made a fast exit to my room and fell asleep quickly, my adrenaline rush had finally stopped.

Mildred and I ignored each other all day Saturday. What a relief. In fact, she actually served me food without a side of sarcasm. Glad she was elsewhere in the house, I went and sat with Dad in the living room. His receding hairline had a hint of gray in it, his same steel-framed glasses sat across his nose as he read the paper. He had kept his scholarly demeanor and still looked Clark Kent handsome. He was still my Daddy and I was proud of him.

"Congratulations on retiring, Dad," I offered, hoping to get his attention. "Connor told me about your special dinner this evening at the college. I'm glad I could be here for that."

Daddy pulled the paper down, then gave me a bland look and a nod. "I'm glad you could make it," he replied. "How long has it been? Let's see . . . 1970, so almost fifteen years. I hope life's treating you better these days. I know your marriage wasn't very happy."

He pulled his paper back up and continued reading.

You got that right, I thought, keeping my expression neutral. *But I couldn't return home, could I? You and Mother made* that *very clear.*

A memory of my last visit and the abrupt kick out the front door raced through my mind. A slow burn started and my temples began to throb. My father turned a page as he went on reading his newspaper. I was ignored and dismissed.

Guess I'll take my fat self up the stairs and do some reading by myself. Fat, fat, fat!

Connor had gone off to visit high school friends and left me alone with two adults who still, after all of these years, didn't have the time of day for me. Disappointment formed a hard lump in my throat and my temple pain turned into a headache. I thought I had Daddy back for a few moments, but I was wrong. The truth was Connor and I had different parents. Upstairs, I lay back on the small bed and closed my eyes.

Dear Father in heaven, You really are my only Father, aren't you. . . I'm glad I can feel Your love. I'm trying to stay civil and unemotional with these people. Please show me how You see them so I don't lose my temper and say something I regret. It's all still so painful. Why did I come here?

I pushed my hands across my forehead, trying to stop the headache and waited for God's impression. I heard no words, but a calm feeling flowed in. I slept and fell into a dream of a small girl with blonde hair crinkled with black. Her eyes dim, her face striped with soot, I felt a longing to grab her up in my arms and breathe life into the cooling body. How many years had it been since I last had that nightmare about that poor girl?

I woke to Connor gently shaking me at five o'clock.

"Wow, you were conked out," he commented. "Uh, sorry to wake you. We have to be over to the college at six, so can you be ready soon? Mom and Dad left already."

I sat up fast, working to throw off sleep, and felt a little dizzy. "Yeah, sorry. Glad you woke me. I'll meet you downstairs in a few."

I jumped up, dressed, freshened my face, and slipped into some flat shoes.

I need to get those flowered tennis shoes when I get back to LA. Sure glad I didn't spend money I don't have on a new outfit for this trip. What a crock! I walked downstairs and out the front door. *Oh boo hoo, get over yourself. Remember, go as a reporter, let others talk.*

The engine was running as I slid in next to Connor. I looked at my driving, grown-up brother, so good-looking in his dark blue jacket, freshly creased jeans, and white button-down shirt opened at the neck. He was an adult now; the little brother part of him was long gone.

"You gotta girlfriend?" I teased pleasantly. "What are you doing for work?"

Connor gave a little laugh. "Yes, Jeanie and I have been together four years, and yes, I'm managing a landscaping company right now. Anything else you want to know? Uh . . . here we are, so it'll have to wait."

We walked into the building together and stood in the opened French doors. The parents left their table near the podium and walked up to us. Daddy took Connor's left arm, Mother took his right, and they walked back to the table together, leaving me in the doorway by myself. They sat down together, lightly chatting. Connor turned to me then and motioned me over.

Reality. The lonely emptiness of childhood filled me as I walked to their table.

It's gonna be a long night. I wonder when the next bus leaves. I took a deep breath to steady myself. *No crying now, Janet. Stay neutral!*

The accolades for my father came and went along with the prime rib, baked potato, and apple pie dinner. At the end of several speeches, Joe Ingalls, the only father I'd ever known, got up and thanked everyone. He reminisced about some college experiences, how wonderful it had been to be a college professor and women's track coach, then sat down to thundering applause.

It was a celebration for my father. No one looked or spoke to me.

Back at the house that evening, I phoned the bus station for the schedule and learned a bus was leaving for LA in an hour. The family talked and laughed in the living room as I packed up my suitcase. I descended the stairs, dropped my suitcase by the front door, and went in.

"Connor, can you take me to the Medford bus station?" I asked, deliberately keeping my gaze on him alone. "There's a bus leaving in an hour."

"Oh! I thought you weren't leaving 'til tomorrow," Daddy said as he stood, wine glass in his hand. He walked toward me, confusion on his face. It was odd to suddenly be noticed.

"I'm glad I got to see you honored, Dad," I replied, "but I need to go. You guys will have a better time without me here and I'd like to get back for work."

And very intense therapy.

"Poor you, feeling left out?" Mother said glibly, a half-empty wine glass on the coffee table in front of her. Alcohol and people from my past. It was never a good mix.

"No, Mother," I said evenly. "Not poor me, just realistic me."

"Come on, sis. I'll take you," Connor agreed as he walked toward the front door and picked up my suitcase.

I gave my father a peck on the cheek and put my head on his chest, wrapping my arms around his middle. His arms came around me then in a snug embrace. I turned to say good-bye to Mildred, but she was standing far away in front of the window that looked out on the back-yard, her back to me.

Nuf said. Thanks for making my leaving easy.

Connor and I drove to the bus station in silence. When we pulled into the parking lot and stopped, I glanced over at him. He stared straight ahead as he shut off the engine.

"Thank you for driving me," I said sadly. Adrenaline was rushing again. "Can't say I'm glad I came, but it certainly was enlightening."

He gave me a wistful smile and took my hand. "I don't blame you for leaving. I saw what happened at the dinner."

Well, that was satisfying, knowing I wasn't the only one caught in reality. *I didn't imagine it then,* I assured myself. *This isn't home.*

Love for my brother blazed up from deep inside me. "Actions tell the truth, don't they?"

He nodded. "They do. We just left you standing there. I'm sorry I didn't say something. I should have–"

"Let me give you a hug when we get out," I interjected, "but thank you for that."

Tears piled up in my eyes. I brushed them away as I stepped onto the sidewalk.

"Listen," Connor said suddenly, "you're not responsible for other people's actions."

My wise brother. Thank you, lovey.

Connor dropped my suitcase at my feet and wrapped his arms around me, pinning my arms to my side, his heart beating fast. A foot taller than me, just like his father, I snuggled up to his chest and closed my eyes as the tears fell, dampening the front of his button-down shirt.

"Take care of yourself, sis. Be safe." He got in the car and drove off quickly.

The next Thursday I sat in Raina's office feeling like the damaged eighteen-year-old all over again. I'd seen the parents with my need for their love and acceptance but got the same disappointment. A huge knot was in my throat and I couldn't speak. I swallowed hard.

"Thomas Wolfe was right, I can't go home again," I mused. "Maybe it never *was* home."

Raina nodded. "You don't ever have to go back either; trust yourself. You're safe right where you're planted for now, totally accepted. Tell me about your journey . . . take your time. "

CHAPTER 28

PUTTING ME TOGETHER

Raina's compassion was something I could count on, but on that day, I had an anger still in slow burn that hadn't shut off since I'd left Ashland.

"Are you always this happy?" I scowled, my eyebrows hunched down over my eyes.

I wanna slap the woman.

Raina smiled. "I guess I am. I've had to work at it. It's been a journey." She paused. "I suspect your trip was lousy."

"Good guess," I said irritably.

"I'm not surprised. It was 50/50 that things would go well, er . . ." She gave me a practical, empathetic grin. "Maybe more like 80/20 from what you've told me. So, what are you going to do now? Your life is yours to control especially after that visit. I like Viktor Frankl's quote, 'Everything can be taken from a man [or woman] but one thing . . . to choose one's attitude in any given set of circumstances, to choose one's own way.' Choice means control."

I glared at her—she was so calm, so pretty, so smart. How I felt right now looking at her just made me sick. I stomped over and glared out the window.

"Why didn't you share that stuff before I left?" I grumbled. "It would have saved me money, not to mention the misery. I would have just stayed here."

"Would you have heard me if I'd shared my thoughts, or even considered it?"

My shoulder muscles tightened and I crossed my arms. I could hear the wall clock ticking away as I tried to ignore her insights.

"You had to find out for yourself, Janet," Raina insisted softly. "The truth is nothing has changed and nothing will. No matter what you do, how much you try to be what they want, you won't get acceptance from those people. Remember? Those are empty wells. They're their own worst enemies, not yours."

My anger began to cool. *Control is mine and always has been . . . right. So why do I feel like dog poop?* I turned and gave Raina a hard look. She looked back with empathy.

How does she put up with me? I can hardly put up with myself.

"Talk to me," Raina simply said.

I took a deep breath. "Okay, honestly? I want to stop feeling like I'm going to hell because I don't like the parents who raised me and I'm breaking the fifth commandment. They don't care about me, if they ever did. I want a full disconnect. I want all the ugly feelings about myself to stop nagging me." I paused for a moment. "Will anybody ever love me?" I shouted.

"Yes, *you* will love you," Raina replied. "And God has *always* loved you unconditionally in your imperfectness. And He won't stop loving you."

Feeling sheepish and broken, I sat, head down, elbows on knees, hands dangling.

"So, let's work on this. Here's your new homework. When you wake up each day, say, 'I'm smart, I brought my worth with me from God and my spirit is strong.' When you lie down at night, tell yourself at least three things you've done that day that you're pleased about, like, 'I brushed my teeth or I changed my underwear.'"

I chuckled. "Sounds stupid, but okay, I'll do it . . . just because you said."

Raina looked pleased. "One last thing, and it's the most important. Before we meet next, write a letter to your mother and tell her everything you've always wanted to say. It's for you, not her. When you've finished, tear it up, stomp it into the ground, burn it, whatever you want. She'll never see it, so write honestly about everything you can think of: how you feel about her cruelty and insults, everything you'd say to her face, even if you want to punch her."

The idea grew on me. *Truth on paper . . . I can do that. I can even swear.*

I was back in my room by seven that evening. Angry, resentful feelings were already surfacing. I'd spent years stuffing them down with food. That Saturday summer morning, I sat at a desk in my room. The sun poured in across the blank paper in front of me, a spotlight waiting for me to fill it. Therapy had opened the heartache I'd been stuffing down with millions of calories. Raina made it okay to explode thirty years of torment. It was an out-of-control fire.

Dear Mother,

No, dear Mildred. You weren't a mother, were you? You were a caregiver, and only because you had to be. It's what Daddy wanted. Did he make you adopt me? At least *he* loved me. Did that piss you off? Were you jealous?

I sat back, staring in awe at my first paragraph. *What now? Oh, just keep going.*

All I wanted was to be hugged, and for someone to say, 'I love you.' At least I could get that from Grandy. Her actions taught me what love really is. What I learned from you was how to be afraid. You called me names, humiliated me, laughed at my faults. I lived in fear of you, but that's what you wanted, isn't it? What's the matter with you? How did you get to be such a freaking controlling tyrant?

I tried to win your approval, tried to be the good girl I thought you wanted, but I never got it right. I got an emotional kick in the teeth for coming to you as a needy thirteen-month-old baby. How dare I! Verbal abuse, neglect, sarcasm, all of it was worse than any slaps you gave me.

When I tried to get some understanding from the school counselor, she was just another adult conned by your hypocrisy. No one saw what went on and no one believed me. I buried my feelings and reactions with food every chance I got, and I tried to keep away from you. Worthless, ashamed, and guilty, that was me on the inside thanks to you. I married to run away from home, but he turned out to be like you, violent and controlling, more thanks for that! Damnshithell on all of it and you!

I wrote for half an hour, all of my open, honest, raw emotions vomited onto the page. Then I tore it up and started again. Once I began, pent-up anger and self-pity poured out in a deluge. I used words I'd only heard from Dave, since profanity described it all best. I screamed at Mildred with my pen. I didn't even stop to eat.

I actually feel sorry for you now, Mildred. I am a smart, compassionate woman with a desire to be an influence for good in the world. It is one gift my torturous upbringing produced in me. And you drove me to find God and his compassion. He loves me just the way I am. I'm sorry you'll never know the real me. But one thing for sure, I will NEVER be like you!

After eight handwritten pages, back and front, I ran out of words and energy and slumped in my chair. Three hours had passed. My face was damp with tears, my spirit numb. I had written in a hurried daze, visualizing Mildred's horrified face, stunned by my truth, shot dead with the weapon of my words.

I took a box of matches and my retribution writing to the driveway. I ripped, tore, and shredded the paper into tiny pieces and dropped them on the concrete. Gathering the remains into a little clump, I struck three matches for good measure and dropped them on the heap. Small flames sparked up and burned through my venom.

"Burn, baby, burn!"

In less than a minute, decades of anger and misery were embers. Embers became cinders, and cinders turned into a heap of dead ash that scattered on the breeze. So much pain made such a little fire. I wanted a bonfire to burn down the neighborhood.

I stomped on the rest with my sensible, clunky shoe, then shoved them on to the lawn. Backing up against the retaining wall, I stared at my achievement.

CHAPTER 29

I WOKE UP

How do you feel, Janet?

H ow do you feel, Janet?
I felt nothing, but at the same time I didn't hear the dictator in my head either. Weird!

Is Mildred's apparition gone for good? Please, God, let it be true.

I put my hands on my forehead to shade my eyes from the noon sun.

"How do I feel?" I mused out loud. "Determined? Raina would say, 'Chutzpah.'"

The familiar pent-up rage that was always with me had disappeared. *Who am I now?* I didn't know. Without anger, self-loathing, and a broken heart, I get to find the real me, who I am without the lies, but *who is that?*

This is a Maya Angelou thing: "True love liberates, it doesn't bind." True love for myself. Your main job is to take care of yourself and figure out what you can do and be.

The celebration exhausted me. I returned to my room, dropped onto the bed, and slept hard—then dreamed.

There was Mama, jabbering into the wall phone at the neighbors like before, silhouetted by the kitchen light. A fireman entered the living room in a black coat and bright yellow helmet carrying a charred bundle. He settled her on the couch and left silently.

From above, I watched the scene, like a shadow. Deep blue eyes stared at me from the little girl's sooty face. Blonde wavy hair and pale skin was layered in a dusting of ash. Her jean jacket was scorched and her blue jeans had a burned hole. She gave me a steady, strong look and I heard her words, "What's *your* problem? *You* know who I am! I'm the one who's pushed you through the fire you've been carrying, the fire of deep longing your adopted mother wouldn't put out with her embrace, her understanding, her acceptance. She burnt you over and over. But you're not a shell of a person. You're a *shero*, Janet—WE are a shero!"

Startled, I sat straight up on my bed. *True love liberates.* I puffed out relieved, warm breaths that flowed from smiling lips. My face crinkled up with pleasure. "Oh Janet," I breathed, "you've had the answers all along. Good one! Shero indeed." For the first time, I laughed and it was at myself.

Next Thursday, I walked into Raina's office with a lighter body, full of enthusiasm, and a glowing face.

"Wow! You look luminous," Raina offered, smiling back at my over-wide grin.

"I feel really alive! Sort of electric. Is this the way *normal* people feel? Whatever *normal* is." I let go a chuckle.

You were right, Orson. Joy is a great, big, electrical experience.

"Normal is whatever works for you."

"I like it. And I'm less frantic too. I'm coming out of a dark cave, Raina, out of all that dank, mildewy smell. All the cold that has bound me down. And you are my guide."

Raina and I laughed together with this new joy.

"I'll accept being a guide, but you're doing the work. Remember that. You must have put the homework into action."

"Yes . . . I did. I wrote all the things I wanted to say to Mildred, then burned up the gloom and pain and turned it into ash. I can't even remember what I wrote . . . I just feel, well, my insides had a purifying shower."

I paused and gathered my thoughts. "And I never want to see that woman again."

"Good! Boundaries," Raina replied. "When you acknowledge your fears they, or the person who brought them, lose their power. God doesn't want you to have people in your life who hurt you, no matter who they are. *Damaged people damage people.*"

Nodding, I looked intently at my therapist. "Mildred never really loved me, did she? Wow, I actually said that out loud. I think Daddy loved me, but he lives with Mildred, and it's easier to go along with her by keeping me out of their lives."

"Good insight," Raina agreed. She walked to the large white pad that still sat on a stand near her desk and drew a line from Mildred to her parents, then a line from them to husband Joe and circled his name. "In Mildred's eyes, everything is about your father. Codependency and enabling were what she learned from *her* mother so she's a master. You were the scapegoat for her childhood anger. Projection, she dumped her subconscious feelings on you instead of dealing with them. And now, you're breaking that cycle because your goal is to NOT be like her with your own children."

Raina flipped over a clean page of the pad and wrote "DON'T" at the top of it.

"Here are a couple of 'don'ts' I want you to use as you continue to progress."

1. Don't believe everything you think.

"Your thought process is changed now due to your burning ceremony," Raina told me. "Bravo! Feelings about yourself came from you-know-who, but it's over now."

We chuckled at that.

"Feelings are just chemicals and the ones you had were false and limiting. Feel the feeling, change the thought. You don't have to do anything with them. You're already beginning to do that." Raina turned back to the paper. "This one you know."

2. Don't be controlled by your fears.

Raina glanced at me over her shoulder. "It takes vigilance. You've got to pay attention to any words that may still pop into your head. Feel the fear, then do what scares you anyway, as long as it's not harmful to your spirit. Push through it."

That's what the dream child said. I've been pushed along to this moment.

"One more." Raina turned back to writing.

3. Don't be defined by your past.

"You're more than the sum of your mistakes, Janet," Raina stated. "We *all* are much more than our mistakes because we belong to God. Fortunately, He knew there'd be mistakes and we'd have all kinds of struggles in life. That's part of the definition. Jesus took care of that. He paid the price for us and taught us how to talk to Him through prayer."

Raina returned to her desk and set down her marker. "That's enough for now; some things for you to chew on. You can take that page with you, if you want."

"You read my mind." I sat composed, hands folded in my lap as I read her powerful list, taking it all in. My soul had been stretched, my subconscious challenged as I learned to consider myself and life in a new and better light. Then a panicked thought popped up.

"What if Mildred or Daddy contact me? What do I do if they want to talk to me or see me? Or what if poor Connor gets in the middle, like he did before? Oh, wait! What about other people I don't want to spend time with, you know? What do I do and say then? I have to have a plan to take care of myself, don't I?"

"Planning ahead is a good idea. You'll figure out what to do with your adopted parents," Raina assured me. "And really, you already know. Most of us have the answers we need, we just have to listen to our intuition, accept it, and act on it. As for others, you can say, 'I'm sorry, I have another commitment.' That could just be washing your hair, but they don't have to know that. You don't have to do anything with anyone anytime you don't want to, ever."

"Good, I like that," I replied. I clasped my hands under my chin and looked at the carpet deep in thought.

"Not to echo what I just said, but I've got a commitment that takes me out of town for two weeks," Raina revealed. "Our next appointment will be three weeks out."

She turned and looked at me. My eyebrows scrunched down and I shook my head in disbelief.

"You'll be okay without me for a while," Raina said calmly. "I have faith in you. Besides, you need some time to yourself, to figure out how to keep going in your new direction once therapy is completed. This will give you a good start."

"I guess so," I muttered, frowning. "Okay, Raina. Uh, wherever you're going, I hope it'll be a good trip," I offered, trying to be supportive. "I'll miss you, but, well—"

The words wouldn't come.

"Spit it out."

I'd worked with Raina every Thursday for over a year, even finding a way to cover the costs. She was a teacher, a surrogate mother, and a safe place for my real self. I was bonded to her.

"Don't believe everything you think," she reminded me.

"Yes, all right. I think . . ." I threw out the words fast, spouting what I'd memorized. "Okay, I'm a grown woman who's given birth, left an abusive marriage, and explored my damaging childhood. I aired the family's dirty laundry with you and a lightning bolt didn't strike me dead. I'm smart and determined. I'm going in a different direction now and making good choices. And I'll go buy tennis shoes with flowers on them by myself . . . at least I plan to." I paused. "Not sure I believe all that, but there it is."

"I second all of it," Raina said, standing and smiling. I stood with her then and we hugged. It was a genuine "I love you" warm hug in stillness. She didn't let go until I did. "This isn't what therapists usually do," Raina said as she turned away and closed her calendar, "but I'm proud of you and pleased you're taking responsibility for your life. Keep going in your new direction while I'm gone and we'll share when I return. We have more to do, but this is great progress."

She handed me the list with my three "Don'ts" and we walked out the door together. "There's one more thing I want you to work on while I'm gone. I want you to concentrate on what was *positive* from your past, what sustained you, what helped you survive, other than compulsive overeating. Grandy, yes, your spirituality, yes, but what else? Think about it, maybe write down all the positive ideas that come to you. You'll have them to read when 'you-know-what' hits the fan," Raina offered.

I drove home in my faded VW square back, Raina's words tumbling through my mind. The poor old car still worked and I was grateful. Basking in the reassurance that there was someone out there who respected me and I respected in return, I knew I'd take the reins and complete all of her assignments.

Yeah, it would be tough. But I had just told myself I was smart and determined. And I would make sure that was the truth.

CHAPTER 30

ACCELERATING

A June sun poured into my rented room, still bright and warm at 6:00 p.m.

I sat on my bed, propped a book up on my lap, and placed a sheet of paper across it. *Okay, feel the fear, do it anyway.* Once again, I began to write:

Mother and Daddy,

I'm so grateful for all you've done for me as I was growing up. I love learning now and I know how to clean a toilet.

While I'm being yelled at, I thought, smirking and telling myself to *not* include it.

However, since I left home, I've been without any kind of support, expressions of love, or even contact from you. You made it crystal clear at my last visit how you've felt about me all along. I won't waste your time describing my feelings. I'll just say I've decided to make my absence permanent, continuing on without you as I've always done. I'm sure your lives will be all you want, since they already are. Mine will be all I want now, too . . . finally.

Love to you just the same, Janet

That weekend, I walked to the nearby mailbox and stood there. Five minutes passed as I breathed deep and exhaled slowly. My life was changing, but this was slamming a door on the past for good. A flash of energy rushed through me.

"Scary, but exciting, take control, Janet," I reminded myself. "You can do this!"

I scrunched my eyes closed and took one more breath. Opening my eyes, I pulled down the mailbox flap, threw the letter in fast, and let the metal lid bang shut. "At least you're out moving, not out eating," I assured myself quietly as I walked home.

A feeling hit me as the summer sun warmed my shoulders and the top of my head. It wasn't a familiar sensation, but it felt so good. Was this control? Well, at least I was moving forward . . . at my own speed.

Is this satisfaction? Whatever it is, it feels groovy, far-out, rad, cool, man!

The Fourth of July came, a celebration of independence all over the US. By 10:00 a.m., everyone in the house had already scattered to go make merry. It was a fab gift, since I liked being alone with my books, rock 'n' roll, and photos of my sons.

Maybe movie theaters will be empty. Ghostbusters is still playing . . . I could use two hours of laughter. No jitters for two hours to think about what might happen since I, well, mailed/nailed the coffin closed. Movies always save me.

I opened the bedroom door to go downstairs, and there, lying on the carpet in front of my door, addressed in Daddy's handwriting, was what I had hoped for . . . and feared. Hands shaking a little, I ripped open the envelope and took out the letter with blue-inked words.

Dear Janet,

Be careful not to burn your bridges behind you. Your mother put the garden in last week and we now have . . .

Blah, blah, blah . . . The rest of the words blurred together. Finally, I read the last line: Love, Dad

I stared at the page, analyzing especially what was not written. With crystal clear intention, I walked to the waste basket, crumpled the letter, and threw it in on top of used tissues and dental floss. A lump of tears formed in my throat, but I swallowed it. There had officially been enough crying over this drama.

Good-bye and have a great rest of your life . . . without ME!

I'd never admit it, but I was heartbroken over Daddy's letter for a hot minute. The truth was, I wanted him to desperately write onto that paper, "What? You can't do this, we (mostly him) love you."

But I never got any of that, because, just like Raina said, it wasn't true. The next day, I gave myself a bit of time to embrace that disappointment . . . and the day after that too.

Then came glorious, brilliant acceptance. It cascaded over me, and I admitted to myself that the childhood love from my daddy was gone. *But you've known that for some time, haven't you?* I told myself with a sad smile.

By day three, the fog was completely gone. Freedom!

CHAPTER 31

ASCENDING

My final clean break came towards the end of therapy as I did contract work for a lawyer.

"How much would it cost to change my last name?" I asked him one day.

A compassionate man, Mr. Lindquist listened to the reason for my request, then replied, "Oh, I can do that without a charge. You have a good reason; you deserve it."

When he said that, a favorite movie line ran through my head: "God is great, Sabu" (*Out of Africa*). Once again, I felt Him taking care of me. *He always had taken care of me.* I just never realized.

My new legal name was Janet Bernice. After all, Grandy (Bernice) was my real mother. She was my security, my example of how to live a good life, how to live with God.

I descended the stairs and went out into the old Hollywood neighborhood. It was getting to be a regular habit. Shaded by a canopy of age-old oak trees, I felt the warmth of God's sun peeking through their tangled branches. My legs pushed me along with a child-like energy, and I fully embraced the peace I felt from my toes to the crown of my head.

Four more months had passed since the letter during which my mind got clear. I had walked off twenty pounds, to match my lighter, bubbly personality.

Will my boys notice? I wondered on my daily walks. *We have to reunite soon . . . really soon. I miss them so much.*

Raina and I continued to explore the freakin' secrets from my past. We focused on mental health issues, and there were a lot of them, each with their own names: depression, borderline personality disorder, and, surprisingly, PTSD. I learned that any traumatic experience can lead to the development of post-traumatic stress disorder.

"It's all the trauma you've shared, Janet. Identifying the roots of emotional trauma is like finding cancer. Cutting out the tumor means gaining new ways of thinking and being."

We worked together for the next six years in once-a-week sessions. Accompanying that process were antidepressants. Raina was right; antidepressants helped. My energy for daily life sky-rocketed with better chemicals and helped me practice newly learned behaviors.

Just as she suggested, I remembered good things from my childhood and wrote them down. I was surprised there were so many. The early days with Daddy returned and I scribbled them into a journal. Even memories of Uncle Ted made me laugh, in spite of his snakes and teasing. My uncle loved me, even though his way of doing it was definitely unique.

If an unpleasant recollection tried to sneak in, I yelled, "Stop it! Disappear!" With practice, the process I'd created worked. Raina was right: taking personal control and making good choices as much as possible were the linchpins of change, freedom, and rebirth.

The dictator in my head, Mildred, never returned. There were no more screaming insults to impact my self-esteem or make me do stupid things.

Was every waking moment of my rebirth a bed of roses? No, it was a normal human life with ups and downs. But now I had tools and chose differently when challenges came: "When you know better, you do better" (John Waterbury CMPC).

Six years of therapy and better decisions led to new decisions. Working as a movie studio contractor became a stepping stone to better employment elsewhere in Los Angeles. The film industry and I had to part company. I didn't drive the right car, wear the right clothes, go to the right parties, or know (sleep with), the right people. Honestly, I just didn't want to.

An improved typing speed and the ability to be comfortable around all kinds of people, even some of the weirdos particular to this town, helped me interview with assurance. I changed direction and got hired to type reports at Coldwell Banker. I even rode the express bus downtown with strangers. I used that time to figure out what I *really* wanted to do with my life, besides being a mother.

I grew to love the power of words and stories of all types. Movies, books, plays: they all taught me about people and life. Yet, I'd have to find another way to use words and stories beyond movies. I needed to escape LA. I hated it! I needed to reclaim life on my own terms, now that I was discovering not only *who* I was, but definitely who I was *not*.

There was one last thing I needed to do before I said good-bye, before I left Raina. There was a long-held goal that I was ready to make happen.

"I want to find my birth mother," I told Raina one morning.

And find out why I was put up for adoption with a woman who didn't love me.

Raina considered the idea, her face pensive as a minute passed slowly.

"Yes, you *should*," she responded, "I think you're ready. But know that the results may not be what you want. How you were conceived, by whom, in what circumstance, even *why* you were given up for adoption . . . any of those truths may not be what you want to hear."

That sobered me. I already knew a mother who didn't want me, so what if I was conceived through an affair, incest, or, God forbid, a rape? I knew about that last one, and adoption too. Still, I had to uncover this last, big freakin' secret! It was time, and I was strong.

Heavenly Father, I prayed that evening, *I'm going to try to find my birth mother. If this is a direction I shouldn't go, please help me to know it. Otherwise, I'm going to go forward and I hope it's with Your blessing. I love you, I love Jesus, amen.*

The next month at church I met Alice, a genealogy expert. Alice's daughter was also adopted and Alice had helped her find her birth parents. I was surprised by her genuine love for her adopted daughter and her genuine warmth for me. "I'd be happy to look into your adoption for you," she offered. "I know how to get around some of the barriers, like sealed files. Let's give it a try."

Finally, a real possibility and definitely an answer from God. My body did what it always did in excitement, rushed a giant surge of adrenaline into my veins so fast I had to sit down. My mouth hung open and my eyes lit up as I listened to Alice describe what was possible.

How will it feel to uncover the secret that has haunted me all my life? Yowza!

The next Friday, with the last of the summer weather burning its pleasant heat into southern California once more, Alice rang me. "Would you like to speak to your mother? She's in California too. She remarried and, like you, she's been searching."

It had only been four days. I was thirty-three and about to speak to my real mother for the first time. My forehead and underarms became damp.

I gulped, then did my best to find my voice. "Uh, yes, whoa, YES!"

That afternoon, the black phone receiver hot in my hand, a raspy female voice came through the wires. "Hello, Janet. This is your mother, Kathleen."

Used to this common reaction now, I allowed the tears to flood my eyes. Her words crossed years of longing I couldn't admit out loud.

Kathleen continued, "Your sister hired a private detective for me to find you some years ago, but he lost track. I even asked Joe, your adopted dad, if you wanted to know about me, but he said no, that you never asked."

Now that was something I wasn't expecting. *Daddy said no?* A fresh wave of shock hit me, and then fire exploded in my brain. *That liar! Unfair, unfeeling son of a biscuit!*

"Oh, I *did* ask," I quickly assured her. "I've always wanted to know! I searched for you too. I even have my adoption papers, with the father's name. Vasco . . . somebody."

A few seconds of silence followed this declaration and I wondered if I said something wrong. "Kathleen . . .?"

I heard her breathing as she paused for a minute to collect her thoughts. She cleared her throat and then replied, "I hate to burst your bubble, but Vasco's not your dad. We had a son together, but he was unfaithful to me. So, I thought I'd better find a way to support myself and my baby boy. Um, I went back to school. I met this handsome artist, and I fell head over heels for the guy—so sexy, so talented. We had an affair. Then, surprise! You."

I shut my eyes, trying to process all this new flood of information . . . more secrets, more secrets, more freakin' secrets! Only this time, also more truths that I got to embrace or be drowned in. I took a breath. *I know about surprise births, don't I?* I thought with compassion. *We have that in common.*

"After you were born," my birth mother continued, "I took you to see him. But he only wanted an artist's life: no family, no wife. He wasn't interested in you *or* me. His name is Geoffrey Bowman."

Bowman, that has to be English – Shakespeare. I love *everything English!*

Even with my mind whirling, that, at least, brought me some comfort. It was positive news: *I'm a love child, from two consensual partners!*

A month and a half later, I sat with Mom for dinner at the San Francisco Cliff House. Expansive windows looked out at a rippling Pacific Ocean and three jutting rock formations. A man in his forties helped Kathleen hobble to a chair, walking with a cane.

Short gray and silver hair, with a wrinkled careworn face, Mother's crinkled brown eyes were drooped and tired. But I was happy that we looked alike in some ways: across from me was the same slender nose, oval-shaped face, and blue eyes. Mother smiled at me and a bit of energy lit up her gaze.

I've never looked like someone before, but *I do look like my real mother; all children look like their parents, don't they? Wow, it's never been true before, I can hardly believe it!*

The man who had settled Mom at the table approached and extended a hand. "I'm your half-brother, John. It's good to finally meet you. I asked Mother if there were any other secrets we needed to know, but she just gave me a nasty look." He let out a hearty laugh.

I laughed, too, and liked him immediately. I approached my mother, who was still smiling, and took her hand. Leaning over, I kissed her cheek and hugged her with an arm around her shoulder, my head next to hers. I hoped to feel a connection, a sense of belonging, but there was nothing. Maybe it was too soon. I scooted a chair over to sit close to the woman I'd waited so long to meet.

Two sisters and another brother joined us, Karol, Karen, and Erik, the youngest brother who just happened to be visiting from Australia. All of a sudden, I had a real, live family: there were five half-brothers and sisters, including the older brother I'd just met. Yet another beautiful surprise! I'd always thought of myself as the oldest, being older than Connor, but now there was one more son from Mom's first marriage: Mike.

I took in all the information as fast as I could, but quickly was overwhelmed. I'm sure my eyes were the size of half-dollars. This large crowd of people was my *real* family, spouses and their children too. I got to meet and learn to love sixteen human beings in all.

"Are you gobsmacked?" Mom asked with a chuckle. "It's been a long time, but you do look somewhat like your father. Some of his art is in the Museum of Modern Art in San Francisco. You should go take a look."

Mother changed subjects as fast as thoughts popped into her head. "I can't believe I'm looking at you!" she continued. "The last time I saw you, did you know your brother ran into the street as you drove away with the Ingalls? Mike was screaming for them to bring his baby sister back. 'Don't take my sister! Don't take my sister!' I had to go fetch him."

What an amazing realization. Someone cared that I was being taken.

She continued, "Joe Ingalls is my first cousin, you know—er, maybe you didn't know. Anyway, his mother and mine are sisters. Your grandmother is Zella. She ran a boarding house. I stayed with her when Vasco divorced me."

I smiled and nodded, already feeling like my brain was going to burst as she kept talking nonstop. *Take a breath, Mom, so I can take a breath too!*

"She told me I couldn't keep two kids there since she was running a business. One of them would have to go. Zella and her sister, Bernice, put their heads together and decided that Joe and Mildred should take you. They didn't have kids."

What did she just say? Wait a minute . . .

"Aunt Zella in San Francisco? We once visited and she gave me a doll with real blonde hair." That meant that Zella was *Daddy's aunt*, but my grandmother. If that was true, then Grandy was my "grand" aunt. Maybe that's why we called her Grandy.

Through the shocked haze surrounding me, I made a mental note that I needed to write all this information down to get it straight. But there was one thing I *did* understand: Daddy and I *were* really related. A chuckle ripped through me and I grinned. That would totally frost Mildred!

A brother stood up and raised his glass. "I propose a toast to the sister we didn't know we had. I'm sure this family is crazier than the one that raised you," he quipped. Everybody laughed and they all nodded, except me because I knew the truth.

I stored away the one-of-a-kind memory when he proclaimed loudly, "Welcome! Here's to our long-lost sister!"

* * * * * *

In 2013, Daddy died from a brain tumor. I learned about it six months after the fact. His obituary listed only his birth son and wife. In spite of all that, God showed me His infinite mercy. On a cool morning in February the following year, I walked along a paved path that paralleled a creek. I gazed at the natural beauty around me, admiring the different colors and patterns of trees and plants.

Without warning, and just as clear as if he stood next to me, Daddy whispered, "I'm so sorry, Tiger. I'm so very sorry."

I came to a dead stop, put my hand to my heart, closed my eyes, and let the tears fall, now comfortable with my emotional reaction. Taking a deep breath, I whispered, "Thank you, Daddy. That means everything to me."

Love flowed over and around me. I accepted and received it all; it came from the only man who was my earthly father. Raina would call it closure. I knew it was a miracle.

EPILOGUE

Since meeting my birth mom, I've experienced a carnival of spectacular events, most of them wonderful. God rocks! Power arrived from internally rejecting all the lies and deep down embracing the truth about myself. As a divine daughter of God, I rock too!

My four sons returned to live with me in 1986. While we did have to deal with ramifications from their years with Dave, I loved them through their challenges unconditionally, especially because I never forgot my own childhood of verbal abuse and never being accepted. More than anything, I didn't want my sons to *ever* experience any of that from me. I tried to pattern my behavior after all the positives that had come to me through the years.

Carole and I are friends to this day. She divorced Dave and married Leon, the love of her life. We *did* talk about Dave the first time we got together after her marriage. All bets were off! "I have all kinds of condiments in my storage now," Carole shared, "Dave would only allow me to buy mayonnaise because that's all *he* liked!"

"Oh, sister-friend! We're so much the same! He always said, 'it's my money, I earned it!' So, I have packages of toilet paper in storage because we never had enough money to stay stocked up." We laughed over all that 'til the tears flowed and soda came out our noses.

My sons and I had years of up and down challenges that would fill another whole book. But one thing was sure: they have unique qualities that were not squashed by me. Today I get to love the good men they have become. Each son is now married with children. I thank God for the genuine relationships I have with each of them, their companions, and my beautiful grandchildren.

As for the boy who came unexpectedly into the world in 1981, I wonder about him occasionally and hope he's had love from good parents. Did I tell my boys about that part of my life? Yes. In fact, my youngest son offered, "If he ever finds us, Mama, I'd accept him as my brother. He's family!" That's when I knew behaviors from my adoptive parents had not been carried to my children. I hugged him tightly for his unconditional love.

God was always in the details, the Source I turned to when I needed to go forward. Heavenly Father had put people in my life that changed me in so many ways. The belief and confidence others, especially women, had in me boosted my courage when life was less than perfect and gave me courage to stride into the life that *I* wanted to create.

I returned to the university and learned for myself how to teach others. I worked with nontraditional students and watched how education impacted them for the better. The biggest joy was when someone realized they *weren't* stupid and they really *could* pursue a dreamed-of goal and find success. A professional mentor at Western Governors University (WGU), I mentored students all across the United States. In June, WGU provided a full graduation experience in Salt Lake City for students who could attend. It was at that program when I got to meet one of my Hispanic students, Robert. He was the first in his family to earn a college degree. I mentored him for over a year through his life challenges. I felt a genuine understanding for his struggles, knowing intensely how it felt to be guided unconditionally. With his family, Robert drove all night to attend the ceremony and meet me. What a privilege to be in graduation photos with him and his very proud parents.

With time, I learned to forgive myself for my many life mistakes. I always hoped the people in my life would fulfill my heart-felt needs, my internal empty well. But with time, I realized it was only *me* who filled my empty well and answered my needs, along with a loving Heavenly Father who directed and encouraged me. It took me time to trust Him and let go of my concept of a father learned in my teenage years. I finally realized, God was waiting there for me all the time. I am no longer an empty well, I am a beautifully overflowing one.

I still wondered about writing that moved readers or an audience. How does it happen? What makes a book or play a classic? Stories in film, books, or poems, they all still grabbed me and never let me go. I didn't know why something I read made me cry or cheer. So, when the opportunity came to pursue a masters in English, I couldn't get into those classes fast enough.

With my sons on their own, I entered graduate school at Weber State University (WSU). My academic adviser was Merlin Cheney. He directed me to classes that *only* focused on what I loved: literature and writing. He taught many classes himself, truly the wizard Merlin, a spellbinding professor of English. A benevolent face with a Roman nose, Dr. Cheney had a fringe of white hair that he kept closely cropped. When he entered a classroom, he usually wore a tweed sweater, a matching tweed hat, and wire-rimmed glasses. He was classy, like an English gentleman, with his kind face and approachable demeanor.

A favorite quote of mine was from C.S. Lewis: "We read to know we are not alone."

Dr. Cheney said the same, but a little differently: "It's the common humanity. We read about the mistakes or successes of others. We don't have to go out and experience those choices for ourselves. When writing is good, it grabs your soul. It lets the reader, or viewer, follow the hero's journey and learn."

His classes were different too. He didn't lecture. Learning was the student's responsibility. We explored, we *did* the research, we *wrote* the papers, and we *presented* them to the rest of the class. I took two classes from him, three from Dr. Donna Cheney, his wife, and counseled with him regarding classes as I continued forward towards graduation.

On graduation day, May 7, 2009, Dr. Cheney draped the master's degree hood around my neck and said, "Congratulations, Janet, you did it!" Then I heard my grandkids holler from the balcony, "That's my Nana!" I waved as I crossed the stage, tears drenching my cheeks, of course, and beamed a wide smile. When I divorced Dave, I never dreamed I could come this far in my new life.

My relationship with both Cheneys would continue for the next twelve years. We visited often and had long late afternoon talks about Thomas Hardy, Orson Welles, and even Winston Churchill. Then, when Donna passed away, Merlin, heartbroken, continued to visit with me. I brought him dinner and DVDs I thought he'd enjoy watching like

The Darkest Hour. It was a time I looked forward to as well.

The more time we spent together, the closer he and I became. And I was flabbergasted. I had dated a few times, but as soon as I talked about film plots or character motivation in books, boredom raced across my date's face. One snowy afternoon I told Merlin, "I love having someone to talk to who is interested in what I'm interested in. I never thought I'd have these kinds of conversations."

"I never thought I'd find someone other than Donna who would have these interesting conversations with me either. I really look forward to our visits," he replied with a kind smile.

I felt my feelings of friendship deepen into something more. I hadn't felt that way for a long, long time, and even then, these flutters in my heart weren't just girlish notions or seeking someone to take care of me. No, I was a healing, independent creature who had accepted herself and was learning to live with all her imperfections and the adventures of my journey.

Merlin was a Latter-day Saint like me. I was intrigued, listening to his stories about working as a minister at the Weber County jail, a volunteer calling he held for eight years. He saw everyone as a human being, never mind their crime, ethnicity, or skin color. He told me, "There are two kinds of people, those we love and those we don't yet understand."

Then Merlin relayed a story.

"One late Wednesday evening, I was on my way home from the jail when I saw a man walking down the road in flip-flops, shorts, and a tank top. You know, if someone is arrested in the summer and let out of jail in March, they come out dressed the way they went in," he explained. "Where are you going? Can I give you a lift?"

The man got in and shared how he had no place to go and no way to earn a living. He could hardly speak English and couldn't read. This *did not* sit well with Merlin. He knew it was no accident that they'd met on that cold winter night. With many phone calls, he helped the man find a place to stay and, later, get training to drive a forklift.

"I told him, 'the day you don't show up for training or call in sick, it's over. I won't be able to help you with anything after that.' It was his one shot, you know? The man finished his course and went on to have a decent life."

Merlin expanded that humane service to include WSU students who came to the jail and taught ESL classes to inmates while receiving degree credit for their instruction.

"A majority of folks I worked with out there really *couldn't* read or write. They did whatever they could to survive; what choice did they have?" Merlin asserted.

What a difference between this warm-hearted man and Dave. I didn't need a man in my life . . . but with Merlin, I felt things I'd never felt in my past relationship. Safety. Respect. Intellectual equality. The desires to grow and learn and give unconditionally to one another. That was *love*, right? And, as time passed, those feelings didn't go away.

I took some time to myself when I was home, got really quiet, and then prayed aloud. "Dear Father, I have romantic feelings for Merlin Cheney. Totally unexpected, Father. I told myself I wouldn't marry unless you brought someone into my life because I don't trust myself to make a good choice. So, is this it? Maybe not. He did have a wonderful fifty-plus years with Donna, after all. Whichever way this goes, I am leaving it in Your hands, Father. All good comes from Thee and I accept whatever happens. In Jesus' name, amen."

On a Saturday evening in March 2019, Merlin and I went to dinner, conversing about books and life as we always did. It fed my soul and heart in ways I never thought possible. As we walked to his car, he said, "Can you come back to the house and visit a little longer?"

I gave him a massive grin. Of course!

We sat near each other, he in his leather green recliner, me in the adjacent upholstered maroon chair. Then Merlin leaned in and took my hand. "I've been thinking," he took a breath, "you and I make a good team. We love the same things–books, education, the Savior. I would love to take you to England so we can see the birthplaces of authors we admire. However, to do that, we'd have to form some kind of partnership and—"

"Wait a minute!" I uttered, a little astonished. "Are . . . are you proposing to me?"

"Yes, in a very poor way. I love you and want to spend the rest of my life with you, such as it is."

Tears welled up in my vision. I tightened my grip on his fingers and my heart swelled. He loved me and accepted me just as I was . . . just like I loved him. I knew that I could embrace every adventure going forward with this man. *Okay, God, you win! But please, help me breathe!*

That was the finishing touch to my long, therapeutic journey. I learned to love myself and attracted a love I never thought I would find. Another tender mercy, God knew me better than I knew myself. Merlin and I shared together and served together with love. I became a better person being with this man. I'd call it a *Lawrence of Arabia* epic story, just for me.

FINAL THOUGHTS

Don't be afraid to look deeply at your life. Yes, it's true, you are the sum total of how you grew up and what you've done in whatever form, up 'til now. You've done the best you could to survive and live, to the best of your understanding.

Give yourself credit for being smart and determined!

Know that you DO have the ability to refocus and change, no matter your age or background, especially if your desire is rooted in wanting to be an influence for good.

A few life lessons that helped me change:

1. You can't go to an empty well to get your bucket filled—damaged people damage people. Stop looking to them to love you and fill you up.
2. Do not keep people in your life who refuse to treat you with respect, no matter how you know them. **All human beings deserve love and kindness.**
3. Find the best way for *you* to gain life tools and methods for managing life challenges. I needed a professional "guide" who saw my life, and me, without bias.
4. Seek God, in whatever way you see Him/Her. Meditate, ponder, and allow the One who loves you unconditionally to direct your path for good.
5. *Always remember*: **You are loved and are deserving of *being* loved.** Let this be the root of why you go forward.

Matthew 22:39, Jesus said: "Love your neighbor as yourself."

Therefore, learn how to love yourself first! When you do this, you will be able to love others. You don't have to invite damaged people over for potato salad, but you can love them as a child of God from a distance as far away as you might need.

I would love to hear from you and cheer you on! You can reach out to me and subscribe to my newsletter at https://www.healingyourse-crets.com/ or email me at: jbc@healingsecrets.com.

PHOTO GALLERY

Daddy with me at 13 mos.

Grandmother/Aunt Zella

My Birth Mother

Adopted grandparents,
Grandy and Gramps

Me, Alex, Chris, Ben, and Eric

Me at 13 months

Me at one year old

Me and my Lithuanian
grandmother, the
mother of Mildred

Grandy, me, and Gramps ready for church

Merlin, the love of my life, and me

ABOUT THE AUTHOR

Janet Bernice Cheney (born August 1, 1952) holds a master's degree in English from Weber State University and is a John Maxwell-certified life coach. Known as Janet Bernice until marriage to her sweetheart, she taught English online and in the classroom for twenty years. A published author for three years with *Ancestry* magazine, she is an avid genealogist and intense fan of all good historical biography. Defining herself as a creative, besides writing and being an inspirational speaker, Janet is a painter and cross-stitcher extraordinaire.

Janet Cheney describes herself as a recovering basket case. She is also a woman of faith, mentor, abuse survivor, and devoted friend. A proud mother of five and grandmother of nine. Her life revolves around time with family and volunteer service.

https://www.healingyoursecrets.com/
jbc@healingyoursecrets.com
jcheney@substack.com
https://www.facebook.com/Cheney.Janet
http://www.twitter.com/Janet_secrets
https://www.instagram.com/jbernice68

FULL REVIEWS

"In this journey of personal discovery laid bare, Janet Bernice Cheney reminds us that all families have secrets . . . secrets that color the world we live in and that can limit our potential in horribly restrictive boxes. Struggling to discover her real origin story, Janet lets us follow along on her hero's journey of understanding, healing, cutting ties, and forgiveness. She shows what a gift it is to lean on God and the good people He places in our path to help us along the way. You'll walk away inspired to look deeply into your own life . . . and anyway, we all deserve a pair of tennis shoes covered in flowers."
—**Jennifer Utley, Executive Story Producer, *Ancestry.com***

"From the very beginning, Janet was raised in an atmosphere of confusion, uncertainty, and fear. Not much made any real sense except that her life was going to be painful and full of uncertainty. Her life, especially with her adopted mother, seemed almost impossible to make any sense for her. And from there, things seemed to deteriorate. Janet never knew what to expect. She just never seemed to fit in. Emotional abuse, physical abuse, getting married at a young age, drugs, having a baby, more babies, then the death of her baby. Her husband was out of control. Marital problems. Divorce. Codependency. Church, therapy, spiritualty, and insight. In spite of all the above issues of interpersonal, marital, several children, with a husband who didn't have any idea of responsibility or maturity, Janet took control, and she has developed a great amount of insight, sensitivity, and spirituality that will be helpful in reaching others who have had similar experiences."
—**John Waterbury, CMHC, Therapist Retired**

"We should all appreciate the raw and transparent view that Janet shares about her life, in her book, So Many Freakin' Secrets. The hurt and betrayal, the gut-wrenching realities of her life, and especially the total absence of love, avoidance, and neglect from her mother would be the undoing of many, if not all, women. Janet has painfully, yet beautifully, woven the pieces of her life together to tell us how she overcame the hell she was living in, and eventually, with the help of trusted friends, professionals, and her own personal fortitude, has courageously risen above her past, giving us a blueprint of sorts, showing us that there is a way out. A motivating and inspiring read for anyone in difficult situations."
—Georgia Carpenter, Book Promoter and Publicist

It's disheartening to realize how many children are adopted for the wrong reasons only to be abused emotionally and physically. So Many Freakin' Secrets is a well-written story about the author's healing journey. This poignant narrative serves as a beacon of hope for those who have experienced similar circumstances."
—Madison Frederick, International Best-Selling Author of *Untangle the Web of Narcissism*

"I absolutely loved So Many Freakin' Secrets and was so impressed by Janet's strength and courage for how she lived her powerful and inspirational story. The story flowed great and I was sucked in, not wanting to put the book down. My heart ached right along with the author during her struggles and I cheered as she made her comeback. Very well done!"
—Brita Peterson, International Best-Selling Author of *Getting Through Today: How Chronic Illness Taught Me, the Beauty in Being Broken*

REVIEWS

Here are what readers are saying about this powerful and inspirational book:

"Such a powerful and inspirational story. I loved every piece of it, the story flowed great and I was sucked in, not wanting to put it down . . . the book moved me and I got through it in a couple of days. I felt so many emotions, my heart ached right along with the struggles, and I was cheering along as Janet made her comeback, very well done!"
 —**Brita Bigler Peterson, international bestselling author of *Getting Through Today: How Chronic Illness Taught Me the Beauty in Being Broken***

"Your story is compelling. I love that it is written with so much personal style coming through. This woman's been through so much stuff and come out a winner! I read it all the way through because I could barely put it down! I loved this book!"
 —**Circe Dopp, luthier and teacher**

"In addition to uncovering intriguing, life-changing family secrets, you'll find a groovy hippy spirit, a stalwart female soul, and a relatable journey to self-acceptance, inner peace, and real freedom in Janet's story, So Many Freakin' Secrets. Taking on the challenge of transcending the mysteries behind adoption, the heavy layers of Vietnam-era PTSD, and the barriers faced by single mothers, Janet takes her readers through a powerful adventure where rock 'n' roll, true love, and our own gifts shine brightly on the other side."
 —**Hannah R. Lyon, bestselling fantasy author and comprehensive editor**

"Janet is an inspiring soul, an author, speaker, and coach with mad skills and gifts to share. Having lived an extraordinary life of overcoming and finding tremendous joy, she gifts clients with generous wisdom for life and smart tools for even greater living."

—**Bridget Cook-Burch,** ***New York Times*** **and** ***Wall Street Journal*** **bestselling author of** ***The Witness Wore Red*,** **cofounder of SheroesUnited.org and CEO of YourInspiredStory.com.**

www.ingramcontent.com/pod-product-compliance
Lightning Source LLC
Chambersburg PA
CBHW030403130626
46549CB00004B/1609